How I Became a Human Being

A Disabled Man's Quest for Independence

How I Became a Human Being

A Disabled Man's Quest for Independence

MARK O'BRIEN

WITH GILLIAN KENDALL

THE UNIVERSITY OF WISCONSIN PRESS

The University of Wisconsin Press
1930 Monroe Street, 3rd Floor
Madison, Wisconsin 53711-2059
uwpress.wisc.edu

3 Henrietta Street
London WC2E 8LU, England
eurospanbookstore.com

Printed in the United States of America

Library of Congress Cataloging-in-Publication Data

O'Brien, Mark, 1949–1999.
How I became a human being : a disabled man's quest for independence /
Mark O'Brien with Gillian Kendall.
p. cm. — (Wisconsin studies in autobiography)
ISBN 0-299-18430-7 (cloth : alk. paper)
1. O'Brien, Mark, 1949–1999—Health. 2. Physically handicapped—
Rehabilitation—Wisconsin. I. Kendall, Gillian. II. Title. III. Series.
RM930.5.U6 O24 2003
362.1′96835′0092—dc21
2002010451

ISBN 978-0-299-18434-6 (pbk. : alk. paper)
ISBN 978-0-299-18433-9 (e-book)

For Walter and Helen,
who gave me life and saved my life.

Free at last, free at last,
Thank God Almighty!
I'm free at last.

—TRADITIONAL SPIRITUAL

Contents

Illustrations

Preface

or the majority of his life, Mark breathed exactly eighteen times a minute, his air controlled by the wonderful, terrible iron lung in which he lived. That rhythm also limited his speech, sometimes fragmenting it, as he could speak only during the brief, controlled exhalations. Often, there were sudden breaks in his conversation, pauses in the middle of sentences, breaths before a single word. Other times, he rushed a sentence to get it out in time. That rhythm, I think, also affected Mark's written language, keeping it concise, brief—and sometimes a bit telegraphic. In chapter 11, Mark talks about the similarity between journalism and poetry, the need for precision and brevity in both. The journal entries I've seen and his letters and emails to me were similarly pithy, and, in conversations during our fifteen-year friendship, he spoke bluntly and forcefully, but never at length.

As coauthor, my job has been to slow down and expand the stories behind Mark's poetic, journalistic style. Working with Mark, I asked him to explain quick references or throwaway sentences, which often stood for whole scenes or complicated emotions. Our work went best when I was by Mark's side, he relating stories, I writing down not his exact words but his ideas, memories, and feelings.

When Mark died, in 1999, we had a complete draft of a book but not a fully developed story. Where I trusted my own memories or perceptions not to betray Mark's meaning, I have tried to fill in some spaces and to provide transitions and clarifications. In the places where the text remains elliptical, it is because I have not known enough to fill out the outline—sadly, there are many things about my friend that

I didn't know enough about, didn't think to ask while I was able to. And in some instances, Mark substituted fictitious names for real ones, to hide identities.

After Mark died, I asked for one of his mouthsticks—the wood-and-plastic tools he used for typing. I keep it as a reminder of how dedicated Mark was to communication and self-expression, to remind myself to work as hard as he did.

A reporter once asked me why I thought Mark had stayed alive so long. For what purpose? I said that I didn't think Mark needed to define his life's purpose any more than anyone else did; most people's raison d'être changes or remains undefined. There was considerable pressure on Mark to live for something or someone else, to stand for some ideal, to represent some group. One of his achievements was that he lived for himself, his writing, and the people he was close to, refusing to limit himself in political or didactic terms.

Sharing the work of writing Mark's biography has been an honor, and I am grateful to Birmingham-Southern College for a grant toward work on an early draft. I am glad that the book will make Mark's story available to many readers of different abilities and backgrounds, especially to people who live in countries that lack legal support and protection for the disabled.

—GILLIAN KENDALL

How I Became a Human Being

A Disabled Man's Quest for Independence

Prologue

On the day I graduated from the University of California, Berkeley, on the night that Jessica Yu's documentary about me won an Oscar, and at other times, I have been praised for being a hero, but heroism has had little to do with my achieving success at Berkeley or elsewhere. I was the beneficiary of a deep and important change in society. In my first published article, in *CoEvolution Quarterly,* I tried to explain that change: "I still cannot sit up straight, turn my head to the left, or sleep outside of a respirator. But these problems no longer set me apart or mark me as a freak as they did when I was a child and an adolescent. The reasons for this change have more to do with the nature and the quality of society than they have to do with how much responsibility a society will entrust to disabled people."

For centuries, disabled people had been locked up in state-owned or state-subsidized institutions. We will never know how many lives were wasted, how many intellects dulled, how many souls murdered, through that system. The people who began and ran this system were good people who thought of themselves as reformers helping the helpless. But they never asked us what we wanted.

Freedom.

Ed Roberts, Judy Heumann, and Hale Zukas led the change, demanding that society free us from the living death of nursing homes. They and others demonstrated, argued, and fought for attendant programs to pay people to work for us in our own homes. These programs give us the power to hire, train, and fire the people who wash, feed, dress, and lift us. Other changes were begun as well, such as disabled students' programs, state payment for power wheelchairs, and laws forbidding discrimination against disabled people. But attendant programs were the most essential. Without them, I would still be stuck in a nursing home.

These changes have freed thousands of disabled people. However, thousands of others remain in nursing homes, trapped by the failure of Congress and of state legislatures to enact laws that will permit all of us to live, with the help of attendants, outside nursing homes. I have been lucky enough to live in California, a state that has a good attendant program. I hope other states will free their disabled people.

That first published article, "How I Became a Human Being," showed that independent living changed how I am perceived.

> [People] began to treat me as if I were a human being. It's strange to tell because up until then people had made me feel as if I were something else, something less, something not capable of bearing personal responsibility. Because this society has, by unspoken agreement, defined a human being as someone who can bear the major responsibilities required for a self-directed life, I was not a human being. Nor are convicts, children, or retarded people regarded as such. But now that I have been given this responsibility and have proven that I can run my life as well as anybody else, I have been granted that degree of respect which is commonly accorded to a human being. When one of my attendants referred to me as "buddy," it thrilled me because I had not been accustomed to receiving that degree of respect. Such respect came as something of a surprise.

The whole disability revolution has come as a surprise. This book shows how that revolution freed me to become a human being, and how that revolution made a society become more human.

PART 1

Dependent

1

Dorchester

(1949–1955)

I ran everywhere I went. I couldn't understand why adults always walked; running was so much fun. My Keds beating the sidewalks, the air rushing past, friends pounding next to me—I could never get enough of the excitement of fast movement.

As I remember childhood, I woke up eager to start each day. Every morning, I climbed down the ladder from the orange bunk bed I shared with my younger brother, Ken. We ran into the kitchen, where our mother gave us breakfast: usually bowls of hot oatmeal, thick with raisins. Then, no matter what the weather, we headed outside. We ran down the front steps of our brown-and-yellow house, into the life of our crowded, Irish-Catholic neighborhood.

At one end of our C-shaped street, Glenrose Road, lay a small park named after John Quincy Adams. The important-sounding name always amused me, and I loved swinging on the monkey bars, but I never could climb the park's trees. The bottom branches swayed just out of reach, and if I scrambled up the trunk, my legs below my shorts would be covered in red welts and scrapes. So, until I grew older and taller, I had to settle for squeezing through the neighbors' tight hedges. This technique later proved a good way to get away from bullies.

Routinely, the boys of the neighborhood knocked me down to the hard, gray sidewalks, hit me, straddled me, and hit me some more. It was terrible and terrifying and, it seemed, unstoppable. When I told my parents, my father tried to teach me how to fight back.

"Punch 'em in the nose!" he shouted, demonstrating how a blow to center of the face would knock my attackers off balance. My father was a big man, with heavy fists and a craggy face behind Steve Allen glasses. Trying to help me, he bounced around, light on his feet. "Like this!" he said, socking an imaginary enemy. "Hard right!"

It seemed like practical advice, and I was always sure it would work, until I was facing a boy about to hit me. Then I forgot the advice, or realized its impracticality.

I was especially afraid of Arthur, a red-haired tough whose very name (which I pronounced "Ah-fah,") suggested thunder. He terrorized me with his glistening pink water pistol and, more, with his quick, hard fists.

After a beating, I would run home, where my mother would kiss the places that hurt and tell me it was all better. That usually worked. Like my father, she encouraged me to fight back, telling me, "You're older than Arthur, you're bigger than Arthur," but it didn't matter. I never defended myself but always scraped through the hedge and rushed home to safety and comfort.

My earliest memory is of standing amid a crowd on a curb, trying to watch green men carrying big wooden sticks. Loud music played all down the street, and my parents were watching what was happening, sometimes clapping, clearly excited. I wanted to watch, too, but I couldn't see over all the tall people in front of me, so I had to squeeze between their legs for a glimpse of the green men. In the confusion, I became separated from my parents.

When my father found me, I was in tears. To let me see better, he lifted me onto his shoulders, but my feet got tangled, and the height made me feel disoriented. I cried louder, and we went home. My parents told me this event, the marching people, was a "parade" and that everyone loved parades, but I had no idea what was going on.

Years later, I learned it had been an Evacuation Day parade and that the green men carrying sticks had been soldiers marching with rifles. In Boston, March 17 is celebrated as the anniversary of the withdrawal of the British fleet from Boston Harbor. General Washington's soldiers had lugged cannons from Fort Ticonderoga, in Vermont, to Dorchester Heights, in Massachusetts, from which point they could fire on, and destroy, His Majesty's ships. History, American and Irish, gets mixed up together in Boston. As I was growing up, history was as present as the weather, and as familiar as my own name.

We lived in the section of Boston called Dorchester (pronounced "Dotchestah"), on Glenrose Road. Our house belonged to my maternal grandfather, James Kelly, whom we called 'Pop.' Upstairs, where he lived, was a quiet, mysterious place devoid of radios and televisions— Pop, a thin, quiet man, hated them both. But his part of the house was rich in the scent of cigars, and cheerful with the light that entered the big windows. Upstairs, people read, ate, and gossiped amid the old, soft furniture and the sunshine.

Affectionately, Pop gave me his empty El Producto cigar boxes, which I cherished as emblems of his confidence. I never put anything in the boxes or used them for building blocks—they were too important for that. I simply carried them about, carefully and solemnly. With their pretty Cuban ladies, strange foreign words, and dark, dramatic smell, they were Essence of Pop, and I felt honored to own them.

When I climbed the stairs to Pop's place, the first things I saw were Pop's washer and dryer. When it was new, the washing machine had smooth surfaces and flashing lights that fascinated me. Once, when I went upstairs alone to admire it, I turned the washer's big glowing dial. It started up with a roar, and I ran like hell downstairs.

The basement was as mysterious as the upstairs, but in a different way. Cold and dark, it sheltered my mother's old wringer washing machine, the kind Popeye ran Bluto through. Thick wooden walls surrounded the coal bin, a stinky, immense pile of black rocks that had to be shoveled into the furnace by one of the men in the family. Everyone warned me to stay away from the furnace, but there was no need to caution me: even when its heavy iron door was shut, it emitted a fierce, dry heat and menacing rumbles. With the door open, the white flames and terrible heat made it seem the entry to Hell.

On the GI Bill, my father, Walter O'Brien, became the first in his family to graduate from college. He got his bachelor's degree from the University of Massachusetts and then went to law school at Suffolk College—all while working nights at the post office.

In a photograph taken at his law school graduation in 1951, my father is wearing a black gown and mortarboard, beaming confidently at the camera. I am standing there, all in white, in contrast to his black. My head about level with his thighs, I am gazing up with a confused expression at the tall, smiling man. Perhaps I was wondering why he was wearing such a funny get-up, or why he was so happy. I had never understood the talk about him going to school—everyone knew that kids went to school, not daddies.

I was still calling him "Daddy" then. Later, when I was four or five, I started calling my father by his nickname, O'Bie, and my mother by her first name, Helen.

Between attending law school during the day and working at the post office at night, Daddy was not often at home. I looked forward to seeing him, except on the days when my mother employed the threat of Daddy-with-the-belt: then I felt all-day dread. But most evenings he came to spend time with me before I went to sleep. In my room, he would make hand-shadows, including a rabbit that chatted to me. Sometimes Daddy sang sad cowboy songs.

> The other night, dear, as I lay sleeping,
> I dreamt I held you in my arms.
> When I awoke, dear, I was mistaken,
> So I hung my head and cried.

Parents Walter (O'Bie) and Helen with Mark in 1949.

Helen with Mark in
December 1949.

Helen with the boys, Mark
and Ken.

I asked about the meaning of the phrase "I hung my head." He tried to demonstrate, but I was still confused. Why would he do that? What did bowing his head have to do with being sad? Why was he so sad? I had too many questions that night, and he got frustrated and left.

One day, my father brought home a big wooden box that he called "the movies" and that everyone else called "television." Taller than I was, it had a piece of green glass and two knobs on its front, for channel and volume. Once we learned how to work it, my siblings, Ken and Karen, and I watched *Howdy Doody* six days a week, but my favorite was a local children's show called *Big Brother.*

Big Brother, an amiable duffer, strummed a ukulele, showed cartoons, and toasted the president of the United States every weekday at 12:30 P.M. This ceremony began with Big Brother facing the camera and holding an eight-ounce glass of milk, with a portrait of the president of the United States looming over his shoulder. As the organ growled out "Hail to the Chief," the camera would zoom in on Ike, whom I confused with God and the Shawmut National Bank Indian. When the last notes of "Hail to the Chief" had ended, the camera would pan back to show Big Brother holding an empty, milk-glazed glass.

"Ahhh," Big Brother would exhale, refreshed by his drink. And Ken and I would gasp and choke, splattering milk over our chins and shirts, trying to participate in this display of lactic patriotism.

Big Brother lived in a Tudor cottage with diamond-paned windows. It seemed real until the day when moving men walked into the scene and began moving the walls away. Big Brother sputtered indignantly while the men moved in new walls, windows, and even a new fireplace. Perhaps the producers were making a joke, or trying to teach young viewers something about the impermanence of life, but I felt angry and betrayed. That whole English cottage had been a fraud of cardboard sets, so perhaps Big Brother was a fake, too.

All three of us children watched the Walt Disney show, but only Ken and I were fascinated by *Davy Crockett.* Caught up in the first Disney-engineered craze, my brother and I obtained glorious Davy Crockett caps made of cheap, scratchy fur. They fell off all the time. For Christmas, Santa Claus brought us two authentic Davy Crockett rifles, big wooden sticks like those the green men had carried in the parade.

Late that Christmas Day, Ken and I stood on our front steps, fending off a crowd of boys determined to take our Davy Crockett weapons. The fighting was close and bitter, like the Battle of the Alamo. Badly outnumbered, we lost the guns, which seemed terribly wrong and sad. However, the next day, our parents got them back, apparently by use of diplomacy, not force.

When I wasn't outside, I enjoyed being with my mother in the house, listening to her sing and watching her cook. I used to push open the swinging door that led from the living room to the kitchen to watch her. She told me to not shove the door so hard, because that made it swing madly in and out, but I enjoyed seeing the door move by itself, a dead object brought alive by my magic.

While doing housework, Helen sang "I'm Gonna Wash That Man Right Out of My Hair," "Oh, What a Beautiful Morning," and other songs from the 1940s musicals she had seen on Broadway. Her voice, high, clear, and sassy, sounded throughout the house as half-walked, half-danced, her curls bouncing when she tossed her head. My mother was pretty in a classic Irish way, with a small red nose and bright eyes very blue against her pale, freckled skin.

Sometimes she gave me pieces of uncooked bacon, my favorite food for its fat, juiciness, and sharp flavor. Unbaked dough was my second favorite, but it also raised a dilemma—if I ate it all, how could she bake apple and lemon meringue pies? Although generally I was of little use in the kitchen, I did enjoy rolling dough with the big, red-handled, wooden rolling pin.

Mark at the Glenrose Road house, circa 1953.

The kitchen was a safe, comfortable place, and I didn't care that I was becoming plump on bacon and pie and, especially, my mother's mashed potatoes, which made the room smell like the restaurants of Heaven. I played with the mounds of mashed potatoes, making mountains and castles, watching the brown gravy cascade in thick rivers, and eating as much as I could. Frequently, I overate so much that I threw up after a meal. As a plump mama's boy, no wonder I made an irresistible target for the bullies of Glenrose Road.

My father often drove us to Revere Beach, his home town north of Boston, to visit his mother, our Grandma. Her little house, filled with pictures of saints and medallions of the thin, bald Pope Pius XII, smelled like overcooked vegetables.

A widow and the mother of seven children, Grandma was a large, square-jawed woman who had been born on the Aran Islands, off the west coast of Ireland. Despite the frequent visits, her size frightened me, and her gravelly brogue made her seem unusual, even bizarre. I knew no one else with an accent, let alone an accent that would make a person say "Maarsachusetts" and "praist." An affectionate woman, she smothered me in her embraces and embarrassed my father by calling him "Wally" as if he were still a little boy. It felt odd to see O'Bie treated that way. If he was the biggest, strongest man in the world, as he often assured me, why didn't he tell Grandma to quit calling him Wally? Slowly, I realized that he deferred to Grandma because she was his mother, just as Helen was my mother.

Relationships confused me. After Ken was born in 1951, I was told I was his brother. When Ken became old enough to talk, he insisted he was my brother. We fought over our status until Helen told us we were both each other's brothers. This concept took me some time to accept. Similarly, for a long time, I considered Uncle Jim to be my uncle and Uncle Joe to be Ken's uncle.

When I was a preschooler, one of my favorite toys was a set of brightly colored cloth triangles that snapped together to make little tentlike cubbyholes. I would assemble these tents next to the dining room table; playing inside, I felt safe. No adults or bullies could fit through the opening, and I discouraged Ken from entering. When I put my eyes up close to the triangles, the outside world was transformed into yellow, green, or red.

I could spend hours inside this private place, my arms wrapped around my knees, thinking or dreaming, but one day I made the mistake of telling my parents how hot the tent got inside. Alarmed, possibly worried that I might suffocate, they took away the triangles.

Every summer, we went to the beach, actually to several beaches around Boston. The best were trips to Nantasket Beach, south of the city, which had the biggest roller coasters and loudest merry-go-rounds. Most of all I loved swimming, the weightless, cold, wet thrill of it. Exuberant and bully-free, I screamed with pleasure and ran confidently all over acres of sand. My fat little body, seal-like, seemed best suited for water use. Once, running out of the water, I noticed with amazement that I was still wet—thoroughly, deliciously wet. My nipples felt sharp and sensitive, which delighted me, but when I screamed at my mother about this wonderful phenomenon, she told me to quiet down.

For beach picnics, my parents always brought a big thermos of pink Kool-Aid, my favorite, and a basket filled with sandwiches. Once, I made the mistake of asking for one of their crabmeat sandwiches. My father told me that the filling was made of one of those ugly red animals that roamed the beach. Ick! A food phobia was born.

When my mother changed me back into land clothes in one of the little wooden booths, the wet, prickly sand particles fall out of my swimming trunks. Stuck between my toes for days, the sand scratched me, annoyed me, and reminded me of joy.

Mark before polio. Helen holds his sister Karen and their brother, Ken, 1953.

The front of our house had eleven steps. Once I jumped off the third one, sideways, onto the ground next to the staircase. Then I tried jumping off step number four. That went okay, so I went up and up, jumping down and climbing back, until the ninth step, from which I leaped and fell badly. I landed in a heap, twisting my ankle. Though my mother said the ankle was all right, not broken or sprained, she forbade my jumping off the higher steps.

I started kindergarten at age five, but I disliked it, probably because I was no longer the focus of adult attention. The teachers played a game in which, every day, one of the kids got to be "It," the center of attention, the star of the class, for the whole day. For some reason, I never got to be It.

Once a boy pulled my chair out from under me as I was sitting down, a trick he justified and exacerbated by calling me a baby. Only babies wore short pants; I wore short pants; therefore, the syllogism concluded, I was a baby. Babies, being small, helpless, and wet, were the most despised objects in the universe of boys. To be called a baby was the ultimate insult.

But there were humiliations worse than being teased for my short pants or my babyishness. When I left kindergarten to walk home, I would be grabbed from behind, thrown on the sidewalk, and beaten. I told my mother about each of these traumas, and eventually the teacher walked home with me. However, I still hated being separated from my mother, so my parents withdrew me from kindergarten.

Mark at Nantasket
Beach, circa 1954.

Cowboy Mark,
Christmas 1954.

Mark and Ken,
circa 1955.

Social life at home was not always easy, either. My red-haired cousin, Donna, the same age as I, had a trumpet. It was not a real trumpet— it made harmonica sounds when you blew through it—but I wanted it because it was shiny and loud and it looked real. Once I stole it from her. She protested, saying it was hers, and I said it was mine. She challenged me to a race to determine the trumpet's true owner. I accepted fearlessly. After all, she was a girl, and everyone knew that boys were bigger, stronger, faster, and smarter than girls. We ran around the block until my heart pounded hard and my legs ached, but she, a mere girl, got in front and won—more injustice!

I had always ridden a tricycle, but on my sixth birthday, in July 1955, my parents gave me a bicycle, maroon and cream, with little red training wheels. I loved it. Stunned by the color combination, I thought "maroonandcream" was a single word, signifying one magic color.

I worried, though, about one day having to ride my bicycle upright, the way the big kids rode theirs. I couldn't see what would keep the bike from falling over. Coaching me in the backyard, my father said I no longer needed the training wheels. I didn't know why he said this; it always felt as though I were about to tip over and skin a knee, but now, forty years later, it seems obvious. I had ridden the bicycle for long distances without the training wheels touching the ground. He had seen me doing something I thought impossible, and he wanted to show me how skilled I had become, by removing the training wheels. He knew I no longer needed them. But I was too frightened, and, anyway, we both ran out of time. He never did take the training wheels off that bike.

2

Polio

(1955–1957)

It was September 1955, at the end of the swim season, and my brother tells me that our family had spent the day at the beach. I remember only what happened that night, after a sharp pain in my abdomen woke me. It felt like being stabbed repeatedly on the right side and in my belly. Curled on the top of the bunk bed I shared with Ken, I started crying.

I didn't want to get up in the dark, because whenever I walked across my room at night, the toy box went out of its way to trip me. I didn't know why it attacked me, but neither did I know why other boys attacked me. The brutality of the world lay beyond my understanding. Later, of course, I revised my view of the toy box's malevolence— I realized that I would simply lose my way in the dark and stumble over a perfectly innocent piece of furniture. But at that moment, I lay in the dark, squeezing my eyes shut in pain and dreading setting foot on the floor. After some time, when I couldn't take the pain anymore, I lowered the wooden bedrail, climbed down the ladder, and went to my parents, who were watching television and reading the Boston *Globe*.

For a few minutes, I enjoyed being up with the grown-ups in the blue glow of the television. When the doctor arrived, my father told me not to be afraid, and I was not. Mysteriously, the doctor tapped my knees with a little rubber hammer, which hurt. The grown-ups talked, and then my father told me I would be going to Children's Hospital, a big building downtown where they helped boys who were sick. Although I didn't feel sick, I did feel worried: I had had bellyaches before, but none of them had ever caused such nighttime commotion. Besides, I didn't want to leave home.

O'Bie, driving the family through the night streets, told me how he had gone to Children's Hospital when he was in eighth grade, to have his appendix removed. I recalled the ugly scar where they had cut my father's belly open to remove a dangerous part of him. Would they tear my belly open? He said no, they would not do anything to hurt me; they only wanted me to feel better.

The vast, complex building smelled of a blend of urine and disinfectant that I would come to associate with hospitals. Mantled by the fluorescent lights, we wandered from room to room, nurse to nurse, and doctor to doctor. My sister, Karen, cried from being so sleepy, while I felt both tired and astonished. What had happened? It was only a bellyache. I just wanted Helen to kiss the pain and make it go away. I wondered why no one would give me that pink medicine with the funny name, Peppy Bee Bee I called it.

A nurse told me to get on a kind of stretcher with wheels and a mattress, which she called a gurney. That was better; at least I no longer had to walk. The nurse pushed me through long, noisy halls until we came to a room with beds in it. Lining up the gurney parallel to a bed, the nurse told me to roll over and onto the mattress. I did. That was the last movement I would ever make with my whole body.

I fell asleep, and then I went into a coma for thirty days. I have no memories of that coma except that it was hard to get out of it. Every effort to wake up seemed to be repelled by an irresistible force.

When I finally woke up in the big, dimly lit room, I first saw my stuffed bear, Teddy. I was lying inside a strange machine, paralyzed from the neck down, and separated from my home and family. Years later, when I told a psychology professor that I couldn't recall that moment of realization, he said it was probably just as well.

The strange machine in which I was lying was an iron lung—a horizontal metal cylinder on legs, about three feet wide and perhaps eight long, weighing about 650 pounds. I lay in the cylinder on a movable mattress, with my head poking out the end. An adjustable collar fit around my neck to keep the cylinder—the lung—airtight. A motor caused the air inside the lung to change pressure around my body. Decreased pressure created a vacuum that pulled up my chest and lungs, pulling air down my throat. This suction alternated with a release of the vacuum, which allowed me to exhale. This change in pressure, which caused me to breathe, happened eighteen times a minute. Except for the times I have been out of the iron lung, this is the rhythm I have breathed in since that day.

Heavy, wool blankets, warmed in a big, metal steamer, were laid on me. Their wet smell pervaded the air, the dull, persistent pain of muscle spasms throbbed in my arms and legs, and the sobbing of the other children filled the room. The blankets, brown and scratchy, were so heavy that they made breathing difficult. The nurses stopped using them on me but continued to heap the blankets upon the other children, so I stayed familiar with their dank, gloomy smell. They were "Sister Kenny" blankets, developed by an Australian nun who claimed they would prevent further paralysis. The nun was wrong; the blankets only encouraged more paralysis. Not only were they uncomfortable, but the name "Sister Kenny blankets" confused me. Sister Kenny? No, Kenny was my brother; Karen was my sister.

The pain in my limbs was intensified by the physical therapists, whose job it was to stretch and bend my arms and legs as far as they could, and then a bit further. The idea was that their limits could be expanded by vigorous exercise. The physical therapists, moved by the noblest intentions, tormented me twice every weekday, stretching everything every way fifty times. I was always either in pain or in fear of having further pain inflicted upon me. Once, overwhelmed with fright, I pulled the sheet up with my tongue and my teeth so I could hide my head underneath it.

Sure that the physical therapists' only goal was to hurt me, I cried, screamed, and begged them to stop. The therapists must have been very resolute women; in spite of my howling, they continued to exercise me and kept trying to persuade me that the actions were helping.

One therapist, noticing my interest in astronomy, asked me about the solar system during our sessions. Surprised by her interest, I told her what I knew. Being able to explain something to an adult distracted and pleased me. One morning, I became so engrossed in describing the moons of Jupiter that I failed to notice that she was stretching my right foot too far. When I did notice, I screamed, but she continued to stretch my ankle, ripping the Achilles tendon. For months after, I was in terrible pain, which intensified whenever I was moved. From then on, I became terrified of anything touching my right foot. The pain was so terrible that the terror remains to this day, a deep, savage phobia.

Children's Hospital was famous for its polio treatment. From all over the world, people brought their children there, hoping for a cure. Some children saw their parents only once or twice a year, which was one reason they cried all the time.

I was relatively fortunate in that my family lived in Boston. My parents, along with Pop and my uncles and aunts, visited almost daily. However, I saw them even more often than they visited, because the initial fever of polio produced vivid hallucinations, in which they arrived smiling, dressed in their Sunday best. My joy at seeing them would change to terror as they vanished. How could my parents suddenly appear, then just as suddenly disappear? It was terribly upsetting. The nurses and the social worker tried to explain this phenomenon to me, but I never understood. Mercifully, the hallucinations decreased in frequency and intensity over the next two years, weakened to the point where I would only hear my mother speaking softly from the darkness of night.

The nurses, urging us children to eat the hospital meals, claimed that food would make us able-bodied again. For a while, I ate as much of the overcooked asparagus and jaw-breaker steak as I could, but I eventually gave up on that route to health. I never felt hungry, never enjoyed eating, and stayed underweight for years.

For entertainment, I watched bad TV—the only kind available— such as *Superman, The Mickey Mouse Club,* and *Sergeant Preston of the Yukon.* I doubted that I would ever become "one of the leaders of the twenty-first century," the people the Mickey Mouse Club dedicated itself to serving. The twenty-first century was more than forty years in the future, and the future was the last thing I wanted to think about. Perhaps, miraculously, I would stay a child forever.

I couldn't imagine being a disabled adult. Aside from John Collins, the mayor of Boston, who had been disabled by polio, I had never heard of adults who were not able-bodied. The idea seemed as self-contradictory as short giants. Besides, I knew that if I lived another twenty or thirty years, then so would Helen and O'Bie, because they were the only people who loved me and took good care of me. If it is true that no child can picture his parents growing old or dying, then it was doubly so for me.

Big Brother still hoisted a glass of milk to a portrait of President Eisenhower every noon, and the other boys on the ward coughed and spilled milk all over themselves despite the warnings of the omnipresent nurses, who cynically insisted this milk-guzzling was fake, that Big Brother dumped his milk away during "Hail to the Chief." Apparently everything on TV was fake, except for Douglas Edwards, who had been doing the CBS news as long as I could remember.

It is difficult to say which caused more problems to a small, paralyzed boy, shitting or not shitting. First, when I needed what the nurses called a "BM," I had to call for a nurse and ask her to lay me on top of a big steel bedpan, always an awkward procedure. To reach the state of calm needed to empty my bowels, I had to ignore the tumult on the ward as well as the cold, hard steel of the bedpan digging into my lower back. Afterward, being taken off the bedpan was painful and embarrassing. But it mattered little whether I made any contributions to the pan or not. I still had to swallow tablespoonfuls of milk of magnesia, whose dry, sticky taste I dreaded. The penalties for failing to shit every day included the insertion of suppositories, enema tubes, and nurses' gloved fingers. Whatever sense of privacy and dignity I had developed by age six was destroyed. I came to feel that I was a bad, filthy thing that belonged to the nurses. The best I could hope for was to be ignored, and to be ignored I had to learn to be quiet, obedient, and regular in my bowel movements.

One night, I was in a room of Big Kids, perhaps twelve to fifteen years old. Allowed to stay up late, they were watching *I Love Lucy*. I was in an iron lung, lying on a bedpan, where I had been for three or four hours. For some reason, although visiting hours were over, Helen came by. Seeing me, she was upset that I had been left on the bedpan for so long, but I did not understand why. I was becoming used to being neglected, and to the sadness that accompanied such neglect. Dimly, I recall my mother arguing with a nurse and getting her to remove the pan. While I felt grateful to be rescued, I knew it was only temporary, only a fluke. Clearly, I was no longer the center of my parents' attention, and the nurses would continue to control my life the next day and every day from then on.

Visits were the best things that happened. The first time my father was permitted to visit me without wearing a hospital gown, he was so excited he bought a new suit. I was too sick to care about such things, but it must have been a big day for him. More interesting, my father brought me children's books on astronomy. Although I couldn't read, I could enjoy the magnificent illustrations. Pictures of the rings of Saturn reassured me that the universe was still out there, somewhere.

I had no firsthand evidence, because I didn't go outside once during the first fifteen months of my illness, from when I fell sick until I was seven and a half.

Also, my father also brought me catalogs of houses, mostly one-story suburban houses. As with the astronomy books, I didn't need to read them to appreciate them. Staring at the plans for hours, I fantasized about living in split-level luxury amid carpeted stairs, wood-paneled living rooms, and gleaming all-electric kitchens. The houses looked cozy and inviting, especially compared to the hospital.

Some days, my father came to the hospital directly after work to feed me supper and to perform comedy skits for me and the other children. Holding stuffed animals and talking in funny voices, he would joke about the nurses, the hospital food, and his days in the Army Air Corps. He wiggled his bushy brows up and down, singing

> The biscuits that they serve us,
> They say are mighty fine.
> One fell off a table
> And killed a pal of mine.

My favorite routine was the one where he would stand behind a half-closed curtain and lean back so that only his head and neck could be seen. Clutching his throat with his hands, he would gurgle, "Let go! Let go! You're strangling me!" This would get the whole ward giggling, a welcome change.

Looking at catalogs, comic books, and illustrated astronomy books stirred my interest in reading, so when Mrs. Hassey, the hospital teacher, started teaching me to read, I caught on quickly. She used the Dick and Jane series, which bored me profoundly. But the process of learning, if not the content of the books, was thrilling.

One page in *Dick and Jane* showed a blue baby carriage with the mysterious word "THE" printed underneath. Obviously, T-H-E could not be a word. I had learned that much from Mrs. Hassey's phonics lessons. "T" made a tisking sound, "h" made an exhaling sound, and there was no such word as "te-huh-e." Seeing that I was approaching the problem logically, Mrs. Hassey offered help. Over and over, she explained how "t" and "h" together make the tongue-out-the-mouth sound. When it finally sank in, I felt I had solved a tremendous mystery and that I could then read anything.

Further, I was promoted from first to second grade, which thrilled my parents. I couldn't understand their excitement, since I was still in the hospital walloped by polio, and Mrs. Hassey still taught me in my hospital room instead of a real school. Still, I was pleased to have succeeded in something, to have earned praise.

Mrs. Hassey once entered our room and saw my friend Johnny reading a comic book. Furious, she tore the comic off his bookstand and threw it on the floor, shouting that it was evil and stupid. I watched in stunned fascination. What if she had caught me reading a comic book? I read a lot of them, such as the harmless Disneys, and could see nothing evil in them. I was impressed with two lessons— one, the arbitrary nature of adults, and two, the importance of reading only that which was respectable. Unlike children who had use of their hands, I could never sneak comics behind school books, because adults—my parents and the nurses—set up my reading for me.

To help me read, my father bought a bookstand from Jordan Marsh. It was a grand, folding gizmo made of wood and brass, which I used with pleasure for a couple of days. When it disappeared, my father was convinced that it had been stolen. After arguing with a nurse about it, he searched the ward until he found it in a janitor's closet. Indignant, he took it home and painted "MARK O'BRIEN PRIVATE PROPERTY" on it before returning it to me.

Every Sunday, we were visited by a hospital volunteer named Helen, a thin, graying woman with round eyeglasses and a red volunteer's jacket. Because she and my mother had the same name, I called her "Helen-not-my-mother," which tickled her. She cooked French toast and pancakes and fed them to us; she brought balloons, which she blew up and then let fly and squeal around the room. Once she asked me to describe something, anything, that I would like to invent. I said I would like to invent a flying jacket she could wear so that she could fly in through the window.

Although the nurses seemed glad to have someone to help feed us on Sunday mornings, behind her back they always talked about Helen as though she were strange. However, I loved her for being an adult who remembered how to play.

One day, a physical therapist asked another boy on the ward, Johnny, whether he wanted to try sitting on the edge of his bed. He said he would. The therapist put Johnny's legs over the edge, then slowly sat him up. As I watched his skinny legs dangle, I feared Johnny would topple over, but he did not. He sat there for a minute, unsupported, before telling the therapist he was getting dizzy. She let him down, settled him in bed, and then turned to ask whether I wanted to try it. Terrified, I said no. She let me avoid the effort, but I felt I had failed an important test.

For some reason, in 1956, when I was seven years old, I was chosen to be the child who would turn on the Children's Hospital's Christmas tree lights. Since I had been stuck inside I had not seen the unlit fir tree towering in the courtyard outside. Lighting the tree should have been a memorable event, but all I remember was how cold and sleepy I felt lying on a gurney, covered with blankets and waiting for the right minute to push the special microswitch to light up the tree.

The next spring, I was transferred to the Wellesley Convalescent Hospital, a cluster of one- and two-story brick buildings in a leafy suburb. Owned by Children's Hospital, it had many of the same employees, and even Helen-not-my-mother visited.

Most of the patients were in their teens and twenties and lived in an open ward that encompassed much of the floor. They roamed the hospital in their wheelchairs, shrieking, flirting, and listening to rock 'n' roll on tinny little transistor radios. I lived in a small room that was separated from the main ward by folding partitions, dark green, made of a mysterious substance more flexible than wood and thicker than cloth. Whenever the partitions were closed, the room became dark, insulated from the outside ruckus. I shared this room with two girls my age who also used iron lungs. The teenagers baffled and frightened us, and they had little interest in mere eight-year-olds, so we kept to ourselves. All three of us having been weaned, in part, from the iron lungs, we used them only at night. In the darkened room, the girls lay in their iron lungs with their long brown hair framing their heads against the pillows, dark auras surrounding their pale, sick-kid faces.

One day, I was poring over a map of Europe in an atlas propped on my bookstand. Leading an army across the continent and inflicting horrendous damages on the enemy, I was interrupted when a man in a white lab coat, presumably a doctor, approached me and asked in a British accent whether I could tell him where he was from. I pointed my mouthstick at the pink blob of England moored off the green French coast.

"No," he said, "down there," sticking his index finger near my chest. "South Africa."

I was astonished. Not only had I never known of white Africans, but also he spoke like an Englishman. He talked with the girls and me, asking us whether we would enjoy a reading from *The Wind in the Willows*. None of us had ever heard of the book, and we accepted his offer. For the next few months, Doctor Clarke came by five evenings a week to read to us in his serious, subdued voice. I never understood the plot of the book, but years later, when white South Africans were routinely denounced for their immorality, I remembered Doctor Clarke and his kindness.

As a result of physical therapy, my limbs had become more flexible. Then the doctors wanted to concentrate on straightening up my feet, which flopped down parallel to the mattress, as if I were pointing my toes. In order to improve my feet, one doctor put them in casts.

As my feet changed, the casts had to be remade. Every fortnight, I was taken to the cast room, a small, powdery-smelling place full of cabinets, with vials on every counter. I tried to be brave about it, telling the other children that I liked to "get it over with"—a heroic-sounding phrase I had probably learned from my father. Inside the room, the doctor, a genial Southerner, would wrap Ace bandages around each of my legs. Then a nurse would hold my calf and bend back my foot, according to the doctor's instructions. Then the doctor would slather on the wet, goopy plaster. Although the bending hurt, I managed to contain myself when the new casts were being put on.

But at the other end of the procedure, when the hard, old casts had to be cut off, I lost my composure. When the doctor turned on the buzz saw, vibrations shook my leg. Fearing that my flesh would be ripped to shreds at any second, I screamed, "No! No!"

The doctor looked at the nurse. "Have you ever seen such a fish?"

Instantly, I knew what he meant, even though I had never heard the word "fish" used that way. The doctor's tone said it meant "coward." Here he stood, holding the screaming buzz-saw a half inch from my flesh, lecturing me on my cowardice.

"You hate me!" I screamed, flipped out and enraged. "You're torturing me!"

The doctor bore my remarks with patience as he returned to cutting around my toes. "Someday, young man, you'll have to withstand serious pain, and you won't be prepared for it." His condescension seemed to prove that he enjoyed tormenting me.

Another doctor had another plan for correcting my floppy feet. He put them in permanent casts, which itched wickedly during the summer. Straps around the toes of these casts allowed the doctor to tighten and replaster the angle of my feet every two weeks.

As such experiments were run on the girls and me, we began to call ourselves "the guinea pigs." At one point, a box a little bigger than a pack of cigarettes was set near us. The box had about thirty holes, which corresponded to the keys of a typewriter. Given mouthsticks with styluses, we were told to practice typing by poking styluses in the holes. The practice book instructed us to type the combination E-D-F. So, E-D-F, E-D-F, I typed endlessly, bored and sore-necked, repeating the pattern for two weeks. After that, I refused to type anymore.

Also, we had to try impossibly elaborate page-turning devices. These were connected to ceiling projection gizmos, all operated with chin-side microswitches, that flashed the dim, gray words of books up on the dim, gray ceilings.

Because the doctors were trying to get us out of iron lungs, we had to test spacesuit-like respirators. I don't remember the proper name for the spacesuit, but it resembled a big plastic bag. We each lay inside a bag, with hard plastic cages arching over our chests. An external machine pumped air into and out of the bags, the air freezing us while the plastic bag made us feel sticky and hot. Whether the spacesuit worked as a respirator seemed beside the point. Being in it was unbearable. Hadn't anyone noticed this before? Or were we the first humans subjected to this?

Most weekdays, I went to the hospital's classroom. On a gurney, I would be surrounded by a dozen or so other patients in wheelchairs or three-wheeled wooden contraptions called go-carts. Two teachers tried to educate a roomful of kids ranging from eight to seventeen years old. This, of course, proved impossible. The teachers merely asked me questions about the books they had assigned to make sure I had read them. I always had read them; they were never hard, but neither were they memorable.

At the beginning of class, we had to say the Pledge of Allegiance and the Protestant version of the Lord's Prayer, which tacks onto the end of the prayer the doxology "for Thine is the kingdom and the power and the glory forever." My parents told me this version was the wrong one, but that they, too, had been forced to say it in the public schools when they were children. The teachers insisted they were carrying on the Protestant tradition of Massachusetts. I was confused by this clash of authorities but relieved a few years later by the Supreme Court's decision outlawing "voluntary" school prayer. I knew just how voluntary those prayers were. To this day, I wonder what satisfaction the religious right takes in forcing children to pray to a God they do not believe in.

That spring, for the first time in a year and a half, I began going outside regularly. In warm weather, nurses and orderlies pushed our beds and gurneys out to the big concrete deck so that we could join the patients in wheelchairs. I enjoyed the fresh air, the change of scene, and being with other patients. The teenagers' transistor radios blared "Itsy Bitsy Teeny Weeny Yellow Polka Dot Bikini," which always embarrassed me with its sexiness, especially when the teenaged boys started whistling and making wolf howls. On the other hand, the song "Tammy" always made me cry, especially the part where the hooty owl hooty-hoots from above. Best was when the radios played the games of the Boston Red Sox.

That summer, Nancy, a tall, salt-and-pepper-haired physical therapist, taught me the intricate rules of baseball, answering all the questions that had become important to me after Don Larsen had pitched his perfect game in the previous year's World Series. My father taped to my bed a 1957 Red Sox schedule printed on paper as thick and shiny as a milk carton. Nancy drew circles on the dates when the Red Sox won and X's on the dates when they lost. She said that it looked like a person winking after the Red Sox split a double header, but I never got her joke. I was only eight that summer, but I still remember the names of the players and that the Red Sox were in second place most of the season before slumping to a third-place finish. Ever since then, I've kept a baseball schedule taped to my bed or iron lung.

I spent fewer nights sleeping in the iron lung. Instead, I slept on my hospital bed with a green plastic respirator, which the girls and I called a "turtle shell," clamped to my chest. It wasn't comfortable, but neither had the iron lung been, with its foam rubber collars that dug into my neck. The turtle shell's gaskets left pink and red marks on my hips and sides. As with the spacesuit, the shell had a hose and a motor that pumped air in and out. But the respirator worked better and was more comfortable; I could spend a night with it on and feel invigorated the next morning.

As the summer of 1957 faded, I was allowed to spend weekends at home with my family. The girls and I spent fewer nights in our iron lungs and more nights in our hospital beds wearing the turtle shells. After I had shown that I could sleep well five nights of the week in the shell, the doctors decided I could leave. They told my parents they could transfer me to a nursing home.

My father looked into that possibility, but he found that the average life expectancy of a nursing home resident was eighteen months. So, after receiving training in how to take care of me, my parents brought me home in the fall of 1957.

I don't remember the names of the girls, and I never saw them again. My mother told me they both died a few years after I left.

3

Stoughton

(1957–1966)

While I was living those two years in hospitals, my father acquired two things—a car and a house. The car was a 1955 Chevrolet station wagon, blue, with a white roof and long red tail lights. My father and Karen enjoyed talking about the car, christened "Skyrocket," as though it were a horse. Starting the ignition, O'Bie would call, "Hi-ho, Skyrocket!" If the engine rumbled, Karen would say it was Skyrocket neighing for his oats. Increasing the vehicle's usefulness, O'Bie built a wooden rack to hold my ambulance cot in the rear of the wagon, so I wouldn't roll around.

The family had moved to an untrafficked, narrow street called Whitney Avenue, in Stoughton, about twenty miles south of Boston. Our new house, white with blue shutters, had a two-car garage and a half-acre lot of flat, grassy land. My father did a good deal of work on the house. He rebuilt the stone barbecue so that the wind would blow the smoke away from, not into, the chef's face. He poured new concrete stairs for the kitchen door. He planted trees, and, between the twin maples in front, he installed a sign that said, "Walter O'Brien, Notary Public," with a light that could be controlled from inside the house. Also, he added an exterior door and a ramp to my room, so I could go outdoors easily. Along with my room, the first floor had a kitchen, a TV room, and a formal sitting room, all of which I could be wheeled into.

The day I came home from the hospital, homemade signs all over the house said, "Welcome Home, Mark," and "Hello, Mark!" Liberated from the iron lung, restored to my family, I felt highly optimistic. My ability to move fingers and toes seemed to be improving fast: I got in the habit of calling out "NM!" whenever something twitched—"NM" being my medical-sounding abbreviation for "new movement." I was sure the NMs would accumulate until I became "all better," as all the polio kids in Children's Hospital wanted to be.

Upstairs were the other bedrooms and my father's office. O'Bie installed an intercom between my room and my parents' bedroom, saying that, if I ever wanted anything, I should "call room service." The first few days, I think I must have called room service a lot, because O'Bie and my mother then explained that it wasn't really room service, that that had been a joke—and that I should call only for emergencies. Embarrassed, I stopped thinking of the intercom as my special toy.

At that time, I didn't have to be in the iron lung; I could use a portable chest respirator at night. Around seven each morning, Helen would take it off me, put me into a home-sewn hospital gown, lift me onto the wheeled cot, and push me into the TV room. There, with my siblings, I would watch cartoons and *Laurel and Hardy*. Ken always had to leave for school around eight, but Karen, four years old, stayed home.

Karen was a quiet, placid child, very good and not as playful as Ken had been at her age. For long periods, she simply and stared at the TV, her blue eyes nearly hypnotized by the cartoons. While she wasn't wild fun, she was my main companion during the days, and I appreciated her company.

Around nine, my mother would take me back to my room, put me on the bed, and exercise me as the PTs had instructed. Each limb required several different exercises, such as bending the knee, pushing the foot back, curling the fingers, and so on. All in all, it took almost an hour, at the end of which I felt sore, tired, and resentful. She looked tired, too, but we never talked about how we felt, physically or any other way.

After that, she would wash me, set me on the bedpan, and clean me up. These events took about another hour, after which I could read, watch TV, or listen to the radio. Mainly, though, I liked to go outside.

Outside, after school hours, I watched Ken and the other boys play football, baseball, or "guns," a loosely defined game that featured plastic machine guns, our movie-garbled knowledge of World War II, and arguments over which boys had been shot dead. He would push my cot through the dense woods behind our house so that I could watch the battles, and, for my part, I cheered Ken on as loudly as I could.

Although I couldn't fully participate in these games, I enjoyed them and the companionship of the boys, who, though puzzled about how to include me, welcomed me with a simple warmth that I seldom sensed in adults. I knew that the boys must have seen commercials for the March of Dimes and other charities, ads that dramatized and played on the theme of the poor crippled child who could only look on from the sidelines as the other children played. I was embarrassed by such images, which I thought made other people see me as pitiful or sad. I never wanted to be perceived like that. Ken and the other boys were as creeped out by these ads as I was, and they did their best to counter them, treating me as a nonplaying equal.

During one battle of guns, Ken once snuck a derringer under my blankets. Later, at a key point in the fighting, while pretending to help me, he pulled out the gun and killed several Germans. Outraged, the dead Germans argued that Ken and I had violated their trust. After long negotiations—Ken sweating beneath his crew cut, his round face concerned and honest—it was decided that my cot and I were neutral territory and that any weapons found on me would be declared inoperative.

To get me to the vacant lot where the boys played baseball and football, my mother pushed my wheeled cot along a narrow dirt pathway. On one side of the path, a barbed wire fence marked the edge of the Ruperts' property. On the other side lay the wooden fence around Mrs. Wankoski's garden. It would have been much easier for my mother to push me through Mrs. Wankoski's lawn, but our neighbor didn't want anyone going on her property.

The vacant lot, high with yellow grass, stretched three acres to Morton Street. Untended and unmowed, the grass and weeds grew wild and tall. There, the boys played "baseball" with baseballs, softballs, tennis balls, or whatever was available, but without a catcher, because no one had a catcher's mask. The batters derided the pitchers for not throwing the ball high enough for them to hit, but, even so, without a catcher, scores were astronomical.

Sometimes my father joined the game, as did Chuck Yost, the father of our friends Charlie and Rich. When it was their turn to bat, Chuck and O'Bie could blast the ball clear to Morton Street, amazing us with their power.

Despite the neighborly feeling in our new home, we had not left bullies or bullying behind. Charlie Yost, the oldest boy in the neighborhood, dominated the others, regularly beating them up. He was strong and overconfident, but, whenever I argued with him, usually after he had beaten up Ken, he responded with uncomfortable restraint. I could tell that he wanted to hit me, too, but his sense of fair play prevented him. Like the other boys, Charlie had a deep sense of what was fair and what was not fair. Although sometimes they fought physically, the boys resolved most arguments by talking about the dispute in terms of fairness.

We admired and envied Charlie's father. Chuck Yost, dark, hairy, and muscular, had served in the army during World War II and had been shot in the right hand by a German bullet. He sons boasted that if the bullet had entered their father's flesh merely an inch to the left, the hand would have been paralyzed. The thought of big Chuck Yost having a useless hand horrified me. How could he have worked at the shoe factory or smashed those homers with only one hand? Knowing how bad paralysis was, I was glad that it hadn't happened to him.

Next door to us lived the Tolivers, whose backyard was overgrown with ratty grass and old cars, one of them a Model T. A stone wall of unknown age ran along behind our land and the Tolivers', but a big tree interrupted the wall, making a gap through which Ken could maneuver my cot. To the south lay the woods, where the going was rough. An old house stood on this wooded property, but no one knew whether anyone lived there. Naturally, tales abounded that it was haunted. It may have been: after all, everyone knew that the Stoughton gold mine was haunted by the ghosts of Indians, who had been worked to death by English settlers in the seventeenth century.

To the west of the Tolivers' property and the woods lay Avery's field, an immense pasture populated by cows. I seldom went into the pasture, because it was fenced off by barbed wire, but the cows created considerable diversion. Ken and I always joked about how dumb they were. Then one day a truck came and parked on Morton Street to deliver a cow to Avery, and somehow the cow got loose and ran down the hill, into our yard. Amused, Helen grabbed hold of my hospital bed, wheeling it around so that I could see out the door. In her excitement, Helen knocked the light off the wall.

"Can you see her?" Helen asked. "She's heading for the pool! Oh, this is a riot."

I didn't get to see the cow. Three men leaped from the truck, according to Helen's play-by-play, and ran after the cow, which surrendered peacefully. The men escorted her back to the truck and delivered her, I suppose, to Avery's field.

In 1958, the Stoughton public school sent out a teacher to work with me. Pearl came two or three times a week; unlike later teachers, her only job was to teach children who were unable to attend school. She taught me fourth through seventh grades. For all those years, she encouraged me both academically and personally: she praised my schoolwork and laughed at my jokes. I looked forward to seeing her and telling her all my news, whether it was relatively big, like the cow, or something as minor as my sighting of a dust devil in the Yosts' unpaved driveway. Whatever I offered, Pearl responded enthusiastically.

In 1959, Helen and O'Bie began talking about and planning "a trip to Canada," which I assumed would be a pleasant vacation, our first one. My parents drove us in Skyrocket to Sainte-Anne-de-Beaupré, just east of Quebec City, where we stayed four days in a motel beside a highway.

Being in a motel was an adventure in itself. We could watch the trucks roar by on the highway, or look with distaste at the Saint Lawrence Seaway, running low and muddy that summer. The television enchanted me at first, with its French channel and its English channel, but the French was incomprehensible and the English one soon grew boring. Touring around, we could see brightly painted houses, unusual restaurants, Mounties in red jackets, and, most impressive, Canadians who switched effortlessly from speaking French to English. I slept in a double bed with Ken, my turtle shell chest respirator strapped on me, while Karen slept in our parents' room. I felt like a regular kid on a family trip.

Then, on our second day, we went to the cathedral.

The Cathedral of Sainte-Anne-de-Beaupré is an immense Gothic church constructed of heavy gray stone. It towers over the Quebec landscape as its predecessors towered over the countryside in France: awesome and domineering.

After getting me, on my cot, out of Skyrocket, my parents pushed me up one of the wide ramps that led to the interior of the cathedral. Until then I had never seen ramps on a public building, but they seemed like a good idea. Inside, a golden statue of Saint Anne, the mother of the Blessed Virgin Mary, spread her hands in blessing. Signs in several languages forbade the use of cameras. Photographers flashed.

Then I saw why we had come: one huge wall was covered with casts, wheelchairs, canes, crutches, braces, walkers, and all the paraphernalia of disability. Helen whispered to me that disabled people came here from all over the world to seek a miracle from the saint. I suppose that my parents hadn't told me the reasons for the trip before because they hadn't wanted to embarrass me. But then they told me that we could seek the saint's intervention by attending Mass in the cathedral and by applying the holy water to me after we returned home.

Shame, embarrassment, and feelings of worthlessness overwhelmed me during mass. That all these priests, nuns, and other strangers should pray for me, that my parents understood my suffering and were trying to alleviate it, that all this energy should be expended on me, a boy who swore, lied, hated, and sinned as much as any other boy, seemed too much. I cried. I couldn't speak. Helen said I must be exhausted, and we went back to the motel.

The next day, we attended another mass. Angry that I had not yet cured myself, I began to feel that I would never get all better, that I had failed already, that I would never be able to please Helen and O'Bie with one of those "Look!-No-crutches" scenes from the March of Dimes ads. Again, I cried through mass, speechless and confused. Two days later, we went back home.

The statues of Saint Anne we had bought were placed on top of the intercom, and the holy water was stashed in my bureau. O'Bie never touched it, but, from time to time, Helen got out the holy water and dabbed it onto my chest, arms, and forehead in a cruciform pattern. She seemed embarrassed about applying the water, as though she doubted its efficacy. While she put it on, I lay and prayed, despairing and hoping at the same time. As time wore on, Helen applied the holy water less and less frequently, until it stayed in the bureau, a relic of how Catholics behaved before the second Vatican Council.

Later that summer, on a real vacation, we went to Revere Beach, in Massachusetts, and stopped at an amusement park that featured a small roller coaster. Karen and Ken jumped aboard, and I looked hard, hoping there would be a way that I, too, could somehow ride it. There was no way, but the man who ran the place took pity on me and gave me two enormous stuffed animals. One was a teddy bear I never paid much attention to, but the other, a Dalmatian, became the center of my fantasy life.

Ken and I played with the Dalmatian, which we named Happy, in the same way O'Bie played with our toys, making voices and improvising skits. Happy loved fleas and ran a chain of businesses ranging from Lousy Clothes (featuring the jingle "Buy your clothes at Lousy Clothes cuz Lousy Clothes makes lousy clothes") to the Flea-B-S Television Network. Ken also did a schtick about dogshit, which I found funny, but it upset O'Bie, and he forbade any more scatological humor.

In the fall of 1959, the Stoughton public school system instituted an experiment with home instruction by placing speakerphones in my bedroom and in a fifth-grade classroom at Jones Elementary School. I listened in for two hours each day, sometimes participating by talking, and I did the same homework as the other students. The sound quality was terrible—I could hear only the teacher and the kids in the first row. The students couldn't hear me well, either, but I did become associated with the class, and I got to know some other students and occasionally went to their houses to visit.

This two-year school experiment lasted two years and culminated with the sixth grade graduation party, held in a big house that belonged to one student's parents. The kids put on a series of songs and comic sketches on the porch, while those who weren't in the show watched from the lawn below. The closing number featured two boys and a girl singing "Ain't She Sweet," at the end of which the boys chased the girl off the porch. It seemed significant to me that, as teenage lust was setting in on us eleven- and twelve-year-olds, it was publicly demonstrated and accepted in the adult ceremony of the graduation.

The wiring of the new junior high school made it impossible to install a speakerphone, so the graduation ceremony marked the end of the interactive school experiment. This explanation about the phone seems implausible now, but at the time I didn't question it. Although I hadn't liked the racket the speakerphone made, I was disappointed at losing one more link to real life and other kids.

But I gained a new connection to real life in 1960, when a Boston Irishman my father's age, our guy Kennedy, won the Democratic nomination for president. One morning that summer, I was lying in the vacant lot where the boys played baseball, doing nothing and wearing a Kennedy-for-President clip attached to my sunglasses. I was also wearing a wool knit hat. Rich Yost, an enthusiastic Republican and the brother of the neighborhood bully, walked up and pulled my hat down over my glasses so that no one would see the Kennedy clip. When Helen came to get me, I told her what had happened. She complained to Rich's mother, and the next day Rich apologized, leaving me unharmed but newly aware of the consequences of political affiliation.

On election day, I stayed up all night, watching the twelve-inch Admiral television O'Bie had given me that summer. At midnight, Helen came into my room, yawning, and said, "Don't you want to go to sleep yet?" But I didn't go to sleep until one o'clock, my left eye sore from staring at the screen, and the election still undecided. I was fascinated by the succession of states' results, reported one by one. The candidate who won the most popular votes in a state won all that state's votes in the electoral college. It seemed like a gigantic game of Monopoly, with the country as the playing board. Kennedy took most of the eastern states early that night, but Nixon later won enough Midwestern and western votes to make it close. The election wasn't settled until four the next morning, when Illinois reported a narrow win for Kennedy and lifted him over the top.

In those years, my sister, Karen, never seemed happy: I don't remember her laughing much, and O'Bie was her only playmate. He would set her on his knee and sing.

> Pony girl,
> Pony girl,
> Won't you be my pony girl?
> Way out west, way out west,
> Way out west we'll go.
> Giddy-yup, giddy-yup, giddy-yup, whoa!
> My pony girl!

While singing, he bounced her up and down and laughed. Her long hair—down to her elbow—swung in the lamplight. She looked pleased, but her blue eyes never got light and shiny like most children's.

At Christmas in 1960, she seemed especially glum, despite O'Bie's best efforts. I assumed that she had found out the truth about Santa Claus, but even after Christmas she stayed low-spirited. O'Bie and Helen took her for treatment to a hospital in Brockton, where the doctors said that Karen had pneumonia. She was admitted, and, over the next week, more news reached us in terrible flashes: she was in an oxygen tent—she was unconscious—her stomach had collapsed.

On a Sunday afternoon, Ken and I were watching television, and our parents were in my father's office upstairs. We heard the phone ring, and my father answered it, and then we heard O'Bie screaming—a terrible, terrifying howl that I will never forget.

He and Helen ran downstairs, thumping loudly and fast, both of them flushed. I was frightened, because of the scream and because my parents never ran. Then O'Bie told us that Karen had died. The news was beyond terrible: I was shocked and sad, and it was frightening to see my parents so powerless.

That day was January 8, 1961, about two months before what would have been her eighth birthday. Twelve days later, Kennedy was inaugurated as president, but I could not feel happy, and I found his speech wooden and gimmicky. One of the many troubling aspects to Karen's death was that I couldn't forget that the last time I'd seen my sister, I had fought with her. She had stormed out of my room, slamming the door.

When I had first come home, in 1957, Ken and Karen had quarreled constantly. Initially, I sided with Karen, but later I supported Ken. I enjoyed making my sister cry, perhaps because she was thin and weak. Perhaps hurting her made me feel bigger and stronger than she. I enjoyed the rush of power when she got that look of utter despair people get when their last friend betrays them. Of course, I was only a child and had no idea what I was doing. Still, after her death, I blamed myself.

I often wonder what Karen would have been like had she grown into a woman. Would she have forgiven me? If she had, would I have noticed or cared? Or would I have dismissed her love as the irrelevant outpourings of a weird kid sister? And if she and I had grown closer in those years she never lived, would I then have fallen in love with so many women with straight, dark hair? I wonder whether I would have spent so many years searching for Karen's forgiveness in every woman's eyes, her love in every woman's smile.

At the time of Karen's death, my father was working three jobs. As an investigator for the California Industrial Accident Board, he carried a badge in a leather pouch, which impressed me. On the weekends, he

did legal work privately and sold real estate for his old law school pal,
Ray Hodge.

Ray stood about six foot eight, weighed 260 pounds, and had a
cigar butt burning in his mouth at all times. A realtor and occasional
member of the state legislature, Ray introduced my father to the
Stoughton ruling class, which consisted of a dozen men: lawyers, car
salesmen, and realtors who had fought in World War II and who now
drank Miller together and took their wives dancing in the American
Legion hall.

O'Bie bought a lot of things after Karen died, including a car,
another blue-and-white Chevrolet station wagon. It was new, and my
ambulance cot fit well into the back of it, but nobody felt like giving
the vehicle a pet name.

Also, O'Bie bought and had installed an above-ground swimming
pool. I think he thought it would be good for me, relaxing and stim-
ulating, if I could learn to enjoy the water. Trying to teach me to float,
O'Bie stood in the pool with his arms underneath my head, promis-
ing to save me if I began to sink. "Just relax," he said.

Terrified, I sank every time. O'Bie would catch me before I could go
far, and hand me over to Helen, out of the pool.

Although I couldn't float unassisted, we had three inflatable rafts.
The two pink-and-white striped ones seemed flimsy. But the dark
green raft was heavy canvas, and I laid claim to it whenever I was in
the pool. Quite happily, I would float around on it all afternoon, one
foot dangling in the water. Ken and I developed a sort of daredevil
act—he would jump off the ladder over me, somersault in the air,
and splash into the water. One afternoon, he misjudged the dive, his
foot caught the canvas raft, and I was nearly knocked into the water.
O'Bie, angry and perhaps frightened, ordered that there be no more
horseplay whenever I was in the pool. I said I didn't want to go in
anymore if people couldn't play. We compromised; I'd go in the pool
when Ken and his friends weren't around.

I liked it when Ken lent me his *Mad* magazines. Not only did *Mad*
make me laugh, but also it offered the only critique of American
white-bread culture that I knew. Corporations were skewered for their
greed and vague names ("Organization Systems Enterprises"), while
the president was lampooned in a comic strip called "The Tonight
Show Starring Jack Kennedy." Unfortunately, my supply of *Mad*s was
cut off after the magazine ran a plain black cover with the sentence

"Some magazines try to exploit sex, but we at *Mad* never do this." Most of the words were in small white letters, but the word "sex" screamed in mammoth pink. No more *Mad* in this house, pronounced O'Bie. Ken continued to read this forbidden literature on the sly, but I had no sly. Everything I read was set up by my parents and obvious to all.

Despite my mother's best efforts at physical therapy and the satisfactions of a relatively normal family life, my health was deteriorating. Every other month or so, I would suddenly start throwing up and having diarrhea. My parents would cart me back to Children's Hospital, where the nurses would put me in an iron lung and stick an IV in my arm. On one such visit, in 1960, the doctors decided that the turtle shell was no longer effective. Using the shell, I had not been breathing adequately during sleep, and my resulting weakness left me susceptible to every infection that strayed my way, so they sent an iron lung home with me. Consequently, I became sick less often, but going back to the iron lung felt like a defeat. My traveling would be limited, and my neck would be continually sore, gouged by the lung's rubber collar.

At home, my schooling continued. Mr. Rice, a quiet, bespectacled man, taught me history from ninth through eleventh grades. When I asked him why we spent so much time studying the Greeks, he showed me a map of the Middle East and launched into a lecture. "You see how civilization began with the Semitic peoples of Egypt and the Tigris-Euphrates River valleys. The Greeks took what had been developed by them and magnified it, intensified it a thousandfold. Since that time, the Semitic peoples have stagnated, and the Great White Race has carried forth the work of civilization. We of the Great White Race must study our tradition so that we might continue the work of civilization."

Such ideas seemed suspect and weird, but I didn't outwardly object. Having seen maps of medieval African kingdoms in my historical atlas, I suspected he was exaggerating the importance of the GWR However, I was afraid to argue with him or even to question him further, because I was a kid and he was an adult, I the student, he the teacher.

Further, I was sure the GWR would soon destroy itself and everyone else in a game of nuclear ping-pong. I just wondered when this disaster would happen. Sometimes I thought it would be nice if it happened during the day: that way, I could be out in the front yard, see the contrail of the Soviet missile, and watch the giant mushroom cloud sprout to the northeast, where Boston had once been. But would I actually see it? Wouldn't I be blinded by the flash? At other times, I wanted the bomb to hit us late at night. Then the house would be knocked down and set afire, so we would all die quickly. Sometimes it seemed that the best thing would be for O'Bie to build us a fall-out shelter. We could all burrow down, like Dorothy in her tornado shelter in *The Wizard of Oz*. Afterward, we could be pioneers and restart civilization. Except that I'd be dead, of course. Such images and worries kept me constantly depressed.

Not believing anyone could survive a nuclear war, my parents never heeded Kennedy's call for a fallout shelter in every home. They thought that he was hysterical and that he was encouraging hysteria.

During the Cuban missile crisis, it seemed that my horrific fantasies might be realized. Mr. Rice and my mother often talked about the Soviet ships steaming toward Cuba, wondering whether they would fight their way through the naval blockade Kennedy had ordered.

"I don't understand why the Russians would do such a stupid thing," Helen said.

"It's a troubling situation, certainly, Mrs. O'Brien," my teacher replied. "The Russians are a great-souled people, but sometimes that very quality gets them in too deep. I wouldn't become overly concerned, though. Cooler heads will prevail."

One evening, after O'Bie had come home from his new job as an army lawyer, I heard Helen say, "Oh, Walter, how could you drive home during a disaster like that?"

I pictured O'Bie, jaunty, checking out the traffic reports and deftly steering the station wagon around collapsed bridges and burning trucks on Route 128. Just another bitch of a commute. His optimism struck me as absurd, and, for the first time, I thought of him as foolish. Did he really think he could just drive home and take care of everything?

Besides worrying about the state of the world, I always had polio to deal with. Twice a year, my parents took me to Children's Hospital for checkups. I dreaded these visits, afraid that a doctor would order me back into the hospital. On the days of the appointments, I would pretend to sleep late, then whine and try to delay, but Helen always got me out of bed, dressed and ready to go, on time.

My appointment of June 1962 confirmed my fears. The doctor wanted me turned over. I hated to lie on my belly, because the position makes it hard to breathe well. But of course I was turned for examination. The doctor ran his cold finger down my crooked spine, grunted, and said that I had to have a spinal fusion operation by Christmas.

I didn't go in for the surgery until the new year—my parents kept me out for one more holiday. Shortly before I was admitted, O'Bie told me that Helen, then thirty-six, was six months pregnant and that he didn't want her to lift me anymore. I hadn't known she was pregnant. If I had known, I would have tried not to have her pick me up, but she had always seemed happy to lift me or to wheel me and the cot outside. I went to the hospital for the surgery in January 1963, when I was thirteen years old.

Children's Hospital had shut down the Wellesley Convalescent Hospital and moved the patients to the little two-story hospital next door to it, the House of the Good Samaritan. Good Sam had two big rooms, one for little kids, the other for teenagers. I had the bad luck to be assigned to the room with the little kids, six or seven of them, mostly younger than I.

One of the little kids had an autographed picture of President Kennedy. His mother knew one of the president's aides, who had asked him to sign the picture. Although the autograph was illegible except for the boy's name, the owner bragged that it said, "To my good friend Terry Donahue, from John Kennedy." I was amazed that such a spoiled-rotten kid as Terry could have such a prize.

Overlooking the ward was a big pewter relief statue of the baby Jesus. Jesus stood over a twenty-one-inch TV, which presided spiritually over the room. On the big TV, we took turns picking the channels. One boy had his own little color TV set, the first I'd ever seen. On it I tried to watch a launch of one of the Mercury space shots, but the picture was terrible.

Besides having TV for entertainment, we were visited a few times a week by a volunteer who came to sing and to play her guitar. I especially loved hearing her play "Scarlet Ribbons," with its beautiful melody and lyrics. The song was about a parent who overhears a child's prayer for red hair ribbons, which appear out of nowhere the next morning. I wanted to believe that faith would be rewarded and that miracles could and did interrupt the predictability of life. I wanted the surgery to work.

The morning of my operation, I felt brave going in. While I was under anesthesia, the surgeons took out sections of bone from my arms and legs and put the pieces on my lower spine, where it curved. The curvature of my spine, called scoliosis, makes it hard for me to breathe and impossible to sit up straight. The surgeons also put an iron rod down my spine to straighten it, in hopes that I could sit up enough to use a wheelchair.

When I came out of surgery, seeing stars on the acoustic ceiling tiles, I wondered if I was dead. My right leg was in a cast, and I was in terrible pain; it felt as if the bones had been beaten to powder. Everything hurt, especially when I was lifted. Back in the little kids' room, I felt miserable, and time passed very slowly.

When I was getting better, I could be lifted onto the gurney to go to the big kids' room, which featured a poster, about three feet tall, of the president. I'd gaze up at it. It is difficult to explain now how much we all loved him. It wasn't just the Irish who adored him, but everyone in eastern Massachusetts. He was everything desirable, and he was one of us. His murder later that year shocked me. Not only was it sad, it was so unbelievable. Kennedy was life; how could he die?

My grandfather, Pop, visited me often. Although I would offer him a chair, he chose to stand, hands in his pockets, lips tight, staring into space. Sometimes we wouldn't say anything for twenty or thirty minutes, but his presence comforted me. After retiring from the police force, he had started working as a bank guard at a place that happened to be near the hospital, so he could come almost every day. He didn't visit so often just because it was convenient, though—I felt that Pop really cared about me.

One day he brought a *Saturday Evening Post* with Bing Crosby on the cover, and a nurse said that Pop's eyes looked like Bing's, blue and kind. He was always very well dressed in pearly gray suits. Although he'd been a cop, he looked more like a banker or professor.

I admired him and longed to talk to him, but I couldn't, because everything I thought of embarrassed me. "What was the house like when you were a young man?" Or "What was it like to be in the police force during the Depression?" Everything I thought of sounded like something a character on a dopey TV show would ask his grandpa. Also, we might also violate the family code against shows of emotion.

What if something terrible had happened to him? I knew he had been assaulted twice; perhaps he was still vengeful and bitter about those incidents, or for some other reason wouldn't want to talk about them. There was so much not to talk about: for instance, no one in my family had ever talked about my being paralyzed, except regarding practical, immediate concerns such as who would put me to bed or wash me. We never discussed how being paralyzed had affected me emotionally, or how it would affect my future as a student, worker, or a human being. But Pop visited me, and it helped.

During my recovery from surgery, I got on a gurney every day so that I could be pushed around the hospital. In the evenings, volunteers would take me through the halls. I liked going into the chapel, where it was dark and quiet.

Every afternoon, all the kids had to try to nap, whether we wanted to or not. We all hated it. The nurses would turn me on my belly, and I'd lie in the solarium, trying to breathe. Although they could see that I was suffering, the nurses always followed the doctors' orders, and the doctors had decreed that I be turned over. Usually the pressure on the front of my head would cause me to black out. After about an hour, the nurses would come and flop me over, the gown stuck to my chest with sweat.

Although I was coming around from unconsciousness, I didn't feel bad; in fact, I felt pretty good, but I didn't know why. Sometimes the nurses made jokes about my erections, saying things like, "Looks like someone's been having a good time," but I didn't figure out what they meant till years later.

Late in March, I was discharged and sent home with a plaster cast on my back. Although the doctors had considered putting a cast over my chest, they were afraid that it would restrict my breathing. The only time I could be out of the back cast was when I was on the bedpan or on my belly. The cast lining was scratchy, so Helen put in one of O'Bie's old t-shirts to soften it.

Shortly after I got home, my mother went into the hospital to give birth. I tried to think of names for the new baby, which my mother felt would be a girl. "Brenda" and "Phyllis" seemed nice to me; however, my mother named her Rachel.

Once we were all back home, Helen was able to take care of me and my new baby sister. I don't know how. She did a good job; I never felt neglected, and Rachel tells me she never did either.

In 1965, the army needed a lawyer in Sacramento, so O'Bie decided we would move there. We got some California newspapers and talked often of the move, but the place didn't seem real.

On New Year's Eve, my parents invited in everyone they knew, including Ray, my father's brothers whom he hadn't seen in years, all my mother's relatives, Pop, Grandma, and the neighbors across the street. It was my parents' farewell party, and it went until late. I stayed up, too, in my room, having haphazard conversations with half-drunk adults who wandered in to see me as I lay listening to Jean Shepherd on WOR. Two weeks after the party, we left Stoughton.

4

The Move

(January–April 1966)

The plan was simple. My parents would put me into Good Sam while they drove with Ken and Rachel out west to Sacramento, and then I would be brought to the new house later. Afraid of change, I did not particularly want to move to California, but I looked forward to being reunited with the family in a week or two.

Before I left, the students at Stoughton High School voted to give me a school pennant and a letter, like the ones athletes wore on their jackets, an orange "S" with black trim. This gesture surprised me, since I didn't know anyone at the high school except my teachers. But I knew the neighbors, my parents' family and some of my cousins, and I knew the geography and history of the area. It was my home, and I had the sense that Massachusetts was the center of the universe. I couldn't imagine living anywhere else.

Helen and I went through my belongings, deciding what to take and what not to take. When she held up Happy, my old stuffed Dalmatian, she said, "You don't want this, do you?" By then, Happy was torn and dirty, and I hadn't played with him in years, so I agreed to let him go, along with an old stuffed lizard and many other toys. Also I threw out all my board games—Risk, Monopoly and the rest—because I never played with them.

One morning in January 1966, O'Bie and Ken lifted me in my hospital cot into the car. As we drove up narrow Whitney Avenue and turned the corner of Morton Street, I could see the house with the blue shutters receding, and I knew I'd never see it again.

It felt strange being at the House of Good Sam when I wasn't sick.

Again, Pop came to visit me almost every day after he got off work. He generously brought me magazines: *Time, Newsweek,* and *U.S. News and World Report.* Although I seldom had time to read all three magazines, I enjoyed reading about national politics and world affairs, and I liked the book and movie reviews.

In the hospital, I thought the other teenage boys were showoffs and jerks. They wolf-whistled at the nurses, pretending to be wildly attracted to them. I wondered why they were doing such bizarre things to these women, especially since the nurses were there to take care of us. One boy always said, whenever he met a new nurse, "How tall are you?" She'd say five-seven or whatever, and he'd say, "I didn't know they stacked them that high, ha ha ha."

Once a week we were shown a movie; one was a Jerry Lewis film in which the opening credits rolled over a background of a fan dancer. At the end of the credits, she pulled the fans apart, and the words "Directed and Produced by Jerry Lewis" covered her more interesting parts. One of the boys shrieked, "Wow! Rewind the film!" He insisted on seeing it again, on the off chance that, the next time, she would be completely naked. Amazingly, the volunteer did rewind it. At such times, I felt as if the other boys were having a contest to see who could act the most mindlessly horny.

My father had gotten me a book on reproduction from the library. It was very detailed at the microbiological level, but I couldn't figure out how the semen moved from the male organs to the female organs. A friend of my brother's filled us in on the macrobiological level, although he had the wrong orifice in mind. My brother giggled, but he clapped his hand over the other boy's mouth, saying, "We're not supposed to talk about that."

Two or three evenings a week, Mr. Grey, my English teacher, came to visit and instruct me. He had taught me at home during eighth grade, and during one of those home visits Helen had asked him whether he had a girlfriend. He had said, "Ahh, women aren't attracted to horse-faced guys like me." In fact, he did have a long face, with locks of wheat-colored hair falling on his forehead like a mane. He was gawky-looking, and his long, straight teeth made him look solemn.

Now that he was coming to the hospital to teach me tenth grade, he asked me to call him Pete instead of Mr. Grey. I felt awkward doing so at first, but his casual, bemused attitude soon made it easy for me. For some reason, we got along much better the second time he was my teacher.

I am grateful to him because he first got me interested in Shakespeare. For instance, he had me memorize speeches from *Macbeth:*

Tomorrow and tomorrow and tomorrow
creeps in this petty pace from day to day
to the last syllable of recorded time.
And all our yesterdays have but lit fools the way to dusty death ...

Mr. Grey talked about how the speech reflected Macbeth's despair, and he asked me whether I ever felt that way. Sometimes I did.

Both of us loved *Macbeth* for its language. I'd always been daunted by Shakespeare because the words and poetry seemed so difficult, and it seemed like such an adult thing, something over my head. But I found that I needed only to master a few archaisms and read the footnotes. I loved hearing Pete read, in his resonant tenor. He read with conviction, and, when he finished, he would ask me how I felt about that passage.

He offered to teach me the Greek alphabet, saying I had a fine mind and I should use it. We started with Alpha, Beta, Gamma. One evening, as I was trying to recite Lambda, Mu, Nu, a nurse brought in the supper tray.

"I'll feed him," he said. After she left, Pete surveyed the food. "Lord, this stuff is worse than McDonald's."

"What's McDonald's?"

"You never heard of McDonald's?" he asked, twisting up his eyebrows. "All the kids go to McDonald's after school to inhale these little greaseburgers and grease-fried potatoes. You've never been to McDonald's? I bet they have McDonald's in California. Let's see if we can get you to Omega before your mind is ruined by your first greaseburger."

Later that day, he said, "Tell you what. Chilson and I were going to drive out to Colorado this summer to see his family. Why don't we just drive on out to Sacramento to see you and your folks?"

I thought that was a good idea, though I was surprised to learn that he was friends with Chilson, the Catholic priest who once a week came to see me.

Pop gave me the news that my parents, brother, and sister had arrived in Sacramento eight days after they left. They were relaying information to me through Pop because it was difficult for me to use the hospital telephone. Its massive headset, of the kind Lily Tomlin would later make infamous, squeezed my head like an iron brace. Also, the nurses hated our using the phone, because they had to stand by the patient, doing nothing during the call.

The week after my family's arrival, Pop told me they'd rented a house and had been calling the March of Dimes every day to get an iron lung. O'Bie's plan was to have the air force fly me out to McClellan Air Force Base in Sacramento as soon as the iron lung was delivered to our new house. He had arranged this with the air force; as a federal employee, he was entitled to do so.

Weeks went by, and nothing happened. Pop kept saying that they still hadn't received the iron lung. Though I didn't know what was going on, I suspected that the March of Dimes was screwing up. After all, the March had practically disowned the disease, saying that it had "conquered polio" when the vaccine was released. Now it was raising money to fight birth defects and had dropped all mention of polio from its advertising—also, I assumed, it had dropped iron lungs.

Iron lungs have never had great PR, since they are heavy, ugly, and unwieldy. Even the cutest kid does not look like a poster child in an iron lung. For the most part, the only lungs still in use are descendants of the ones developed in the 1920s and 1930s, which were first used successfully in the Children's Hospital in Boston.

Finally, I decided to call Jim Westover, who hosted a talk show on WEEI at 7:30 P.M. In that short time after the show began and before I had to go into the lung, around eight o'clock, I called and complained to Westover that, for want of an iron lung delivery, I was stuck in Good Sam while my parents were in Sacramento. A few minutes later, a nurse said the hospital was getting a lot of phone calls about me. One was from a man who offered to let me call my parents using his credit card. I hadn't talked to them since they left, so I phoned them, and my parents told me how upset they were with the March of Dimes. Every time they called, the chief of the Sacramento office of the March promised that my parents would get the iron lung any day, but nothing happened.

The following day, one of the nurses told me that the March of Dimes had called to say that it would get an iron lung to my parents within twenty-four hours. Impressed by my power and by the power of the media, I wished that I had phoned Westover sooner. The nurse also told me that there would be a representative of the March on the Westover show that night to defend its reputation. This caused me a good deal of excitement. I certainly wanted to hear people talk about me on the show, but the Westover show came on at 8:05 P.M., while Jean Shepherd was on another station at 8:15. I was in an agony of indecision.

I loved Shepherd's forty-five-minute monologues about growing up in Indiana. His gleeful tales of the anarchy of boyhood made me laugh, and they offered a sharp critique of the failings of adults. Shepherd's spiels, conveyed in his confiding, just-you-and-me-buddy tone, demonstrated the power of radio to put stories right in your head. Soon, I would be leaving for California, where I thought I might never hear this artist of radio again. So, that night, I listened to Jean Shepherd. But Pop told me that the March of Dimes man had caught hell from Westover's callers.

My Grandma came to visit, and she told me I would be going to California in two days. It was the last time I would see her. The day before I left, I received a farewell gift: the nurses had chipped in and bought me Arthur Schlesinger Jr.'s book about Kennedy, *A Thousand Days*. I was very moved by their gesture and their awareness of my interest.

An ambulance took me to Westover Air Force Base, where a crew from Channel Five filmed my departure. I was put in a propeller plane that had carried soldiers back from Vietnam and to military hospitals throughout the United States. The plane disappointed me: it went only about 250 miles an hour, and it was tiny—you could see the walls of the fuselage curve in, because the plane was only about ten or twelve feet across.

The air force nurses flying with me offered me a choice: I could lie on a stretcher that was attached to the wall so that I could see out the window, or I could be put in a Huxley respirator that lay on the floor. Though the Huxley was smaller and less comfortable than an iron lung, it was portable, supposedly—if there were four very strong people to do the lifting. The Huxley collar hurt a lot, so during the flight I mostly stayed in the stretcher. A nurse offered me lunch—a pastrami on rye sandwich with pickles. It was my first taste of rye bread, and I liked it. We stopped for the night at Scott Air Force Base, east of Saint Louis. The nurses carried the Huxley, me inside it, out of the airplane, down a flight of stairs, and into a bus that had had the back removed. The bus ferried me to a base hospital, where medics took me down a long ward with room for about forty beds, most of them empty. The loneliness of the place added to the strangeness I felt at being in a part of the country I'd never visited before and in being so far from either home, on either coast. Despite the novelty of flying and the new sensations, I was frightened. I was two thousand miles from my parents, in the company of strangers, and utterly dependent on them.

The few other patients were watching a big color TV, and I couldn't sleep that night. The collar was bothering me, and the nurses, fooling with it, kept me awake.

The next morning, they loaded the Huxley back in the airplane, and I stayed in the respirator more than I had the previous day. That leg of the trip was twice the length of the first, and it felt longer because it took so long to cross the big western states. Lunch was the only break from the loud monotony of flying, and I relished each bite. Lying in the little plane, buzzing above the landscape, I thought about and admired the patience of the early western settlers, who had needed two weeks to cross these states in ox-drawn wagons.

I wanted so much to get to Sacramento, but it was not until late afternoon that we landed at McClellan Air Force Base, north of the city. After the plane taxied to a stop, my family climbed aboard. Rachel looked much older than she had three months earlier. Walking and talking, she seemed much more like a child, less like an infant. She smiled and chirped how happy she was to see me. They all were, and I was comforted to see them after three months of separation.

I was loaded into an air force ambulance, which followed my family's station wagon to the house they had rented in the suburb of Orangevale. Upon arrival, I was put on the ambulance cot I'd always used, which seemed safe and comfortable. Our new home impressed me—a big ranch house with pastel interiors, air conditioning, and, in every room, built-in radios that doubled as intercoms. My parents invited the air force nurses who had flown with me to join them for coffee and pastries. Both nurses were black. I had never seen my parents entertain black people in their home before, and I thought it might be awkward for them, so I thought they must have been very glad to have me home. I was very glad to be there.

5

Sacramento

(1966–1976)

In his teen years, my brother Ken spouted Ambrose Bierce–isms. My favorite was "If I owned Hell and Texas, I'd live in Hell and rent out Texas." That was how I felt about Sacramento. Flat, hot, and yellow, Sacramento was the opposite of four-season Boston, with its green, rolling hills. In our new home in California, there weren't many trees around—certainly no old trees—no old buildings, and no ocean within reasonable reach.

After I arrived, the first problem we encountered was where to put the iron lung. It was too big to fit through the hallway that led to the bedrooms, and my parents didn't want the lung in the living room. They decided that I would spend the days in Rachel's room on my hospital bed, and at night commute to the iron lung in the garage. My father sealed off the front door of the garage, but, aside from that, it was your basic garage, with a concrete floor, wooden walls, no insulation, and no ceiling.

I didn't mind sleeping in the garage so much as taking the trips back and forth. Every evening, my parents would push me on a cot to the end of the house, where a door led to the garage. It had two deep stairs, and, while my parents tried to carry me down, Rachel always insisted on "helping," which meant holding onto the cot and actually tipping it sideways. Routinely, I screamed at Rachel to let go, and my father snarled at me to leave Rachel alone. I was always scared, and she was always enthusiastic, and my parents were always grumpy, trying to do the job.

Once I was settled in my lung in the garage, one of my parents would bring out my radio or TV. Most nights, I watched TV with the door into the house ajar; I had an earphone so that the noise of my television wouldn't interfere with my parents' TV watching. I could see my father's green recliner and the blue beer can on the table next to him. Some nights I listened to the Giants on the radio, or, if there was no game and nothing on TV, I listened to talk shows on KGO. If I needed help, I could call my parents. Eventually, they'd turn off whatever I was listening to and retire to their bedroom at the opposite end of the house.

In the mornings, my father left for work around six. At seven, Helen would lift me out of the iron lung, carry me up the steps, and set me on the cot. I weighed about fifty pounds at the time. She would push the cot into Rachel's room and transfer me onto my hospital bed, where I could read, watch TV, or listen to more talk shows. Whatever I wanted to do, my mother had to arrange for me—set up a book or turn on the radio or television. I still had the bookstand that arched over my chest, and I turned pages with a mouthstick. Reading was difficult because I couldn't turn my head to the left; indeed, I could hold it straight ahead for only a few seconds at a time. My head naturally turns to the right, so, when I am lying on my back, my right cheek touches the pillow.

I had a subscription to *Life,* but I found it very difficult to get through because of the big, floppy pages. Photography has never been my favorite art form, and, after glancing at a picture of Nelson Rockefeller, I just wanted to get to the next page. But I loved *Life's* reviews, as well as the columns by Shana Alexander and Louden Wainwright Jr.

In one column, Wainwright referred casually to "the summer I had polio." The *summer* he had had polio! Having had polio for years at that point, with no cure in sight, I felt angry and jealous, reading about how sad he had felt, lying stuck between hot sheets while other people drove off in their cars.

Since listening to radio was easier than reading magazines, talk shows remained my daytime obsession. Along with baseball and prime-time TV, they constituted my secondhand life. Between talk shows on the radio, I heard songs by Barbra Streisand, Louis Armstrong, and Frank Sinatra: these were the background music as I looked out the window and watched other kids walk home from high school. The romantic songs helped me fantasize that a high school girl would casually strike up a friendship with me, but nothing like that ever happened. In fact, I never talked with anyone in that neighborhood.

In July, my old teacher Pete Gray and Bert Chilson, the priest from Boston, visited us as promised. By then, we had set up the same above-ground pool we had had in Stoughton. Though surprised at the sight of a priest and an English teacher jumping up and down and splashing each other in the water, I enjoyed their company immensely. Pete sneezed a lot from the California pollen and pollution, but he didn't complain. He spent a good part of the visit sitting with me and talking.

A month later, Helen read me a letter from a neighbor back in Stoughton. She was crying as she read that Pete Grey had died in a motel room in Illinois. He had lain down on his bed while Bert went into the bathroom, and, when Bert came out, he saw that Pete was dead. Although only in his mid-thirties, he'd had a heart attack.

Frightened and in tears, I asked Helen whether Pete's hay fever had contributed to his death. She said she didn't know. I was worried that the stress of his visit to California had exacerbated his condition, and I felt terrible about his death. He had been my best friend.

I had never had a friend my own age. My teachers had been friendly, but Pete had been closer than most. For one thing, he had not seemed afraid of me. Besides taking an interest in my life and ideas, he seemed to have faith in me, to believe in my future, in a way that no one else, not even my parents, did. Pete talked about developing my mind, not in terms of going to college but in terms of reading and thinking.

One of his gifts to me was the recommendation of *A Separate Peace,* a novel with a tender beauty and a wisdom that astonished me. Viscerally, I understood the guilt the protagonist felt when his friend died—some of that same feeling arose in me when my sister Karen died and then again after Pete's death. My guilt kept making me feel like a terrible person.

Pete had asked me to write to him. I had looked forward to doing so and perhaps developing some writing skills in the process. After he was gone, I knew I would miss that opportunity. I didn't have a typewriter, and I doubt that I could have used one, but I could move my right thumb a little, and I pretended it would be enough movement for me to write.

Later, I dictated one letter. Helen helped me send it to Peter Rodino, chair of the House Judiciary Committee, urging the impeachment of Richard Nixon. That was my sole written communication beyond schoolwork: otherwise, all my writing stayed in my mind.

During September, I became fascinated with the Brasil '66 song "Mas Que Nada" and the 1966 National League pennant race. While both offered a nearly unbearable degree of tension, only the song gave a satisfying release, with its pounding refrain of "Ebau! Ebau! Ebau!" On the last day of the baseball season, Ken and I listened to the radio as the Giants beat the Pirates. Later that day, the Dodgers were playing the Phillies. If the Phillies had won, the Giants would have been tied for first place with the Dodgers. But the Dodgers beat the Phillies two hours after the Giants game had finished. Ken and I had never before followed a pennant race, and this sudden, sad end to our team's season left us silent and deflated.

October brought fewer days of ninety-degree-plus temperatures, but Sacramento was still uncomfortable. Harry Geise, the TV weatherman, who had fought in the German army during World War II, refused to use the word "hot" unless the temperature hit 108 degrees. Apparently, he had learned how to make the best out of a bad situation. Geise and everyone else in the Sacramento media ignored the choking gray haze that came every October when the rice farmers burned their fields. We who lived in the area would suffer burning eyes and throats, but no one on the news ever commented about the atmosphere.

In our neighborhood, every other telephone pole sprouted blue and red posters saying "Viva Pat Brown." As Massachusetts liberals, we felt confident that the jolly governor would defeat the upstart self-righteous actor, whom Ken dismissed as "Ronnie Re-run." But the same month that we moved into our new house, Ronald Reagan was elected governor.

For some time, we'd been having a new house built. O'Bie had driven us out to the lot so often that I was surprised to see it as a completed dwelling, rather than as piles of dirt and naked wooden beams. The builder had converted most of the garage into a room for me; the rest would be O'Bie's workshop and storage area. But when we moved in, the garage wasn't done, so I stayed in the living room, a large, pleasant space with pale yellow carpet, tall windows, and a railing around a sunken part. At night I could see the white cubes of the doorways to the kitchen and to Rachel's bedroom glowing in the dark.

As always, I liked going into the backyard and onto the patio. Otherwise, the only times I went out were to lie on my cot in the driveway and watch the kids play at the elementary school across the street, so close I could hear them talking. On days when I went into the backyard, usually Helen got me up, and then she and Ken would push me along the outdoor path, which was raised and narrow. Each of them always held one end of the cot, but somehow, one day, it tipped over, and I fell face down on the gravel, terrified, and dizzy. Helen was very upset, but Ken took charge. He quickly righted the cot and put the mattress back on it, and then the two of them lifted me back on. I continued out to the patio, shaken but okay.

My room, the biggest I ever had, was completed two weeks later. Filled with light from two windows, it had a door leading out to the driveway and another leading into the utility room and the main part of the house. When my mother did the wash in the utility room, I could hear the washing machine bumping and rattling. Also, I could also hear my little sister, Rachel, jump the deep step into the utility room and then see her jump the identical deep step into my room, her blonde curls flying. Landing on the linoleum floor, she would run around my TV, put her chin on my mattress, and say, "How-dee!" Whenever she left the room, she'd say, "Back in a flash, with the dee-oh dash!" Though I had no idea what this meant—I assumed she had picked it up from TV—I was always charmed by it.

When my sister and I watched reruns of *Star Trek*, she asked me whether what we saw on the screen was real. I said the actors and the sets were real, but what they were doing wasn't. Thinking about her question, I realized what a difficult philosophical query it was. Surely the story was real, as real as *Macbeth* or *Moby-Dick*, but it wasn't real in the sense that it presented actual events, the way Walter Cronkite's scripts did. But then again, wasn't the Cronkite news edited, shaped to fit the desires of CBS, the sponsors, and Cronkite? I had to give up answering Rachel's questions; instead, I settled back to watch Captain Kirk phaser-beaming Klingons.

In the evenings, my father would put pillows under my head, back, and legs and then put the bedpan under me. After wiping me off, he would take the bedpan and empty it in the bathroom. One evening, while he was taking a long time cleaning out the pan, I pushed my left leg down so that I could rub my butt against the bed. It was very itchy behind my balls. I kept rubbing and rubbing until I ejaculated, though at the time I had no idea what was happening. Although I had long been familiar with erections, I'd never suspected there was anything beyond them. When my father returned, he looked annoyed. Silently, he cleaned up the mess and put me in the iron lung.

After that first time, I orgasmed as often as I could, despite anticipating the mute disapproval of one or the other of my parents. But then I noticed that I was becoming more and more tired. I kept falling asleep during the day. Eating supper seemed such a great effort that often I couldn't finish. Feeling guilty and not wanting to be constantly exhausted, I tried to stop masturbating. It was very difficult, but after a few months I was able to stop entirely, and my energy level returned to normal.

The first year we lived in Sacramento, Ken and I were very close. During ballgames, he would bop into my room and ask, "What's the sitch?" short for "What's the situation?" and meaning "What's the score, who's pitching, and how many runners are on base?" I would fill him in, and often he would stay and listen for an inning or two. He confided in me that the other kids in high school were ridiculing him because of his accent, calling him "Boston" or "Gomer." But he soon became involved with the high school debate team, where he excelled. He was gone most weekends for debate meets, and in time the mantelpiece in the living room was covered with trophies he had won. I envied Ken for his public recognition and for his freedom to travel, but mostly I envied him for his girlfriend, Kris, the sister of his debate partner.

With my color TV off, I could see the blue sky through the window, and sometimes I saw Ken and Kris, their heads bouncing as they walked past. Kris had a long, long braid that swung behind her head, the bottom fastened with a bright red band. I once saw Ken touching her ponytail, and I was jealous. Besides being envious of Ken, I felt angry at myself because I felt I would never have a girlfriend. Ken, too, had grown his hair long—almost Beatle-length. He looked like a real teenager, the kind I felt I would never be.

I was so alienated that I even avoided listening to rock 'n' roll, fearing its sexuality, hating the screaming DJs. And I associated that music with teens. But one day, Ken asked me to lend him seventeen dollars to buy the Beatles' White Album. At that time, Ken and I each received allowances of a dollar a week. I was able to save my money because I never went to stores. Still, seventeen dollars was a lot of money to both of us, but Ken said he would let me listen to the first playing. I sat in the living room with Ken and a friend of his, listening to side one of the blank-jacketed LP, which he called the White Album. Ken had to explain to me that "Why Don't We Do It in the Road?" was a takeoff on the Stones. He said he especially liked "Dear Prudence," which struck me as whiney and repetitious, although I didn't say so, perhaps out of gratitude to Ken for enabling me to be Teenager for a Day. Near the end of side two, I asked O'Bie to take me back to my room. Putting me in the iron lung, my father said, "I don't think these Beatles will last long."

Otherwise, I generally avoided the Beatles and all rock until I was twenty-one, when KZAP-FM began broadcasting in Sacramento. KZAP was the first station I had ever heard with mumbling DJs. The mumblers sounded intelligent and cool compared to the screamers, who sounded like clowns. KZAP's studios were on the seventh story of the Elks building, which was inhabited by businessmen. One of the DJs said that, while taking the elevator up, he had heard his fellow passenger grump, "God-damned long-hair commie faggot hippies," over and over again. Such was my teenage life, identifying with hippies while avoiding actual hipness. I never took drugs, because my parents controlled everything I ingested—it wouldn't work to say, "Mom, would you go out and get a tab for me? No, not the Tab with the bubbles." Besides, I feared messing up the one part of me that worked, my mind.

On weekends, my father would put me on the cot, and then he and Ken would lift it up the stairs and bring me into the TV room so that we could watch sports together. When the Green Bay Packers played the Dallas Cowboys in Green Bay for the 1967 NFL championship, the announcers kept saying it was fourteen below zero. Striving for an authentic game atmosphere, O'Bie, left the sliding glass door open, which let in the Sacramento winter—all fifty-two degrees of it.

On Christmas, Helen and Rachel would lift me and my cot into the living room, where Rachel would unwrap my presents, as well as her own toys. Mine were paperback books, about which she expressed great excitement.

"Oh, boy!" she squealed. "What's this?"

"That's Plato's *Republic*," I said. "That's *Dubliners*."

"That sounds really great!"

Rachel once gave me a lovely crayon drawing of a smiling sun looking down on an orange, lopsided house. I put it up on the wall. After she went to school, they taught her the correct way to draw, and all the life went out of her art.

We never ate dinner as a family. My mother cooked a meal for me at about four o'clock. While she fed me, we watched *The Mike Douglas Show,* and then she cooked for Rachel at about five. Rachel was a very fussy eater: at one time the only foods she would eat were vanilla ice cream and potato chips. (It turned out she had diabetes.) Then Helen made a third supper for herself and O'Bie. Ken came home at unpredictable times, so he made his own supper—usually canned chili.

I felt guilty about all the work my mother did to take care of me. My father fed me on the weekends or when he had vacation, and when I was eighteen, he took over giving me my weekly bath. But, in general, my mother washed, dressed, cooked for, fed, and saw to me. I think O'Bie, too, was anxious that Helen might be overworked.

Since I couldn't contribute to the household physically, I wanted to take care of my mother emotionally. For instance, I worried about her reactions to TV news. Once we saw a story about an oil well fire in Louisiana, and she got very tense. "There goes the price of gasoline!" she said. But, with little knowledge or help to offer, I had no idea what to say.

Music and reading seemed to relax Helen. Sometimes she listened to the radio when she fed me, usually an easy listening station, or she would read the *Sacramento Bee* or a best-seller from the library. Seeing how she enjoyed reading fed my ambition to be a writer.

Mostly, in the interests of helping my mother and father, I tried as hard as I could to be a good boy, which meant being quiet and obedient. However, I didn't always succeed. Once when O'Bie lifted me, he hit my head on the iron lung twice. I lost my temper and yelled, "Can't you do anything right?" I felt terrible and apologized the next day.

People who impose their will on others do so either by force or by withdrawal, and I couldn't do either one. My behavior could be called "learned helplessness." I didn't feel I could control anything except my mouthstick and my mind, so I didn't try to control my environment, chart my future, or disagree with my parents. What was there to argue about? They were doing the best they could in a difficult situation, and they had total control over my life.

As in Stoughton, the Sacramento Unified School District sent out teachers to tutor me after school hours. I was tutored for a year before it was decided that I could take the GED exam, which I passed easily. A school administrator came out to award me the GED, accompanied by a state assembly member and a reporter from the *Sacramento Bee*. It was spring of 1968, and we talked about the upcoming California primary. The assembly member said he supported Robert Kennedy in the presidential primary against Eugene McCarthy and a pro-Humphrey slate. Although still too young to vote, I felt I had to make a choice. I said I sympathized with McCarthy and resented people saying he was just a "stalking horse" for Kennedy. "That doesn't make any sense," I told the reporter and the assembly member, surprised by the certainty in my voice. "No one runs for president as a favor to someone else." But my heart was still with the Kennedy family.

I wanted to see Robert Kennedy when he came to Sacramento to shake hands at the Aorin Mall, but Helen refused to take me, saying, "It'll be mobbed." I supposed she was right—the photos in *Life* showed Bobby sweaty, without a jacket, his right hand at the center of the dozens of extended hands trying to touch his. Still, I very much wanted to see him. However, part of being a good boy was going along with my parents' wishes and suppressing my own. I had no recourse, and I couldn't think of any way to express my anger or disappointment.

The morning after the California primary, Ken walked into my room about quarter to seven. This was no surprise: he was the first one in the household to get up, and he often offered to turn on my television. He knew I would be awake, since I usually woke at sunrise. As he walked in, he pointed his index finger to the side of his head. "They shot Kennedy. This part of his skull was shot off. Mastoid, I think they call it." I thought he was making a sick joke. We had already had one Kennedy shot. But when Ken turned the TV on, I saw it was true—Bobby, cruciform on the pantry floor, soaked in blood.

I watched TV constantly for the next two days, following Kennedy's condition. I nurtured fantasies of seeing him bandaged, one arm paralyzed, appearing at the Democratic Convention, accepting the nomination.

When I saw Frank Mankiewicz, his thin hair blowing in the breeze, announce the death of Robert Kennedy outside the hospital, I wanted to move to Australia. Forlorn, I watched the funeral in Saint Patrick's Cathedral in New York, and I watched the train moving south, carrying

Bobby's body to Washington. The train moved very slowly because people all along the route were mobbing the tracks, throwing flowers, waving, crying, burning candles. I think it took the train four hours just to get to Philadelphia, a sadly segregated city. North Philly is black, and the south is white, yet the train stations of both areas were mobbed.

O'Bie said the TV had been on too long, and it was time to give it a rest. Angry, I protested, but there was nothing I could do. He turned it off. A few hours later, my television back on, I saw them bury Robert Kennedy in Arlington National Cemetery next to his brother. A chorus sang "The Battle Hymn of the Republic" as I silently cried, knowing that our last hope for ending the Vietnam War and our unacknowledged racial war had been destroyed.

As the years passed, I kept up my education in whatever ways I could. Ken lent me paperback books of Shakespeare and Dostoevski, which I enjoyed, although I had a hard time with the Modern Library version of *The Idiot*. It had the phrase, "agenbite of inwit," which amused some of the characters in *Ulysses* but just stumped me. I quit reading it, but, fortunately, someone got me a better translation. Reading Dostoevski gave me the idea that a writer has to be honest about himself. I thought that Dostoevski's understanding of various types of people could have been gained only through introspection.

I thought that I could use the knowledge gained from introspection to write novels with lifelike characters. But the prospect of being so open frightened me. What if everyone saw how sick and weird I was? I didn't think I could bear the rejection and the disgust that would follow, yet I couldn't think of any other way that I might be able to earn a living.

Even if novel writing was my best hope, though, I wasn't at all sure that I could write. First, there was a simple mechanical problem: the only instrument I'd ever used for writing was an IBM typewriter, and I hadn't even been able to reach all the keys with my mouthstick. The other doubt went deeper: I felt that I had had no experience, nothing to draw upon as a writer. I'd never traveled, fought in a war, been in love. I felt I was the opposite of Hemingway's ideal of the writer as adventurer. I wondered whether I could imagine what it was like to be able-bodied and whether I could write about able-bodied people accurately.

While I was fantasizing about writing, some days I watched seven straight hours of television. Watching TV helped me to feel more like a normal person, because I was doing what everyone else was doing, and I could talk about what I had seen. But mostly I was just filling up time.

One of the interesting shows was *Ironside,* on Thursday nights; the main character was the only disabled person on TV. The premise was that a chief of police, paralyzed by a gunshot wound, worked as a consultant to the San Francisco police. He used a wheelchair, he had a live-in attendant, and he seemed energetic and strong. Still, the situation was ridiculous; among many other impossibilities, the attendant worked twenty-four hours a day. In real life, I didn't know anyone disabled. There weren't any prominent disabled people, except Roosevelt, and even he had hidden his disability and tried to pass as able-bodied.

Frequently I would put up with watching a TV show just to avoid asking O'Bie to change the channel. Such requests always annoyed him; it would have been better for me to have a TV with remote control. So to avoid asking the favor, I watched *Dragnet* so that later on that channel I could see *The Dean Martin Show.*

Often I fell asleep watching prime-time TV, and I noticed that I looked forward to evenings when there was nothing on that I wanted to see. Also, I noticed that if I didn't watch TV in the evening, I felt more energetic the next morning. So, I began to cut back my TV viewing.

When I stopped watching *The Game of the Week,* Helen became concerned. I told her it hurt my eyes and that most of the games involved teams I didn't care about. The last TV series I watched was *Upstairs, Downstairs,* in the early seventies.

Watching so much television in my teens and early twenties had helped me to escape my life. Quitting TV, on the other hand made my life seem more real, as if it were something that demanded my attention.

Paying attention to my life, I noticed more about my parents. They worked hard, O'Bie at his job, my mother in the house, and both of them in the yard in the Sacramento sun, mowing the lawn, cleaning the pool, and so on. I could see them aging. They became more forgetful and less confident in taking care of me. I wondered how I could get away from home, where I could go, who would take me, and what I would do.

My learned helplessness was turning into a deep depression. Feeling that I had no future, I withdrew from the world, angry at its cheerful pretense of normality. I prayed. None of my questions seemed to have answers. In 1975, I was so depressed that when Ken told me—with excitement—of the World Series being played by the Boston Red Sox and the Cincinnati Reds, I couldn't make myself care. Baseball writers agreed it was one of the great World Series, but all I could think of was "vanity of vanities." Nothing interested me.

In 1972, we moved again, this time to a new house on an acre lot in rural Placer County. Again, my father instructed the builder to convert half the garage into a room for me. In the old place, I had had most of the garage space. My new room would be longer, but narrower. Still, its big sliding glass door offered me a view of the street, the front yard, and some horses across the street in a corral. I seldom left that room.

One of the few times I went out was to go to the dentist. O'Bie and Ken carried me and my ambulance cot to the second story of a mall, where the dentist's office was. O'Bie carried me through the crowded office and put me in the chair. After the exam, he picked me up and took me back out to my cot. Then he carried me back down the long flight of stairs. All that lifting frightened me more than the dental work.

I stayed in my room for most of four years, reading a little and listening to the radio. During the Watergate hearings, I tried to listen to the San Francisco FM stations, which were broadcasting live coverage, but they were very difficult to pick up in Placer County. I'd turn the sound up as loud as I could, so I could hear the faint rustle of voices over the static.

On TV, I watched the House Judiciary Committee vote in favor of impeaching Nixon. A few days later, I watched the inauguration of Gerald Ford as president. I felt encouraged when Ford said, "Our long national nightmare is over." Perhaps my letter to Peter Rodino had had some effect.

In May 1976, Ken graduated from the McGeorge School of Law in Sacramento. Everyone went to the ceremony except me. I hadn't expected to attend, nor was I sad that I couldn't. I had not gone to his high school or college graduation, either, and I was used to his doing things without me. My parents left in the morning, saying that they would return about one in the afternoon. While they were gone, I read *The Doors of Perception* and listened to Miles Davis on the radio. In the afternoon, I attempted to read Aldous Huxley some more, but there was no longer anything interesting on the radio. By the time my parents returned, after four, my bladder was about to burst.

After that incident, I felt ever more desperate to leave home, but I didn't know what to do. I saw something on TV about the Disabled Students' Program at the University of California at Berkeley. It seemed ideal to me, but I was so passive, I didn't mention it to my parents.

I didn't know it at the time, but, while I was being passive, my father had read about the Disabled Students' Program in the *Sacramento Bee,* and he spent much of the summer of 1976 trying to get me into the program. In August, he showed me pamphlets from the Kaiser Rehabilitation Center in Vallejo. He told me that they could strengthen me so that I could sit up straight in a power wheelchair and thus attend classes at Berkeley. Having already undergone one painful and useless back operation, I didn't believe that there was anything Kaiser could do to fix my spine or my posture, but I didn't say so. I wasn't surprised that my father had decided on my future without consulting me: that was the way my family worked. I felt sad at having to leave, but also relieved, because I wanted to get out before it was too late. Kaiser seemed like my best—if not my only—chance to move out and become independent. So I wanted the change, though I was afraid of leaving home.

One day in early September, we all got up around six. My mother gave me my favorite breakfast—warm Hostess donuts and orange juice—but, before I could finish, O'Bie said we needed to go. He looked strained, as if he'd been awake much of the night. As he put me on the cot, one of my arms and one leg smacked the surface hard and bounced off.

"God damn!" I complained.

"Shut up." O'Bie shoved me into place. "We've got to get going."

"Walter—" Helen interrupted.

He snapped, "The ambulance will be here any minute."

It arrived almost immediately. O'Bie opened the sliding glass door and pushed me and my cot down the driveway and into the street, where he helped the ambulance attendant put me inside. O'Bie and Helen followed the ambulance in their car, and I was on my way, leaving home.

6

Kaiser
(September 1976)

The ambulance attendants pushed me into the Kaiser Rehabilitation Center, with O'Bie and Helen walking behind. Despite my trepidation, I noticed how clean and new the building was. The low, acoustic tile ceilings, up-to-date medical equipment, and spacious patients' rooms impressed me.

As I was wheeled into a brightly lit ward, I saw several empty beds, as well as my iron lung with about a dozen nurses clustered around it. A strong-looking woman with blonde hair pulled into a bun introduced herself as Mrs. Forrest, the head nurse. After chatting with her a little, my father opened the iron lung and lifted me inside, demonstrating how to open and close the machine.

The iron lung was the same one that the March of Dimes had delivered for me ten years earlier, so I was comfortable physically, but emotionally I was going from somewhat nervous to quite terrified. Helen had given me such good care that I was convinced that she was the only person who could do so with ease and delicacy. Now she was leaving, or I was leaving her, and I would have to trust my body, in fact my life, to these strangers, people who had never before seen an iron lung.

As my father switched on the machine, he asked, "Any questions?"

There were none.

"If you have any, ask Mark," he said. "He's the real expert, and he'll always let you know if he's dissatisfied. Won't you?"

Embarrassed, I couldn't think of anything to say, so I nodded. Helen, her pink suit a little rumpled, her makeup a bit smeared, stood back and remained quiet. As they left, she approached me, trying to smile. "I'm sure you'll be okay," she said. "Just have the nurse call us if you need anything." As she bent over to kiss me, I saw the new room reflected in her small, round earrings.

"I'll be okay," I said, as confidently as I could.

"I'm sure you will be," she said, straightening. "Just call if—well, any time."

My parents left the room, waving and giving last-minute encouragements, and then I was alone in the strange, new place. More tired than frightened, I fell asleep and slept until supper time.

When I woke up, I was surprised by how good, hot, and plentiful the food was—there was more roast chicken, green beans, and salad than I could finish. Afterward, I stayed in my iron lung, but the other patients left the room to go to a party across the hall. Mrs. Forrest, the head nurse, came in, drew up a chair, and sat to the left of me. I told her I couldn't turn my head to the left, so she moved to where I could see her. Like everyone, she held her head upright while mine was horizontal, so our eyes didn't meet. Also, she was very tall and broad-shouldered—even more than most men.

"You're not watching TV," she said.

"No. Is it mandatory?"

"No, nothing is mandatory in this place, except pooping."

I told her I was nervous about being in a hospital for the first time in ten years and asked whether I would have to spend time on my belly, as I had in Children's Hospital in Boston. She said no, that I could refuse any treatment I didn't want. She went to the nurses' station and brought back a copy of the California Patients' Bill of Rights, a law that forbids the hospital staff to force any treatments on patients who are sane and of age. Slightly reassured, I settled in for the night.

The next morning a nurse woke me at 7:25 A.M. "Good morning, Mark. Can I take your temperature?"

She explained that she would supervise my care, but that my actual feeding and bathing would be assigned to a male nurse. Though I'd never heard of such a system and though it seemed unnecessarily complicated, I didn't object. The male nurse was supposed to get me washed and on a gurney by 9 A.M., but there weren't enough gurneys to go around, so he never came that morning.

I stayed in bed, bored and disappointed, until Terry Tanaka, one of the physical therapists, came to meet me. About my age, she was

small—only about five feet tall—and I quickly saw that she was forth-
right, witty, and attractive.

Terry took my foot between her small hands and moved it a few
inches while she explained the technique that had been invented by
Kaiser Vallejo's chief of physical therapy. "We try to avoid pain, because
pain just causes the body to tense up in reaction. We try to loosen the
muscles and extend their range." As she spoke, she gently lifted my leg
up and down. "If I hurt you, even a little bit, tell me. Pain is a sign that
we're doing something wrong." I was relieved, because I had always
associated therapy with pain.

In fact, putting up with pain had been a test of machismo and matu-
rity. I had always been accused of being childish if I failed the test by
complaining or yelping. Usually I kept my mouth shut, suppressing my
cries, but that had taken effort away from the therapy. I hated to lose
control and scream, and sometimes, when I did, therapists would further humiliate me by calling me names, in their smug, adult manner.

Terry and I spent that day establishing a baseline measurement, to
see how much I could move my limbs. She found that I could move
the fingers on my right hand about half an inch each way, and I could
move my right thumb in and out a little bit, although not enough to
operate the joystick on a wheelchair.

I couldn't move my left arm or hand at all. I could hunch my
shoulders and turn my head almost straight, but not to the left. I could
wiggle some of my toes about a quarter of an inch up and down. I
could push my left thigh down on the mattress enough to raise my
back a little, and I could rock in bed. I could tighten a muscle in my
right thigh, and I could pull my right foot back a tiny bit. Both my feet
lay parallel to the ground, pulled down by gravity. My left hand lay
curled, palm down, and my right hand lay open, palm up.

After Terry left, the male nurse lifted me on to a gurney and taped
a cardboard schedule where I could see it. He explained that I had three
more appointments outside my room that day: one with a teacher,
another with an occupational therapist, and the last with another physical therapist. They would check off each appointment on my schedule to show that I had made it. He told me to get to my appointments
any way that I could, to be aggressive about "getting rides," which
meant having someone push my gurney. A nurse would take me off
the ward each morning and to my first appointment, but after that I
had to hitchhike. Afraid of the responsibility, I doubted that I could

actually tell people what to do. I didn't think of myself as a person who gave orders.

My first stop, at occupational therapy, disappointed me. The OT said she would try to get me a typewriter so that I could write, but in the meantime she accused me of "frog-breathing" and asked me to look in a mirror so I could see what I was doing and stop it. She parked me by a full-length mirror on the wall and left me there for half an hour.

"Frog-breathing" was the catchword in a fifties medical fad that had been taught me in Children's Hospital. At the time, I dimly understood it to consist of using the tongue to pass air to the back of the mouth. I never did get it right, and my efforts to master it had made me look as if I was gasping and swallowing air. By the time I reached Kaiser, it had gone out of fashion and, evidently, become undesirable.

Not only did I not understand what I was supposed to be doing, but also this was the first time I had ever looked in a full-length mirror, and I hated it. The sight of myself—bony, pale, twisted, and wearing only a hospital gown—made the dream of going to Berkeley seem more ridiculous than ever. When the half hour finally ended, the OT put me out in the hallway, where I waited a minute until I saw my nurse. It was relatively easy to approach him, since I knew him already. "Hello, excuse me," I said, but he didn't hear me at first. "Hello!" I said, as loudly as I could. Once I'd gotten his attention, I asked, "Could you take me to the teacher's office, please?"

"It's kind of out of my way," he said. "But, okay, I guess I got it coming after that lecture I gave you this morning."

All my appointments were on the same floor, but some were far away. It was such a huge building that I hadn't been able to even get a good look at it when I arrived, and trips to various appointments took me through labyrinthine passageways.

The teacher, a small, quiet woman, asked me what kind of occupational goals I had in mind. When I confessed that I wanted to write, she said that I could dictate stories to her. This idea pleased me, because I wasn't sure when or if I would get a typewriter from OT. Right away, I started dictating a story based on my trip to Quebec and the cathedral at Sainte-Anne-de-Beaupré.

Afterward, I got a cleaning woman to push me to the physical therapy hallway, the doors of which were labeled with letters. In the room labeled "M," I was greeted by Susannah, the number two physical therapist, a woman about forty years old. Susannah had a simple, straight figure and a flat cap of dark hair. As she lifted me off the gurney and onto the examining table, I noticed that she wore a light cologne. "Terry tells me you were terrific in bed," she said with a Groucho Marx leer. Embarrassed, I closed my eyes and said nothing.

She put a folded towel into a bucket of crushed ice and then held it on my right shoulder, so cold it stung. "Oh, God," I whimpered.

"Just hang in a few more seconds. This will accelerate blood flow to that muscle group." When she took the ice off, I felt shocked and stimulated. She began to move my arms up and down, slowly, and then in a circle. She used the ice on other parts of me that day and every day after that, but I never got used to the shock. My skin didn't numb up; it just got colder and colder.

That day was like most weekdays in that I didn't have any breaks except lunch. The schedule was a huge change from my previous life, and I enjoyed the stimulation and activity.

The next day I had physical therapy in a new place—the gymnasium. "Wait till you see it," the nurse told me. "You ain't seen nothin' 'til you've seen the gym." Entering it, I saw a huge mural of the disability symbol, except in this version, the stick person was rising out of the wheelchair. *They're crazy*, I thought, *they think they can get people out of chairs*. But apparently others were encouraged by the mural: a middle-aged, English-sounding patient pulled alongside me in his wheelchair, saying, "Well, let's have a go at it."

Bright blue mats were scattered about the immense, polished hardwood floor. Terry, energetic as always, put her slim, strong arms under my armpits and lifted me down to a mat near where another therapist was exercising another patient. Then she scuttled around me, bending my legs, lifting my back, doing everything she could think of to see how my body worked. I was wearing one of the hospital gowns my mother had sewn, while Terry wore a white blouse and shorts. At one point she had my head on her lap. Looking up at me, she said, "Do you realize what my husband would say if he saw us like this?" I was embarrassed again. The other patient nearby, a lawyer who had suffered a stroke, was gossiping with his therapist about his mistress. The atmosphere was aggressive, good-humored, and more grown-up than anything I'd ever experienced. But I was even more embarrassed after Terry put me back on the gurney, saying "I don't care if your mother made that gown for you. Your genitals were hanging out. Ask the nurses to get you regulation pajamas." She spoke brusquely, and I didn't know how to respond.

Later that week in M Room, Susannah put me on a metal exercise table. We'd been doing exercises for about ten minutes when she'd stopped to readjust her hair band. Sweat filmed over her forehead, and I realized how hard she was working. As I gazed at her, she called over a PT from the corridor. "Art, I want to try something here, okay?" Art came in to help, and Susannah explained to him, "I'll put his legs off the side ..."

Horrified, I realized that she was attempting to sit me straight up. My legs were off the side of the table, and she and Art held me by the shoulders as they lifted my torso into a vertical position. I screamed.

"He's sitting on his hoo-hoos," Art said, moving my testicles out from under me.

"*Hoo-hoos?*" Susannah said. "Is that what you tell your kids to call balls?"

A moment later, dizzy, I stared straight into Susannah's calm pale blue eyes. It had been decades since I'd looked anyone straight in the face. Overwhelmed by exhaustion, fear, and dizziness, I said, "You know, you look kind of like Abe Lincoln." As they lay me down, I added, "Before he grew his beard, of course."

"I'll overlook that in the interests of medical science. Art, get a chair."

A wheelchair? I had never believed that I could use one. The therapists in Boston had said that if they gave me a wheelchair, I would lose my incentive to walk again. In the Boston of my childhood, willpower was all-important. If you wanted something badly enough, you could have it. This maxim included curing yourself of paralysis.

But now Art was pushing in a pale green wheelchair, and there was no time for me to object as Susannah lifted me into it. The landing was soft, but my thighs hurt from being stretched too far.

"Your breathing doesn't look good," Susannah said, as she lowered the back of the wheelchair to a more comfortable angle, about twenty degrees. Dizzy, triumphant, and yet afraid that I would slip out of the wheelchair, I returned to the ward, pushed by Susannah. In twenty-one years, I'd rarely sat up that high except for occasional forays into my father's big green recliner.

At the ward, nurses stopped and pointed me out to each other, smiling and pleased.

"Wow, they've got him in a wheelchair!"

Someone said, "Oh, you look comfortable," but I wasn't. It was very difficult, but I knew how important it was for me to be able to use the chair. Instantly, I felt how much more prestigious it was than a gurney. A person in a wheelchair can travel through most buildings and streets, whereas people confined to beds and gurneys are condemned to live in hospitals: gurneys are too big to maneuver in houses, offices, and stores. Also, a person in a wheelchair is sitting, which is closer to standing than lying down is and thus is perceived as more adult.

At the end of the day, I was back in the iron lung, waiting for supper. A tall, beautiful woman walked into the room—she had huge gray eyes and straight, swishy blonde hair past her shoulders. Amazingly, she introduced herself. Her name was Jill, she was a social worker, and she needed to talk to me. I told her that I would like to talk, but it was almost time for me to eat. A nurse brought the tray and asked Jill if she could feed me. Jill glanced at the clock on the wall—4:45 P.M.—and said she would.

As she gave me spoonfuls of lasagna, she told me that I was scheduled to see her in her office the next day. "It's important that we talk tomorrow. Have you been making all your appointments?"

Between bites, I assured her that I had been. She talked about the Kaiser Hospital in Vallejo, saying that it was the rehabilitation center of the statewide Kaiser Permanente group of hospitals and that it attracted patients and students of physical therapy from all over the world. Leaning forward, her movie-star face earnest, she changed the subject to the importance of everyone working together as a team. She reminded me that my work wasn't just physical therapy, that I would also work with the doctor, the OT, and herself, the social worker. I told her that I very much appreciated the physical therapy and that it seemed the only thing that could help me. As the clock neared 5 P.M., she asked the nurse to finish feeding me. He agreed, but, as she left the room, he muttered, "If she's so patriotic, why doesn't she finish?"

The next day, I stayed up in my wheelchair during lunch, for a total of forty-five minutes. I had been determined to make it to the one-hour mark, but I kept passing out. Though I could not stay longer in the chair, I had to stick to my schedule, so the nurses moved me to a gurney. As the time for me to meet Jill approached, I realized there were only two nurses on the ward, so I asked a doctor to take me to my next appointment. To my surprise, he did.

Jill's office had just enough extra space for the gurney to fit. With all the plants and books, the room looked like a cross between a medical library and a rain forest. After greeting me, Jill said she needed to know some things about me to work out a plan for the team.

"We have a lot of information from your medical records," she said. "But we need to get more information about you—how you work, your life these past nineteen years. Let's start with your home life. Did you get out of the house much?"

"Back in Massachusetts, when I was little, yeah, sure. I went out a lot, almost every day."

"But not in California? Not so much? Why not?"

"I don't know. I didn't know anyone in the neighborhoods where we lived ... and it was getting harder for my parents to lift me."

"Did you have any friends after you moved to California?"

What did she think, that I had a great social life? "I like to think of my family as friends."

"But outside your family?"

"No. No, I don't know anyone outside the family."

"You weren't connected with the local high schools or anything?"

"Well, no." I reflected miserably on my life. Why hadn't I been? It had never occurred to me.

"No girlfriends?"

I began to cry. This woman was tearing at me, and I was upset and angry that she would even ask about romantic relationships: I thought it obvious that girls would not be attracted to me. For a while, we didn't speak.

Finally I said, "Is that all? Would it be okay if I just left now?"

She looked at her watch. "No, we have almost ten minutes left to talk, and I'm just curious how you survived such a situation, such isolation."

Sweating, and feeling like a specimen, I nervously rubbed my feet together. *God, I want to leave,* I thought. Did this count as a treatment I could refuse?

"Well, I don't know. I mean, I don't know what you want me to say. My parents took care of me as well as anyone could."

"Let me tell you something, Mister O'Brien. I see a lot of people come through here, and I can't remember one of them who has been as isolated as you say you've been. But you seem quite okay. I admire that. Do you consider yourself religious?"

"Yes, I guess so. I try to pray." I was crying again. I felt as though she were turning me inside out, but I was afraid to tell her to stop, because she seemed to be the authority figure at Kaiser. But what was she doing? I hadn't expected any psychotherapy stuff. I was moved by her concern, but I was also upset, because no one ever talked to me as intimately as she did. I felt disoriented, weepy, and sorry for myself.

"Would you say you are a very religious person?"

"No, not very. I don't know what you mean; I don't go to church or anything."

"Well, I'll drop that. I ought to ask you about something else. We need to know what every patient's goals are. Do you think you could tell me what your goals are, what you expect to gain from being in Kaiser?"

That shook me up further. Goals? What the hell was she talking about? I wanted to be able to sit upright in a wheelchair that I could control. That was what O'Bie had said would happen at Vallejo, and that was what I needed to go to Berkeley.

"I want to be rehabilitated. I want to be able to use a wheelchair that I can operate."

"Anything else?"

"No, that's what I came here for."

She flipped through some papers for a minute. "I know, Mr. O'Brien, that's what everyone comes here for, more or less. They want to be able to walk or use their arms better or something medical like that. Maybe, from what you've told me, you'd say that a reasonable person would want more out of their lives than a wheelchair. Something like friends, a lover, a job, an apartment. Do you know what I mean?"

I couldn't control my crying.

"God damn, Jill. You know I want all those things, but I can't think a million years ahead of now. You're asking me so much, I don't know ..."

"I'm sorry." Reaching into her drawer, she pulled out some Kleenex and got out from behind her desk so that she could wipe my tears. "I didn't mean to upset you. We just need to get as full a picture, physical and emotional, of our patients as we can. But I think we've both had enough for today. Now, remember, we have group on Thursday afternoons. You'll be there for group, won't you?"

Figuring that group wouldn't be as intense and upsetting as our meeting had been, I agreed, and she pushed my gurney back to the ward, the silence broken only by the squeaking of the wheels.

That weekend I practiced staying up in the wheelchair, fighting through waves of exhaustion. To distract myself, I'd stare at an object until it seemed to glow. I remembered Aldous Huxley, in *The Doors of Perception,* using the German word *Istigkeit* ("Is-ness"). As I stared at the back of a woman who was standing at the nurses' station—blonde hair, green dress, dark stockings—I concentrated on those words— "blonde hair, green dress, dark stockings"—over and over, my head about to burst with *Istigkeit.*

Later, waking up in the iron lung, I realized that I had passed out from exhaustion and that a nurse had put me back in the lung. I don't know why I passed out, but the pressure on the top of my head and the overwhelming *Istigkeit* of everything seemed to make me lose consciousness. Fainting was inevitable. After coming around, I would wait a few hours, then get up in the wheelchair again to sit by the stereo in the hallway and listen to music, often the Moody Blues.

A surplus of *Istigkeit* wasn't the worst of learning how to sit up. The worst problem was my tendency to slip down in the wheelchair. One morning, while I was waiting in the PT hallway, suddenly I was nearly horizontal, and the wheels were looming above my elbows. Feeling nothing under my feet, I screamed, "Help!" I was convinced that I would soon slide to the floor, break my legs, and ruin my rehabilitation.

Susannah, standing behind the wheelchair, grabbed my shoulders and hauled me up. "Falling out of the chair is a risk you'll have to take if you want to use one," she said. I accepted that risk: the prospect of staying in bed the rest of my life was more terrifying than the risk of breaking my legs.

Daily I worked at staying in the chair. I was very frustrated that I would pass out after just an hour in the chair, especially because I was surrounded by people who stayed in chairs as much as they wanted to, usually all day. I couldn't explain to them or to able-bodied people that merely sitting up exhausted me. Because of the curvature of my spine, it was hard for me to breathe unless I was lying down. Also, I felt stabbing pains in my thighs because the muscles were so tight. It was a difficult, isolating, other-worldly experience.

One day, again while practicing sitting in my chair while parked the hallway, I saw an orderly talking to his wife, who was a nurse. They had two children who apparently went in and out of hospitals all the time. This couple's life seemed to be centered on hospitals. I saw them as emblematic of hospital culture; some people got their emotional needs met through hospitals. The model of life that such people subscribed to said that anything wrong with you was a disease, and all you needed was a good doctor or a good hospital to fix you. To get into the culture, you had to get a known disease, submit yourself to a doctor's will, and become a patient, passive and trusting of authority. This couple got a lot of attention because they and their kids were in hospitals all the time; they got computer readouts, prescription drugs, and time with doctors; it seemed dramatic to them. Always having hated hospitals, I was spooked by their willingness to surrender their lives to the Great White Healer. It was like watching someone do something I can't stand to think of, like handling snakes. It gave me the creeps.

Gradually, though it was terribly difficult, I could stay in the chair longer and longer—up to an hour and a half, after a few weeks. I was proud of myself and invigorated by all the treatment, but lonely and trapped in my head. When Ken visited me, I assailed him with one of my cockamamie theories of how the body works. I'd come up with a new one every day, all demonstrating the inevitability of my partial but brilliant recovery. I was certain that I would be able to sit up straight, use my right hand enough to operate a joystick, and go buzzing across the Berkeley campus. As Ken listened graciously to my rant, I realized how much I missed his wit, my sister's exuberance, and my parents' affection.

I also missed being able to read as much as I had at home. My bookstand had to be placed over my chest, and in those weeks I was usually either sleeping in the iron lung or forcing myself to endure the rigors of sitting up, which made it impossible to use the bookstand. I read only during the few hours I spent in a hospital bed. Not having the company of books made me feel even more isolated.

There was a seventeen-year-old boy on the ward who was only partly conscious. He couldn't talk, and he writhed and rolled constantly. The physical therapist wanted him to spend time in his wheelchair every day, but whenever he was in it, his catheter would get pulled out. The nurses would have to clean up the mess and hold him down while they reinserted a catheter, and eventually they would put him back to bed, where he could be more effectively restrained.

I talked with the boy's father, who explained that his son had been injured in a car accident a year before. He was a quiet, patient man, who visited often, but he was obviously tiring out. Once he mentioned being grateful that his employer continued to pay him through all the time he had to take off to care for his son. When I asked whom he worked for, he said, "Lockheed Missile and Spacecraft. We make missiles for the government."

The first time I went to group therapy, I was nervous. I was the only person there on a gurney. All the other patients were sitting either in wheelchairs or on regular chairs. Jill led the discussion, which centered on what we all would be doing in the future. The letters "DSP" were spoken frequently, and I learned that they stood for the "Disabled Students' Program" at the University of California at Berkeley.

I'd heard of that program: O'Bie believed it to be my destination. It also seemed to be the destination of everyone else in the group. I worried that there would not be room for me.

After an hour, I felt the group had been completely useless: sixty minutes of chitchat. But at the end of the session, Jill said she'd been impressed by what I had to say. Having thought that I'd said nothing interesting, I was surprised. She encouraged me to talk more in future sessions.

On weekends, there was nothing for me to do except sit in my wheelchair for as long as possible. Sitting in the hall, bored, resentful, and uncomfortable, I struggled to stay awake. To break the monotony, I observed others, and sometimes I was pleasantly rewarded. Once, while I was sitting in the hall, a family came to visit a patient in a different ward. A little girl no more than three feet tall ran out of the room and to Mrs. Forrest, who picked her up and held her high in the air. Gazing into each other's eyes, they laughed deeply, as though sharing a secret about the goodness of life.

Weekends dragged. I much preferred the activity of the week, when I would receive physical therapy twice a day. Terry would ice a muscle group for as long as I could stand it, then start stretching muscles. She and the other PTs talked about stroke victims recovering part of their movement as a result of this treatment. Polio had left my muscles tight, and the therapists hoped that increased flexibility would help.

"Harder! Harder! You're not trying hard enough!" Terry yelled, deepening her voice, beings as abrasive as she could. I would respond by using my own anger to generate energy, pushing down the leg they were lifting, hoping to push her down to the mat. I wanted to show them what I could do, how much I had improved.

The therapists weren't always abrasive—sometimes they would gossip and joke. I loved how spontaneous they were, how they seemed to feel free to express themselves. Also, I enjoyed the attention and relished being treated like an adult. One day, I was waiting for a ride back to the ward, and Terry was leaving work. It had been cool outside, about fifty degrees, and she was wearing an enormous parka—very thick and furry. It made her face and shape nearly invisible.

"There goes Chu the Chill," Susannah said.

"What?"

"Oh, she's always had an unreasonable fear of the cold. Back before she got married, she was Terry Chu and we always called her Chu the Chill. Still do. Somehow, Trembling Tanaka doesn't make it."

I was interested to learn that someone who seemed so healthy and together as Terry could have any eccentricities or problems.

Once, when I was working on the mat, one of the male PTs grabbed Terry, picked her up, and carried her off, grunting like a caveman. She shrieked and laughed. I laughed, too, just watching. I've never seen people who liked their jobs so much.

After a session I felt tired, but glowing and happy. Having worked hard and succeeded, I felt proud of myself and my progress.

My most visible improvement was that after three weeks, I could stay up in the wheelchair for two hours at a time, up to three and a half hours total in a day. I felt insanely happy, and I could breathe better than I had in years. I looked forward to each day; except for weekends, when there were no appointments, every day was exciting.

Further, my spirits were lifted by the progress I saw all around me. Sal, a twenty-five-year-old man, was living in my room when I was admitted. He seemed very cool; even his posture was laid-back—he literally leaned against the back of his chair. Initially he used a push-chair and, like me, had to be pushed everywhere he went. But somehow, in a few weeks, they improved his hands so that he could use a joystick. Once he got an electric chair, he became a speed demon, buzzing down the hallways, spinning around corners, grazing nurses without actually hitting them. It was wonderful to see.

Three weeks after I arrived, I saw Jill again in her beautiful office. She asked me whether I had ever thought of what lay beyond Kaiser.

I hadn't, but I said, "I suppose I'll go to Berkeley."

"You may not be ready for Berkeley. I think it's time we considered other alternatives, other situations for you."

"Why? I like it fine here."

"Well, basically, we're a training facility. You've noticed how you see physical therapists from all over the world here."

That was true. I'd met student therapists from India, Brazil, and Sweden.

"The PT staff is overworked," she continued. "And we need to move people in and out as fast as possible so that we can train the students in as many ways as possible. Now, you like the therapy, don't you?"

"Yes, I do. I wouldn't want to go to another place that had the old stretch-till-it-hurts."

"I understand that. I certainly wouldn't want to go into a situation that was less ideal than what we have here. But, you know, other places have therapists who have been trained here in our technique. I've been talking with social workers at other hospitals in California, and there are three or four I think I could recommend to you."

"But I don't want to leave." The weeks of being treated like a person had made me bolder about voicing my opinions. Also, I felt desperate. "There's no reason for me to leave. The therapy has helped me a lot. I like this place; I like the spirit of the people who work here. Everyone's so gung ho and optimistic. I like you, I like Terry and Susannah in PT. I like the nurses."

"Of course you do. We've all come to like you, too. But I need to tell you that a time may come when we'll want to transfer you to another facility. I want you to keep that in mind, and especially think of the Fairmont Hospital in San Leandro. I've talked to the people there, and they're very good. Very smart, aware, caring people. It's the closest of the places I've checked, about fifty miles from here, if you want to have as short a ride as possible."

"Well, I'm sure I would, if I left."

"'If,' Mark? 'If'? I'm afraid it's more a matter of *when* than *if*. Just think about it. Talk to Terry or whoever about it. I think it's something we'll have to work on."

The thought of leaving Kaiser depressed and worried me. I had happened upon my one chance to regain the use of my body, and now that chance might be taken away from me. At my next appointment, I lay on a mat in the gym, and Terry knelt next to me, looking down.

"Hey, kiddo, you look kind of down. Are you sick?"

"No, no, not sick, it's just that . . . Jill's been talking weird to me."

"Weird? Weird how? She hasn't reverted to Pig Latin again?"

"No," I said, annoyed. "No, she wants me to go to another hospital, a place called Fairmont. Have you ever heard of Fairmont?"

"Fairmont?" She flicked her hair off her face. "Yeah, I've heard of it. It's okay, I guess. But I wouldn't want you to go there. You should tell Jill you won't go there unless you can come back to Vallejo."

I thought about that for a few seconds.

"Hey, kiddo, see these knees?" She slapped her knees. "They used to be Chi-knees, now they're Japa-knees."

Unamused, I stared at her.

"Hey, you must be sick, you didn't even groan or anything. I think I should take you back to the ward."

The following Thursday, I attended another group session in the conference room. Instead of talking, this time we watched a movie about disability and sexuality. The movie consisted of four or five able-bodied men joking and laughing about how they once lugged their crippled friend up a flight of stairs to a whorehouse. I found it embarrassing, and I suspected it wasn't just my shyness but that there was something wrong with the film.

After the movie, a doctor talked about disability and sexuality. I forget most of what he said, but I will always remember his closing line: "You may think you'll never have sex again, but remember . . . some people do become people again."

What? I wasn't a person in this doctor's opinion? I thought I had been. This whole disability-and-sexuality talk had been a catastrophe; I just wanted to get the hell out. But before I could, Jill approached and asked whether I had gone outside since I arrived at Kaiser.

"No."

"I was thinking, maybe instead of meeting Tuesday in my office, I could pick you up on the ward and take you outside, if it's warm enough. Would you like to do that?"

I had been so involved with the physical therapy and my efforts to stay up longer in a wheelchair that I had forgotten there even was an outdoors. "That sounds terrific," I said. "I haven't been outside in ages."

The following Tuesday, in my fourth week at Kaiser, Jill took me outside. The ward was on the third floor, but the building was built into the side of a hill, so we could go out the third floor doors into a parking lot.

Outside, the sky was clear blue; it was a cool day, in the sixties, with a light breeze pushing paper and bits of Styrofoam around the parking lot. In the glass wall of the building, I saw Jill, tall and stunning in her teal pantsuit, her blonde hair gleaming in the sunlight, pushing a nearly flat wheelchair containing me, bony and deformed.

She found a bench, positioned me so that I could see her, and sat down. After a little chat, she said, "You really have to think about the future, and you need to think about it pretty quick."

"I'm not sure I want to leave. Terry and Susannah don't want me to leave. Mrs. Forrest doesn't want me to leave, either. I feel secure here."

"I know you feel secure here, I know you're attached to your physical therapists, but you have to work with the whole team. It's not just PT; it's also your doctor and your social worker. Have you seen your doctor since you came here?"

"Only once, and he didn't seem very interested in me."

"That's just it. I've talked to Dr. Eggers and Mrs. Weiss, the doctor and the social worker at Fairmont. They are very concerned about your condition, and they think they can give you more help than you're getting here."

"Oh, Jill, I don't think I can get any more help than I'm getting here. I'm feeling better than I ever have."

She paused, ran a hand through her hair, looked up, and sighed, as though she were trying to think of something to say.

"All right, I'll admit that you're getting good PT here. But the PTs at Fairmont have been trained here. I talked with one of them, Brett, and she very much wants to work with a polio person. She had very high marks when she was a student here, and I think she'll do her best to help you. And another thing is . . ." She looked at her hands in her lap for a second, then met my eyes. "If you don't like it there, you can come back here within twenty-four hours. I've arranged that with Mrs. Weiss. I know how attached you are to the PTs here. So if you don't like it there, just ask a nurse or someone to call Mrs. Weiss. She'll call me, I'll call the ambulance company, and you'll be back here. That's a promise."

I looked at Jill and thought about my first session with her, how cruel she had seemed. But then I remembered how much we had talked since then and how she'd encouraged me to speak in group. I felt I could trust her, but, more than that, I think I wanted to please her because she was so pretty. I had never seen such a gorgeous woman. "Okay," I said. "I'll go."

I was sad the day I left Kaiser. A nurse told me that she wished I weren't going because I had made so many friends there. I knew she included herself among them, and I felt flattered. But I had made my decision. Jill took me out to the parking lot, where an ambulance picked me up and drove me to the Fairmont hospital in San Leandro.

7

Fairmont

(September 1976–September 1978)

I knew I was in trouble as soon as I saw the air conditioning units sticking out the windows of the buildings of Fairmont Hospital. The buildings looked nice enough: white stucco with Spanish-style red tile roofs. But a few—only a few—of the windows had square metal boxes jutting out. Coming from Sacramento, I knew that any place with window units did not have central air conditioning. Also, I knew how hospitals worked: there is a hierarchy, in which patients are not at the top. The doctors would get the air conditioning, while the patients would suffer in the heat.

Two ambulance attendants wheeled me to a side entrance, down a ramp, and into a dark, crowded basement. In the gloom I could make out exposed plumbing and wiring, rusting green oxygen tanks, broken Hoyer lifts, and other old equipment. We crossed to the elevator and went up to Ward C-2.

It was all the same as the basement—wiring and plumbing everywhere, not hidden in the walls. The ward was painted a foul, pale green, a color often seen in institutions: Gas Chamber Green. A big room with a high ceiling, the ward held four patients, one in each corner. Six tall windows covered in chicken wire let in traces of sunlight and hot air. I wondered whether the chicken wire was supposed to prevent the patients from escaping. And I had been right—no air conditioning.

When the ambulance attendants lifted me from the gurney to my bed, I noticed that the mattress was marshmallow soft. The therapists at Kaiser had stressed the importance of sleeping on a hard surface for strengthening the back muscles.

The attendants left me lying so that I could see only the small part of the room that lay to my right. In the next bed, something lay covered with a sheet. The cover rose and fell where a chest might be, but I couldn't see a head. From time to time, a nurse came along and lifted a feeding tube up from the sheet to pour a can of something—liquid protein, I later learned—down it.

On two televisions, soap operas were turned up loud, but the real-life conversation was minimal, and the few people who did speak sounded bored. A young black man talked in a deep voice about going to physical therapy once or twice a week. Someone answered him with soft, unintelligible mumble.

Many people came to see me that first afternoon. I had to tell them all to stand on the right side of the bed, and I told every one of them I wanted to see Mrs. Weiss, the social worker. She was the one whom Jill, the social worker at Kaiser, had promised would arrange my return to Kaiser in twenty-four hours if I disliked Fairmont. I already disliked it and was ready to go back.

A thin, nervous woman with a trace of a German accent introduced herself as Miss Fichte, the head nurse. She clasped a white plastic bracelet to my right wrist.

"What's this?"

"A patient ID," she said. "You'll wear it all the time."

"Why?"

"Well, so the nurses can identify you."

This puzzled me; the nurses already knew who I was. However, instead of pressing the issue, I told her I needed to see Mrs. Weiss. Miss Fichte said I could not see Mrs. Weiss until the next day. That would take me beyond the twenty-four hour trial period, but I had no recourse.

I was put into the iron lung early, in mid-afternoon. For the rest of that day—and for many, many days afterward—I had nothing to do except eat supper and listen to the competing televisions. Cut off from my family, alone, and at the mercy of the nurses, I felt afraid.

The nurses looked around fifty, too old for this kind of work. One of them talked about how much she hated white people, and I got the impression that she was not fond of men, either.

Around six, a nurse came in, pushing a cart. She asked me whether I wanted a sleeper.

"What's that?"

"Sleeping pills. You know, Chlorolhydrate, Dalmeny, Darvon. You want one?" I said no, I would not have any trouble sleeping. Exhausted, I fell asleep shortly after she left.

In the middle of the night, I was woken by a black orderly. Wearing a hospital gown over his uniform, he held up a urinal. "Needest thou this goodly vessel?" he asked.

I did need it, but I could not tell whether the orderly was teasing me somehow or if he was crazy.

In the morning, yet another nurse, a tall, watery-eyed black woman, came to me, looked at the iron lung and said, "Tell me how I get you out of this thing."

I had to explain it to her, which was difficult because I cannot gesture. I was angry that the hospital had not instructed any of the nurses in how to work with the iron lung. Obviously, I would have to train them myself. Adding to my discomfort and dissatisfaction, Head Nurse Fichte said the nurses could not put me into my wheelchair, because Fairmont had not received the Kaiser doctor's orders allowing me to use it.

I finally got to see Mrs. Weiss on my second day. A short, gray-haired woman, she wore a lab coat over a paisley dress. As soon as she was introduced, I told her what Jill had told me and that I wanted to return to Kaiser.

Weiss looked worried behind her glasses, but she said she would not send me back.

I couldn't believe it and protested that Jill had made clear what the arrangement was.

Firm and angry, Mrs. Weiss said, "I'm not responsible for fulfilling other people's promises."

Outraged and out-argued, I did not know what to do.

Two full days later, Fairmont finally received doctor's orders from Kaiser, and they let me get into my wheelchair. I asked a nurse to raise the back of it, but she said no, Doctor Eggers wanted me to stay flat. All the men on the ward had Doctor Eggers assigned to them, but I had yet to set eyes on him. I told the nurse I wanted to call my mother, so she took me to the nurses' station, there being no phones on the ward. The station was a small cubicle crowded with filing cabinets, furniture, and medicine chests. The nurse dialed for me and held the phone up to my head while other people sidled around me, squeezing in and out of the cramped space.

I asked my mother to call Jill at Kaiser and tell her to get me out. My mother did not recall who Jill was, so I reminded her, repeating that Jill had promised that I could leave Fairmont if I did not like it. I could not say much with the nurse listening, so I told my mother I would call again another time.

When I told the nurse I wanted to call Jill, she said, "No, we don't want you to badmouth this place anymore. No more phone calls for you!"

Having failed with Mrs. Weiss, I hoped to persuade Dr. Eggers to send me back to Kaiser. I met him a few days later. A thin man in a dark, vaguely nautical blazer, he stood three feet away from my bed, holding his hands behind his back. The conversation was very one-sided. He said, "You're not going back to the Kaiser and that's that."

Shortly after that, Miss Fichte told me my blood sugar level was extremely low. I told her my sister has diabetes. A few days later, after some tests, Fichte said I did not have diabetes, but that the low blood-sugar level could have been caused by my being extremely angry. I was.

At Kaiser, they routinely had put me in my wheelchair until I passed out, then put me back in the iron lung to recuperate. Then, when I was ready again, they would lift me back into the wheelchair. That way, I had gradually adjusted to longer and longer periods in the chair.

So, at Fairmont, after my first hour and a half in the chair, I asked to return to the iron lung. My nurse said she could not do that; it was policy that a patient could be lifted only once a shift. Naturally, Miss Fichte would not consider a change in the policy. So I had to get up in the morning and stay up until the evening shift came on duty about three. I do not know how I stood it—it was very hard. I lay on the hard wheelchair, listening to the televisions and the languid gossip of the nurses. There was nothing to look at, no one to talk to. I wonder how I kept my sanity.

I had very few possessions—some clothes my mother had bought, a radio-cassette player, two posters, some classical tapes my brother had given me, two bookstands, textbooks, a few paperbacks, my mouth-stick, toiletries, and a Norelco shaver. Out of my SSI check, the hospital gave me a twenty-five-dollar monthly allowance. Most of this had to go on personal items that the hospital did not provide, such as a washbasin, soap, shampoo, and toothpaste. Trapped, with inadequate care and no money, I was poor and in fear much of the time.

Perhaps that is why I felt so close to God. A deacon from a Catholic church came to give me communion every week. I saw a priest occasionally, maybe once a month. The priest—a big, talkative guy with a goatee and round, rimless glasses—looked like a nineteenth-century intellectual. Sometimes he would speak in German or Spanish with me. One day, he found me reading *The First Five Minutes*, by the physicist Steven Weinberg, which I had borrowed from the Fairmont library.

"¿El primero cinco minutos de qué?" he asked.

"El primero cinco minutos del universe," I replied.

"Ah," he said, popping his eyes in wonder, "¡Una explosión grande! ¿Y qué dice el actor sobre el tiempo antes de explosión?"

My limited Spanish could not support the weight of any more metaphysics. "The author says there was no such thing as time before the Big Bang."

The priest smiled at me as though we were both in on a hot secret. "I'm sure you don't think there can be an effect without a cause."

"No, I don't think that."

"Well, you and I know that. It just takes some people a while to understand that for themselves."

Two weeks after my transfer to Fairmont, my father visited, bringing a Sony Trinitron television as a present. For the first time, he admitted that he and my mother could not take care of me anymore now that they were in their fifties. Instead, he reminded me, he hoped I would go to Berkeley. He thought that at Fairmont, I would gain strength enough to drive a wheelchair around the university campus.

I was skeptical, doubting that Fairmont would help me do anything, but the idea of going to Berkeley—going anywhere, in fact—was exciting. Despite our enthusiasm, though, the idea of actually going to Berkeley seemed impossible.

After turning on the TV, O'Bie fiddled with the tuning and color knobs. My eyes hurt as we watched the Reds play the Yankees in a World Series game. My father turned up the color to such intensity that it hurt my eyes, but I did not object. It had been kind of him to bring the set, and anyway I felt too defeated.

A meeting was held on the ward to discuss my future. I was allowed to attend, along with my occupational therapist, Andi; my physical therapist, Brett; and Mrs. Weiss. There was also someone I hadn't met before, Casey. With high cheekbones, straight black hair, and maroon jacket, Casey was, it turned out, my Department of Rehabilitation counselor. I found myself staring at her glossy hair while she argued that I was an ideal candidate for the Berkeley program. The others were more cautious, saying that I needed to strengthen my body before I could leave. Though of course I rooted for Casey, I felt that the medical people were right in their gloom. Perhaps my admission to Berkeley would take longer than Casey thought, but I was cheered by her optimism and glad to have her on my side.

When the mystery under the sheet in the bed next to mine was revealed, it turned out to be Lawrence, a white guy my age whose brain had been injured in a car crash. His eyes were open, but he didn't speak. His father, a quiet, silver-haired teacher, visited him every evening to talk to him, massage his feet, and do anything he could to try to bring Lawrence out of his coma.

To this end, he bought Lawrence a television and a radio. Soon after he arrived, the father would turn on the television, then the radio. After a couple of minutes, he would turn up the volume on the television, then the volume on the radio, then the volume on the television, and so forth until the room was blasted by noise, and a nurse would ask him to turn it down.

After a few months, Lawrence emerged from the coma, roaring "Fuck you!" loudly enough to be heard at the other end of the building. Sometimes, Lawrence would insult a nurse, screaming, "Scum of the earth, scum of the earth, *scum of the earth!*" until his voice cracked.

At other times, he would sound frightened. "Nurse," he once implored in a loud quaver, "help me fart!"

To this request Miss Fichte replied, "Now Lawrence, there are certain things you have to do for yourself."

Not watching my television made eating difficult for me. The nurses were used to watching the patients' televisions while they fed them. The soaps and the reruns of *Medical Center* relaxed the nurses, and they would sit down with a patient for twenty or thirty minutes. But I seldom had my television turned on, so the nurse feeding me would stand, shift her weight, and fidget. One lunchtime, a young nurse tried to feed me a four-course meal in about five minutes. She poked the fork into my mouth rapidly, while chattering nonstop. The chicken tasted good, but she was stuffing my mouth too fast. When I started coughing, she asked Miss Fichte for help. The two nurses quickly decided that I had a medical problem involving swallowing, and Miss Fichte said she would have the kitchen serve me pureéd meals. From then on, I was given only liquefied vegetables and ground meat. I was not consulted about the decision.

Two people helped me survive the first three months. One was Brett, my physical therapist, who worked with me once a day. The physical therapy department was downstairs through a long tunnel. H Building, built in the 1960s, had acoustic-tiled ceilings and beige walls interrupted by elevators painted a gaudy, too-bright yellow.

Because she had trained at Kaiser in Vallejo, Brett offered the same kind of therapy as that hospital did. That much, at least, of what Jill had told me was true. At Kaiser, the physical therapy involved crushed ice. But at Fairmont, which did not have a crushed-ice machine, they used ice cubes. Crushed ice averages twenty-eight degrees, as opposed to thirty-four degrees for cubes. The colder the ice, the more rapidly it accelerates blood flow to the targeted muscle group. The cold of crushed ice had shocked me, and the therapy that followed seemed intense and energetic. The cold of ice cubes seemed an indifferent sort of cold, good for soft drinks, perhaps, but useless in therapy.

At Kaiser, physical therapy had been the reason for the place—it was actually a rehabilitation center. We had had treatments twice a day, and we were encouraged to get to those appointments any way we could. But, at Fairmont, the nurses complained about having to take me to the PT department for this new-fangled, unproven treatment. Soon the chief PT surrendered to the nurses' complaints and ordered Brett to exercise me in my bed.

Androgynous Brett, slim and bright-eyed in her John Lennon glasses, tried her damnedest to help me. "These exercises and the ice on your wrist will loosen your arm, but remember, if you feel like making a fist, pull your thumb away from your hand." Under her care, I improved somewhat—my arms and shoulders felt looser, my breathing became easier, and, most important, the amount of time I could spend in my wheelchair increased.

But, after a couple of months, Brett had to stop working with me, because MediCal would no longer pay for my therapy. In order to keep paying, MediCal insisted on seeing quantifiable improvements in my condition, such as being able to lift a limb against gravity. My improvement was real, but not measurable in the way that MediCal accepted. When Brett gave me the bad news, she put a hand on my shoulder, and I began to cry. I had begun to think of her as a friend and ally. Now not only was I losing her, but also I feared I was losing my last chance to regain the use of my body.

The other person who helped me survive those first three months was Emma, a student at Mills College who earned credit for volunteering at the hospital. She did a variety of tasks, including assisting Mrs. Weiss, running messages, and visiting the patients in C Building. A smart, articulate woman, Emma had dark brown hair and permanently, mysteriously pink eyelids. She always showed up in jeans and a red t-shirt. Sitting on my bed while I sat beside it in my wheelchair, she would talk for ten minutes, sometimes half an hour, about all kinds of things, anything from growing up in New York City to seeing Bobby Short playing piano to the latest hospital romance. She could and would talk to anyone. To Wilson, the black patient, she talked about the Black Panthers. With Vinny, the soft-voiced Chicano patient, she talked about the Warner Brothers cartoons he watched all day. I was not in love with Emma, but I was in awe of her. She was so active and enthusiastic that I once felt compelled to ask her if there was anything she did not like to do.

"I don't like tennis," she said, cheerfully. "Can't talk while I'm playing tennis."

The days when I saw neither Emma nor Brett dragged terribly. At Kaiser, sometimes I had read in bed with the bookstand arched over my chest. At Fairmont, I was always either in the iron lung or in my wheelchair, and I couldn't figure out a way to set up a book. I lay in my wheelchair at a thirty-degree angle all day and listened to the relentless televisions. I could not hear my radio or tapes because of all the noise. There were always at least two TVs playing different channels. In the evenings, when Lawrence's father visited, there would be three TVs and a radio.

Once I asked an orderly to ask Vinny, the man in the bed on my left, whether he would turn his TV down. I heard him ask Vinny to "turn it down a bit." I could not hear Vinny's response.

The orderly came back, smirking, to report, "Vinny says you can suck his cock."

I gave up on even trying to listen to my radio. I would watch the nurses come and go. I would eat lunch, pee, and listen to the nurses argue with Wilson.

Wilson was a gunshot victim and a great arguer. He would return from physical therapy just before the shift change and say "Suction!" That meant he wanted a nurse to use a vacuum device to suck out the mucus that had accumulated in his tracheotomy, the hole cut in his throat after he had been shot.

"Suction?" the nurse would whine. "You had to come up here right now for a suction? You couldn't wait 'til the P.M. shift came on?"

"You turkey," Wilson would say in his deep, gruff voice. "You're just sitting on your ass, and I need a suction. Jive-time turkey."

Invariably, the nurse would get up from her chair, give him the suction, and continue the exchange. It took me a year to understand that Wilson and the nurses were engaging in a game, an insult exchange some people call "the dozens."

If Emma and Brett were my allies, Nurse Davis was more of an adversary. Mrs. Davis was a smart, stocky black nurse whose face resembled Mao Tse Tung's, and one of Wilson's most skilled sparring partners. Most mornings began with a nurse saying my name and slipping a thermometer under my tongue. But on the mornings Mrs. Davis worked, she switched on the overhead fluorescents as she stepped on to the ward, instantly waking and blinding us. It was like waking up to an atom bomb.

She flashed the lights on us not to hurt anyone but to announce her arrival. Control was her game. She stayed off the ward for the whole hour during the nurses' rotating half-hour lunch times but was careful not to prolong her break so much that other nurses would complain. When she loosened the wing nuts that held the collar on the iron lung, she loosened them as far as they could possibly go before they would fall off and clatter on the floor—it was a strange, unnecessary action, like many of the other things she did.

It was Mrs. Davis who discovered, disclosed, and enforced the work rule forbidding nurses to lift anything weighing more than fifty pounds. I weighed fifty-three pounds, so she insisted that the nurses use a Hoyer lift, a heavy, ancient, awkward contraption. Riding in the thing scared the hell out of me. I dangled in midair, rocking in the canvas sack while the nurse rolled it to the wheelchair, into which I would slowly be lowered.

Once, when using the Hoyer lift, I felt the canvas slipping up the backs of my thighs. I feared I would fall and break my legs, but then someone caught me. It was Miss Fichte, the head nurse. She held me while calmly telling my panicking nurse how to disengage the Hoyer.

Later, Mrs. Davis liked to show off her skill with the Hoyer by twisting and dipping me in the air before setting me, unharmed, into my wheelchair. Once another nurse asked her, "How could anyone as sweet as you hate anyone?"

"Even sweet people are allowed to hate someone."

She appeared to have been pretty once, and whenever I saw her chatting in the nurses' lounge, throwing her head back in laughter, she still was attractive. But she could be mean.

Once she gave me the urinal, asked to borrow one of my *Time* magazines, and sat down about ten feet from me. When I finished, I called so she could take the urinal and empty it. She ignored me until she had finished flipping through my magazine, about twenty minutes later. Whenever she took me to the OT department, she would stop at the double-door entry to the department, set the brake, and leave me there. There I would have to wait for an OT to take me the remaining sixty feet.

It wasn't only I who feared her. Wilson once called her and another nurse "witches." When asked what he meant, he said, "I mean you don't like men."

The other nurse laughed, but Mrs. Davis leapt to her feet and got in Wilson's face. "Wilson Wright Ames, you take that back right now!"

Wilson, startled that anyone should take his insults seriously, apologized. She cowed even him.

Strangely, though, Mrs. Davis took pride in her work. Starting my personal care routine one morning and inspecting my skin, she asked me who had been my nurse and bathed me the day before. When I told her, she said, "Looks like she just ran a damp towel over you."

"Just about," I said.

She then gave me a thorough washing.

One day in December, the charge nurse declared she wanted all the patients who could get up—that meant me and Wilson—in their wheelchairs by eleven, because Santa was coming. This was particularly insulting and preposterous: everyone on the ward was over twenty-five, and belief in Santa Claus was running low.

Mrs. Davis, a Jehovah's Witness, did not even believe in Christmas—to her it was a pagan holiday. Certainly she did not support the Santa plan. To thwart it, she put me on a bedpan about nine and left me there for a couple of hours. I did not care whether I got to see Santa, but it hurt to be on a bedpan that long. The TVs were oddly silent that morning. I listened to Handel's *Messiah* on my radio, feeling surreal because of the music and the absurdity of being caught in the religious wars by being made to lie for hours on a hard, plastic bedpan.

The charge nurse, indignant with Mrs. Davis, finally took me off the bedpan in time to see Santa, who gave me a cassette of Elvis's love songs. I had asked for music by Ravel. However, Vinny relayed word that he wanted the Elvis tape, with no mention of cock-sucking this time, so I gave it to him.

My days ended around six or seven, when, exhausted, I would ask a nurse to pull the faded yellow curtains around my iron lung, and fall asleep. I would wake up again around ten to the sounds of *The Streets of San Francisco* or *Barnaby Jones*. When the eleven o'clock news rumbled through the room, I knew that the night shift of nurses had come on duty. After the late night reruns of *Kojak*, the TVs were switched off, and the relative silence of night settled in. All that remained were the rhythmic whooshing of my iron lung and the rhythmic clackings of the respirators pumping air into Wilson's and Vinny's throats.

Different rules applied at night. If I needed a nurse, for a urinal or an extra blanket, I would call "nurse" softly, so as not to wake the other patients. If called too softly, I would not get a nurse for hours, because they slept most of the night.

Mrs. Kiley was a night nurse, and whenever Mrs. Kiley came to take away my urinal, she would pull at my dick and nudge a pillow into my balls. The first time she did this, I was first astonished and then pleased that someone had acknowledged my sexuality. I enjoyed her attentions, figuring this sort of playful roughness would be the most I could ever expect. Certainly, I never felt I would have the chance to be sexual within a loving relationship. Aroused, I called her again later that night, but either she did not hear me or she had a one-to-a-customer policy. I thought of asking her to perform other services for me, especially during one night when I thought I heard her spanking the other patients, but I never did.

After I had spent more than three months at Fairmont, in January 1977, three changes occurred that improved my life greatly. First, the occupational therapist, Andi, introduced me to a typewriter I could use. It was a Possum, an IBM Selectric with two microswitches I could hit with my chin. The switches set off a complicated series of beeps, which were translated into the characters of the keyboard. Andi clocked me at eleven characters a minute. It was slow and awkward, but it worked. Better, it gave me an excuse to get off the ward all day. Andi insisted that the Possum stay in her department because, during the one night it spent on C-2, the nurses messed with it and nearly broke it.

I liked being in the OT department. Whenever I went there, I would ask Andi to cut off my patient ID, which I called my slave bracelet.

As soon as she noticed, Miss Fichte would put a new slave bracelet on my wrist. Finally, I told her I did not want the damned thing.

"We need you to wear it," she said.

"Why?"

"Well, without it, the med nurse might give you the wrong medication and you'd get sick. We wouldn't want that to happen."

"But," I pointed out, "I'm not taking any medications."

"You may well be taking some medications in the future, and, in that case, we'd need to be able to identify you."

"But you already know who I am, every nurse on the ward knows who I am, I know who I am. . . ."

"But if you're unconscious—" she began.

"If I'm unconscious, getting the wrong meds'll be the least of my worries."

Without acknowledging what I'd said, Miss Fichte put another bracelet on me. The next day I once again asked Andi to cut it off, and Miss Fichte never mentioned it again.

The second positive change that January started with a visit from Roger, a muscular man in a wheelchair, who introduced himself as the disabled students' counselor at California State University at Hayward. He told me I could take CSU courses without leaving the hospital. Students would tape the lectures, bring them to me in the hospital, and administer the tests. With some excitement, I picked a psychology course and one on the history of Christianity. Doing the schoolwork stimulated me, but more important were the visits of the students.

My first tutor from Hayward was Carol, an eighteen-year-old math major. Pretty, bubbly, and fearless in the creepy hospital, she would walk on the ward around 6 P.M., giving us two hours before I had to go to sleep.

"Good to see you," she would say, settling in next to the iron lung and depositing her books and a cassette recorder on a hospital table. We usually chatted about school, her family, and my day before starting the cassette of that day's psychology lecture.

Carol gave me a secretarial stand to hold my books, but we could not figure out how to use it. This was a problem, because I needed to read the assignments.

One evening, she surprised me by inviting me to a picnic for Hayward's disabled students. I was delighted at the prospect of getting outside the hospital for the first time in six months, but I was even more pleased that Carol wanted to spend a spring afternoon with me. At the picnic, I felt bewildered at being in a social setting with Carol and worried that the wheelchair might tip over on such bumpy ground. But Carol handled everything well. Returning to Fairmont, I told her I was tired but happy.

She said, "That's the best way to be."

I began to notice how much I enjoyed looking at her face, especially when she was quiet and relaxed, while reading. At those times, her face seemed softer, more childlike and vulnerable. I thought I detected then the real Carol that lay beneath the cheerleader personality. Her face looked exotic and beautiful, with dark, expressive eyes.

One evening, she told me she had been reading Steinbeck's *The Grapes of Wrath*. Glowing with enthusiasm, she said, "It's really terrific."

Feeling a delightful loss of control, I said, "I love you."

"I never knew things got so bad in this country during the depression."

"I love you."

"These people were so poor. They lost everything."

"I love you."

"You really ought to read *The Grapes of Wrath*."

I took the hint and shut up.

Later, Carol won a scholarship from the Japanese American Citizens League and transferred to the University of Arizona. When she left at the end of summer, I felt the world would end.

Mrs. Weiss congratulated me for signing up for classes at Cal State. Since there was still time for me to apply for the 1977 fall quarter at UC–Berkeley, she offered to get the application forms for me. I saw Berkeley as a great academic opportunity, and, more important, the

Berkeley Disabled Students' Program offered me the only way out of Fairmont and into a life of my own.

My new Cal State tutor, Charlotte, helped me fill out the application for Berkeley. As part of the process, I was required to write an essay on why I wanted to attend the university. I knew that typing it myself on the Possum typewriter would take too long, so I dictated it to Charlotte, who typed it at home. We were both sure it was terrific.

When my parents visited that month, I told them about my problem with the bookstand. My father got one of the hospital tables, placed it to my right, lowered it to eye level, and put my psychology textbook on it. With my mouthstick, I could turn the pages. For the first time since Kaiser—more than three months—I could read! This development was the third revolution in my life that January.

Emma once spotted me reading a book about Kant for a philosophy class. She pointed a finger at me and said, "Scholar!" So I became the ward scholar, reading philosophy while the other guys watched *Big Time Wrestling*.

In OT, I used the Possum typewriter to type up Simon and Garfunkel lyrics, like "Mrs. Robinson" and "The Fifty-Ninth Street Bridge Song." One day, Andi said she was tired of reading lyrics. "Type me a novel!" she commanded. So I tried, drafting a first-person autobiographical novel that I would later revise and call *Ceilings*. It was not a good novel, but I tried.

Typing wore me out, especially in the afternoons, but if Andi saw that I was not working, she would push me back to the ward. I had to take breaks, but whenever I heard Andi's heels clicking down the hall, I would start typing again. After a few months, she let me stay in the OT department all day, taking me back to C-2 only at lunch, when the department shut its doors. So with spending less time on the ward, taking classes, and reading again, I found that life became somewhat better.

Being around the therapists in OT was infinitely preferable to being around the nurses all day. One of the frustrations about living at Fairmont was that labor was sharply divided between the nurses and the therapists. For instance, I could not ask a therapist to bring me a urinal; only nurses could do that. But there were other significant differences, too. The therapists were in their twenties, white college graduates, energetic, and ambitious. The nurses were in their forties and fifties, racially mixed, high school graduates, and defeated. The nurses worked harder because they were responsible for the drudgery of patient care—washing, lifting, changing sheets and diapers. The therapists were paid better, which inclined my sympathies toward the nurses, until one nurse took out her frustrations on me while getting me dressed.

In June, I learned that I could attend classes at Cal State in person, because a new van service could take me to campus. Excited, I signed up for classes. The first day, I wore the spiffy green pajamas my mother had given me. The driver from the van service looked at me, looked at a nurse, and asked, "That guy's going to Cal State?"

I was and I did, in my pajamas. One of my tutors pushed me around campus and helped me with my writing class. I enjoyed going to the university immensely, in part because the students, professors, and the staff of the disabled students' center treated me much better than I was treated at Fairmont.

However, on my return, Mrs. Weiss chewed me out for leaving the hospital before clearing it with her first. Since Fairmont had been sued so often, it had insurance problems. She feared that if I were injured en route to the university, the hospital would face another lawsuit. So then I had to get official approval from her before leaving.

Roger, a Cal State–Hayward counselor, told me to quit wearing pajamas to class, a suggestion that instantly made sense to me. So I needed to start wearing shirts and pants. However, getting dressed presented a problem, because I can't have my arms raised above my shoulders. It takes time and attention to put a shirt on me without causing a lot of pain.

Usually people managed to dress and undress me without incident, but one afternoon one of the older nurses, annoyed by my attitude, roughly raised my right arm too high. It hurt like hell, and I screamed and cried.

The next morning, other nurses asked me who had injured my arm. Fearing further retribution, I refused to tell them, but they said they already knew; the information about who had taken care of me the previous afternoon was in the charts. It was like living in a totalitarian state; everyone knew everything about you—the last time you shit, how long you slept, what you ate, how much you had peed, who had been your nurse. Of course the others knew who had hurt my arm. That nurse resigned the next day, and I did not miss her.

To be fair, I must say that most of the nurses were good-hearted and tried to help me. But I always feared one nurse, Mrs. Ashby. She admitted to being half crazy, but I think she was underestimating.

Mrs. Ashby was as crabby as Mrs. Davis, but incompetent. Always wearing a baggy hospital gown over her uniform, she walked in a flat-footed shuffle and frequently complained that her feet hurt. Maybe the pain in her feet caused her terrible temper. One morning, she responded to Lawrence's *"Fuck you!"* by throwing a basin of water over him. They alternated, Lawrence roaring *"Fuck you!"* and Mrs. Ashby sloshing him. As the other nurses gathered around this barbarous scene, I thought Ashby was finally going to be reprimanded. But when Miss Fichte came by, she just laughed off the whole thing.

Mrs. Ashby's approach to patient care consisted of wandering around the ward holding up a wet washcloth, gossiping about her family and the other nurses in a voice that ranged from conspiratorial stage whisper to maniacal shriek. When short of material, she would improvise.

Once Mrs. Ashby announced that Paul, the orderly, had red sores all over his chest. When I asked him about this, he unbuttoned his shirt and showed me his chest, which was perfectly normal. When Paul later called Mrs. Ashby a lying bitch, she said nothing, turned, and left with a look of regal dignity.

I was supposed to be in my wheelchair every weekday morning at 10:30, either for school or for OT, but I was usually late on the mornings that Mrs. Ashby worked. Whenever I reminded her that I had to get up, she would scream at me that she had other patients, that I was always harassing her, and that if OT wanted me so badly, why didn't they get me up? Once I appealed to Miss Fichte, who washed me and put me into my wheelchair herself rather than confront Mrs. Ashby.

One afternoon, my tutor Charlotte and I sat in the back of the van, listening to the radio playing the disco hit "The Hustle" as we breezed along the overpasses, the setting sun bronzing the suburban houses. I wanted to tell Charlotte something about the place we were headed for, Fairmont Hospital, but I needed a quick, one-syllable word because I had to shout over the music and the freeway noise. Hearing myself call the hospital "home," a word I had been avoiding for a year, I felt horrified.

To celebrate my twenty-eighth birthday, in July 1977, my mother and my sister, Rachel, visited and brought lunch. We went outside and settled at a picnic table amid a small wooded area on the hospital's grounds. When my mother asked whether I wanted to start eating, I said no, I wanted to wait for my friends to arrive. I felt odd saying "my friends," because I had never had any before. I feared I would sound as though I were bragging and that my bragging would be punished by something, perhaps by the loss of my friends. My tutors, Carol, Tara, and Charlotte, arrived late with Charlotte's friend Tish. Charlotte and Tara brought their guitars, and we sang "Angel Baby" and other songs Tara called "oldies-but-moldies." Tara teased me about my Boston accent, calling me "Mahk." We had cake, and Rachel and my mother laughed at everyone's jokes. It was a good birthday.

That summer, I visited Berkeley to see Zona Roberts, the director of the Disabled Students' Program. Her office was a crowded room over Berkeley's famous Top Dog, an organic hot dog restaurant. I was pushed up a steep ramp to get to the office. She sat to my left, where I could not see her, but I was too nervous and too bent on making a good impression to ask her to move. Her questions were not difficult ones— mostly things like why did I want to come to UC–Berkeley, and how did I see myself handling the workload?—but talking to someone I could not see was odd and disconcerting. She did not exactly say that I would not make it into the program, but neither did she indicate that I would.

I left her office feeling discouraged, wondering how different I was from Ed Roberts, Zona's son, who also used an iron lung. One of the first disabled students to attend UC–Berkeley, he had then founded the Center for Independent Living and was later appointed director of the California Department of Rehabilitation. I wondered when I would get my chance.

One afternoon in October 1977, I was sitting in the hospital's corridor to escape the roars of the competing televisions. Staring at the oxygen tanks and feeling the time crawl by, I was startled to see Carol, my tutor, who I thought was in Arizona, emerge from a door, run to my side, bend over, and kiss me. She kissed me! The first woman outside my family to kiss me, and it was Carol! For the whole time we chatted about her trip, I was nearly incoherent with ecstasy.

When I was little, the Children's Hospital had bathed me by using a very sturdy canvas sling and a large tub; I had enjoyed it. But it had been years since I'd wanted to go in the tub, and I was afraid of water. The device the Fairmont nurses used to immerse the patients into the tub made me even less enthusiastic. A metal frame hung in the air, and from it hung a dark-green net made of webbing, like that on lawn chairs. This rickety affair was attached to a base with wheels. Whenever I saw Wilson return from a bath, dripping and sagging in the net, I wondered why he would let anyone do that to him.

One day, two of the most unpleasant nurses, Davis and Ashby, came to my bed. One of them said, "We've decided it's time you had a bath, young man."

"I don't want a bath."

"That's too bad. You'll feel a lot better afterward," one said. "Pretty soon, you'll be wanting to go to the bath twice a week, like Wilson does."

Ignoring my objections, the nurses went ahead and put me on this bathing contraption. I argued the whole time—"You can't do this! The California Patients' Bill of Rights says you can't force me to do anything against my will!"

"What about nurses' rights?" Davis snapped.

As they pushed me toward the bathroom on the other side of the ward, I continued to protest as loudly as possible, until we ran into Head Nurse Fichte. She calmly told the nurses to put me back to bed, that if I didn't want to go in the tub, they couldn't force me. Later, Fichte made a few jokes to spare the nurses' feelings. The nurses never mentioned the incident, but they never brought the contraption near me again.

Wilson had the bed in the opposite corner of the room from mine. A Black Panther who had been shot in the spine, he was the only other patient on C-2 who wanted to get better and get out of there. He had studied at Berkeley after being shot, but he had suffered a relapse. He wanted to go back to Berkeley and become a junior high school counselor. Up in his tall, green wheelchair every weekday, he spent hours in the PT and OT departments, lifting weights to strengthen his arms.

In the late afternoons, he would return with sweat stains under the arms of the blue hospital pajamas, his dark forehead shining. Although his biceps were becoming stronger, he lacked fine motor skills and used special splints to feed himself. He could use these splints only while sitting in his wheelchair, but he drove his wheelchair with style.

Returning from PT, he would execute two graceful arcs, one forward, one back, so he could watch Vinny's TV while he fed himself supper.

Although I admired him, we seldom spoke, perhaps because our voices were so weak, perhaps because we were too busy pursuing our programs for leaving the joint, perhaps because he thought of me as a spoiled, suburban, white boy.

Friends from his old neighborhood in Richmond dropped by to see Wilson. Once he asked them whether "turkey" was still current as an insult word on the street. At Christmas, his friends gave him a bottle of Harvey's Bristol Cream. Wilson had a nurse distribute cups to me and the other patients. Although I hated the taste, I appreciated his generosity.

One afternoon, my tutor and I ran into Wilson downstairs, away from the ward. Wilson's arm often hurt him badly, I thought from exercising it so much. Wilson was proud, but that day he begged Charlotte to rub his arm, which she did. Thanking her, he said that the nurses, on the doctor's orders, would not massage his arm. He added that they would not give him any pain medicine and, further, that "that goddamned turkey Eggers" would not even examine him.

A few days afterward, I heard a nurse exclaim, "Wilson, if you won't eat, you'll die!" A day later, they took him to intensive care. The next morning, I saw a nurse packing Wilson's belongings. I asked her why.

"Didn't anyone tell you? Wilson died."

"You don't seem very upset."

"Oh, I loved Wilson, but we all have to die."

I think Wilson starved himself to death. It was his only escape from the pain and from the hospital's indifference. Seeing how dangerous a place the Fairmont was, I became more determined to get out with my life.

Shortly after Wilson died, I was rejected by Berkeley for the second time. My tutor Charlotte took me to a pay phone downstairs so that I could phone Zona Roberts and ask why. Zona said she thought another year at Cal State would strengthen me academically. I was stunned, horrified, and angry. Another year at Cal State meant another year at Fairmont. Although I loved the school and the people I met there, I could not endure the thought of living another year in that dangerous hospital. I protested, but not much; I did not want to offend Roberts. But after we hung up, I cursed her.

Charlotte sympathized, telling me I could apply again and that I could survive another year in Fairmont. Charlotte had heard that Roberts did not want any more respirator people in the Disabled Students' Program because a person on a respirator had died in a Berkeley dorm. That didn't make any sense to me, because Zona's son, Ed Roberts, who had founded the program, used a respirator. Ed had even lived in the same spot in the exact same room in Fairmont that I now occupied. All the nurses had told me that I was the next Ed Roberts. I didn't want to be the next Ed Roberts, but I did want to go to Berkeley.

Mrs. Weiss, surprised by the rejection, asked to see my application. Afterward, she told me politely that my essay was clichéd, trite, and sentimental. She offered to help me write another, and we resubmitted my application in time for the quarter that would begin in January, 1978.

Meanwhile, the OT department contracted with Bill Rich, a wheelchair vendor, to make a motorized wheelchair for me. The award of the contract was no surprise: Rich was married to one of the therapists. The wheelchair Rich made, a kind of electrified gurney, did not impress Andi. She said, "It looks like a cat box on wheels."

I thought it looked more like a coffin: flat and upholstered in layers of shiny, dark blue vinyl. I operated it by touching a joystick with my chin. Despite its looks, it zipped around inside the hospital nicely, except when the joystick fell off, which was often.

Andi tried to teach me to drive it in the parking lot, which more closely approximated real-world conditions than did the linoleum inside Fairmont. On asphalt, though, the wheelchair proved a disaster—underpowered, fragile, and plagued with electrical problems. The university required disabled students to own power chairs, and I knew this clunker could never work at Berkeley. Still, I studied a map of the Fairmont complex that I had taped to my iron lung, hoping to learn my way around.

C building was shaped like a dumbbell. At one end were the wards, C-2 on the first floor, C-3 and C-4 on the second floor. C-2 was divided into a men's wing and a women's wing, with a long corridor between them. Along the corridor were a ramped exit and small offices and storage rooms, then the outpatient clinics. I drove the length of the corridor several times a day in the clunker, growing as familiar with the hall as Mark Twain had been with the Mississippi.

On the men's wing, we got a new patient: Cissy, a woman in her forties, with polio and an iron lung. One of her grown daughters visited daily, and she was friendly to me. One night, after her daughter had gone home, Cissy stayed awake all night, calling for a nurse every twenty minutes in a high, thin, frightened voice. By sunrise, she was desperate.

"Speak French! Speak French!" she begged a nurse.

"Orange juice?" the nurse asked. "You want orange juice?"

Driving to OT in the power gurney that morning, I wondered why the woman had wanted to hear French. I imagined that the reason was that French was the most beautiful language the woman had ever heard, and she wanted some beauty if she were about to die. Perhaps the woman thought angels spoke French.

At lunchtime, as usual, I left OT and drove back to C-2 to eat and use the bedpan. In the ward, Cissy's daughter was sitting by her mother's lung, her face wet and red from crying. She glanced at me but did not speak, and I knew that this was not a good time to intrude. I drove back to OT, but my need to urinate had become desperate by three o'clock. Reluctantly, I drove back to C-2. A nurse met me out in the corridor and told me the woman in the iron lung had died and they were still cleaning up.

After this second death, I became desperate to leave Fairmont. Dr. Eggers had said he would let me out only if I could move into a facility that offered twenty-four-hour care, as the Berkeley disabled students' dormitory did. My third application was rejected the following spring, even though the Disabled Students' Program had a new director. I despaired. Would I have to live out the rest of my life at Fairmont? That would not be long, given the average life expectancy at that institution. Even if I managed to live, what would I have to live for? Trips to OT? I felt that my life was over.

After I received that rejection, Mrs. Weiss asked to see the letter. All I had read was the "we regret to inform you" part, but Mrs. Weiss showed me that the letter said Berkeley could not admit me because there were too many people in my declared major. Mrs. Weiss asked, "You declared 'Undeclared,' didn't you?"

"Yes."

"Well, they must have made a mistake."

She called the Disabled Students' Program. I was typing in OT when the secretary told me that Casey had called to say that I had been admitted to the University of California. The wheelchair requirement had been waived for me.

"Is that good?" the secretary asked.

Overwhelmed with relief and excitement, I could not say anything. After a few seconds, I managed to say, "Yes, that's good. That's very good."

Andi heard the news and came rushing over, saying, "Great!"

"Yeah, but September's three months away," I complained.

"Shit," she smiled. "Three months is like the day after tomorrow in this place."

That was true: some people were in there for life, and I was to escape. Two days later, I received a postcard. On the back was a note from Casey, written in red:

"You will be admitted to the Davidson Hall dorm of UC–Berkeley at 12:01 A.M. Wednesday September 6. CONGRATULATIONS!!"

I had the postcard taped to the iron lung to keep up my spirits during my last months at Fairmont.

A few weeks before I left, Mrs. Davis asked whether I really wanted to live at Berkeley. I said, "Of course."

She leaned over me. "All those hippies addicted to drugs? You want them to take care of you? They'll steal all your money."

I did not say anything, but I figured that that would be better than having my life stolen from me by a hospital addicted to MediCal payments. And I noticed that Davis and Ashby were showing me more of something that resembled respect—even, perhaps, admiration.

One day that summer, Frances, the new director of the Disabled Students' Program, came to Fairmont along with several attendants who worked for the program. Red-cheeked Frances watched from her wheelchair while Miss Fichte showed the attendants how to work the iron lung. I was in my wheelchair, watching. One of the DSP attendants got inside the iron lung to see how it felt. I appreciated his attempt at empathy until, swinging his legs to climb out, he nearly slammed into my chest.

The DSP attendants, men and women in their twenties, did not wear uniforms. To my relief, they wore jeans, t-shirts, and sneakers like regular people. If these were the drug-crazed hippies who would take all my money, then I could hardly wait. I could not keep from staring at one of the hippie-attendants, a woman with short, blonde hair and a beautiful, oval face. When the iron lung demonstration was completed, Miss Fichte suggested we go to OT to look at the Possum typewriter. The woman with the beautiful face introduced herself as Jessie and asked whether she could push me to OT Surprised and flattered, I said yes. Once we got there, Jessie read some of my writings and said she enjoyed them. I knew I was going to like Berkeley.

Mrs. Weiss told me that Dr. Eggers kept losing the papers he needed to discharge me. She had done the paperwork herself, she told me, because she believed in independent living for disabled people. She also said that at Berkeley, I would "discover women."

My Cal State tutor Tish helped me pack the night before I left Fairmont. It was more work than I had anticipated, and we did not finish until nine, well past my usual bedtime. I had resolved to ask Mrs. Kiley for some further sexual favors that last night, but I slept deeply through the shift.

The next morning, a nurse told me I had lipstick on my forehead. I felt sure that Mrs. Kiley had planted that kiss. I was flattered, but chagrined that I had missed my last chance to see her.

On my last morning at Fairmont, two nurses got me up without using the Hoyer lift.

After they lifted me, one of them said, "You never belonged here in the first place." I could not have agreed more.

I had lived in Fairmont for one year, eleven months, and some days. Phil and Artie from the Disabled Students' Program came to help me leave. They took me and my stuff out the door, down a ramp, and into a van, and I left that place forever.

PART 2

Independent

8

Year One

(September 1978–June 1979)

T hat Thursday, September 6, 1978, the van took me along Highway 580, which cuts through the wooded hills above Berkeley and Oakland. The hillsides were full of huge trees, much bigger than the saplings that lined Sacramento's streets. After about twenty minutes, I began seeing houses—mansions that had been converted into sorority and fraternity houses. The size and age of the structures, as well as the giant trees and cooler air, reminded me of Boston. Soon we were passing gas stations and stores, apartment buildings and people.

When we stopped, Artie pushed me in my wheelchair on to the lift and lowered me to the street, saying "Here we are, Davidson Hall. How do you feel?"

I wasn't sure. Not overjoyed. Mostly I felt uncertain about how to deal with these new people who weren't nurses. Dimly, I feared they would hurt me. I didn't know Artie, the Latino man of about twenty-three who had driven me here, but I had to trust him—he was an SA, or Special Assistant, a university employee who helped the disabled students in the dormitories. He pushed me up a curb ramp and into the ten-story, blankly modern dormitory. The lobby had a ceiling at least twenty feet above the floor. We passed telephones, an elevator, upholstered furniture, and posters for everything: LSAT courses, dating services, Cal football, travel in Europe, and the Ms. Gay America pageant. Chaotic and unsettled, it seemed like a hotel in a war zone. The two of us entered the elevator, my wheelchair just barely fitting.

Once upstairs, we went down a corridor whose only decor was a mural of a Cal bear—the UC mascot—smoking a joint. We turned into 1B, my room, about ten by fourteen feet, with a large window overlooking College Avenue. Unfortunately, the iron lung was lined up so that the window was on my left, so I could not look out the window. I could, however, see my room and out into the hallway.

Right behind us came several other Special Assistants; there was always at least one on duty in the dorm. They usually hung out in an office downstairs, but as I arrived, most of them came crowding into my new place.

"Did you tell him about it yet?" one asked. Someone told me how the iron lung had been lifted up on a crane and swung through the window frame. "A bunch of guys held that sucker in place and disconnected the cable that held it and whomp! it fell on the floor. You should have heard it." They seemed excited, not perturbed, by the lung.

I asked Artie to get my hospital table, wash basin, and other necessities from the van. As he went off, two SAs lifted me into the iron lung. Pretty soon, I was set with the hospital table next to me, adjusted to the right height and holding the telephone, a most marvelous device. After everyone left, I examined the phone, which had several parts: a regular telephone, a speaker box, and a switch I could turn on with a light tap of my mouthstick. An operator would come on, I would say the magic words "manual line," and then she would ask what number I wanted and dial it. I called everyone I could think of—my brother; my parents; my tutors; and Carol, my old tutor, at her new place in Arizona. I had been missing her and was disappointed that she could not talk for long.

Still, I was thrilled that I could contact people easily and that I could hear them once they got on the line. When I was growing up, if a relative called, one of my parents would take me to the telephone and hold the hard, cold receiver to my head. It was awkward, and I could barely understand the soft, metallic voices. Now I was in control, and I relished it.

Frances, DSP's cheerful, ruddy-skinned director, came to welcome me. Like me, she had had polio, but, unlike me, she could control an electric wheelchair. She looked at the cardboard sign on my lung—someone at Fairmont had drawn a note in purple crayon to instruct the nurses to take me to OT every day at 10 A.M. and 1 P.M. Even after the crane journey, the sign was still attached.

"Well, you won't be needing that anymore," Frances said, taking down the note. "Now you're in big-time OT."

She asked whether DSP's mechanics would have to maintain the iron lung. I told her no, the Lifecare foundation would take care of that. Lifecare had owned, rented, and maintained most of the iron lungs in the country since the March of Dimes went out of the polio business. She blew out a breath, saying, "Good."

Later, Ivy, another SA, came to my room. I hadn't met her before, and she didn't seem especially welcoming. Brusquely, she asked, "How do you like the telephone?"

"I like it fine. I've been playing with it half the afternoon."

"I know!" Her voice was loud and nasal. "I've been trying to get through. It's time to eat. Is there anything I can get you?"

"I don't know. What's available?"

"We have a refrigerator in the SA office with the usual stuff: cold cuts, tomatoes, bread, juice, cheese, beer . . . what do you want?" Waiting for my answer, she folded her arms across her chest. Her posture seemed military to me—unnecessarily rigid. Her hair fell in sharp bangs over her small eyes.

"How about ham and cheese on wheat? With mustard and pickles, if you have any." It was pleasing to order my own meal. Simple as it was, it was what I was hungry for, not what someone in the kitchen had decided hours or days or weeks ago to make for everyone in an institution.

Later, while Ivy fed me, she told me that two SAs would be on duty that night and for the next week but that I should hire my own attendants as soon as I could. The SAs, she said, would give me names of possible workers. "We'll work for you as long as you don't have people, but it's best to have your own attendants. That way you can control your life better."

I already had hired two attendants on one of my preparatory trips to Berkeley, but when I phoned them after my arrival, they both said they'd taken jobs with other disabled people. I was angry that they had let me down and nervous about conducting more interviews.

The interview process I used was perfunctory and nerve-wracking: I just asked people where they lived and whether they'd had experience being an attendant. Regardless of the answers, I hired every applicant, because I needed attendants.

When Ivy left the room that first day, closing the door behind her, I was in my own room, and it was dark. It was the first time in two years I'd been alone in my own room, with a closed door and the lights out.

Above me, plastic stars that someone had stuck to the ceiling glowed, green and soft.

The next morning, my first at Berkeley, Jessie came to do my morning routine. I remembered her as the pretty, hippie-ish woman who had volunteered to push my wheelchair when the SAs had come to Fairmont. Now, businesslike but also kind, she opened the iron lung, pulled me through, and washed me. She was not a nurse, she was close to my age, she was gorgeous, and I lay naked in front of her. Embarrassed and hating myself, I told her I was constipated. I lied so that such a beautiful, considerate woman would not have to wipe shit off me. She was wearing a loose blue dress that came below her knees. I knew nothing of fashion, but I guessed that it was not in style, and I liked it—and her.

On Saturday, Ivy called around noon to ask what I wanted for lunch.

I said, "A cheese sandwich on wheat."

"Well, Mark, a cheese sandwich is all very well and good, but you really ought to start to think about nutrition. Don't you think you should have a salad or something else?"

Annoyed, I said nothing. I had taken enough of such condescension at the hospital, and I wasn't going to tolerate more in Berkeley. After a long silence, I said, "Thank you," as coldly as I could, and hung up. A few minutes later, my cheese sandwich arrived.

The next day, Jessie asked me what I wanted for lunch. Again, I said a cheese sandwich, which she brought. Settling down to feed me, she noticed that I was reading *The Magic Mountain*.

"What's it about?"

"Oh, it's about a young German who goes to this Swiss health resort around 1900. At least, that's what it's about on the surface," I told her. Since she seemed interested, I continued. "But what it's really about is a debate between this Italian, Settembrini, who represents the liberal, humanist tradition of the West, and this Spaniard, Naphta, who is—" I relished the unlikely combination of words "—a Jesuit communist terrorist."

She asked whether she could borrow it, so I recommended a chapter of particular interest and asked her to put up a Kurt Vonnegut novel in its place. Vonnegut was a lot more fun than Mann.

"Who's your favorite author?" she asked, putting a corner of bread and cheese in my mouth.

When I'd chewed and swallowed, I said, "Norman Mailer."

"Chauvinist."

"Well," I said, scrambling, "I also like Joyce Carol Oates."

"Who's she?"

"Oh, she writes short stories, mostly, about people in terrible situations, and she makes you feel that you're right there." I chewed another bite while she thought that over. I loved looking at her face and her short, sandy blonde hair. Either she didn't sense my looking at her, or she didn't mind.

"Do you like it here?"

"Yeah, well, kind of. Yesterday I got a lecture on nutrition. I didn't much like that."

"Was that from Ivy?"

"Yeah."

"Well, some of us are more subtle than others."

Later, as she was washing the dishes, she asked over her shoulder, "What are you going to do about Christmas?"

"I don't know. What do I have to do about Christmas?"

"Well, the dorms close during the holidays, for almost a month, and you'll have to find a place to stay. I'd invite you to my place, except that I live upstairs."

I was struck by her generosity. Not many people would be willing to live with a big, noisy iron lung.

The phone rang. It was the other SA on duty, wanting to know whether Jessie was still feeding me. She said no, took *The Magic Mountain*, and left.

That weekend, I interviewed Melissa, a six-foot Texan with frizzy red hair, for an attendant job. Melissa greeted me and then said "Holy shit!" to the iron lung. She cursed, cheerfully and easily, in every conversation we ever had, but her language was expressive and good-humored, never offensive. Having worked as an attendant for years, she seemed trustworthy, so I hired her for the weekday supper shift.

A few days later, Melissa introduced me to Mickey, a thin, squinting young man with long, light hair. I was starting to feel that everyone in Berkeley was slim, young, able-bodied, and strong, but Mickey had had experience with iron lungs, so I hired him to work weekday mornings.

Eager to help, Mickey offered to buy soap, washcloths, and towels for my morning routine. I told him I could get my own, but I quickly came to appreciate his enthusiasm and useful ideas. One I used for years, for washing my hair, involved a cheap plastic rain poncho. Mickey would put a chair behind my head, then tie the poncho to the chair and the iron lung so that when he poured water on my head, the water ran down the trench of the poncho into a basin. Nothing got wet except my head, the poncho, and the basin.

Another innovation: when Mickey lifted me, he put the wheelchair parallel to the iron lung, but with the heads at opposite ends. Standing between the chair and lung, he lifted me, then turned a hundred and eighty degrees. The spin made me dizzy, but I trusted Mickey so much that I didn't protest.

Other attendants came into my life in various ways. A woman named Tess phoned me to say that she understood that I needed an attendant to take me to school. This was the first time that anyone had called me and actually asked for a job. When she said that she had experience as an attendant, a nurse's aide, and an English teacher's assistant, I hired her. Then I was set up with people to do personal care, though at times I felt like a fish swimming in a sea of attendants.

I have the impression that many able-bodied people think that disabled people who live independently do so with the assistance of one devoted attendant, and they assume that this attendant is motivated by romantic love or saintliness. Nothing could be further from the truth, and that scenario is not even desirable. Having a multiplicity of attendants prevents burn-out and provides redundancy. I usually employ five or six attendants. If one attendant gets sick, another can fill in.

Attendants work for money. How they are paid is a matter of great political contention in the state legislatures. California's In-Home Supportive Services program has paid for my attendants in a fair and dignified manner, but, for years, home health agencies have been trying to take over attendant care. Where they have succeeded, disabled people have been denied the power to hire and fire their own attendants. The myth of the One Devoted Attendant serves the interests of the home health agencies; it depoliticizes the issue.

In mid-September, an acquaintance named asked me if I wanted to attend a Cal football game. Ted was a disabled student who had lived in the dorms the year before, a confident, ebullient Spaniard. Frances had been wise enough to ask him to guide shy, neurotic me through Berkeley.

Ted told me that disabled students were admitted free to football games and allowed to sit along the sidelines, close to the field. I'm not fond of football, but classes hadn't begun, and I couldn't think of an excuse to get out of it. Until then, my weekends had consisted of staying in my room and reading. Besides, college football was so American. I thought I should try it at least once.

With my usual negativity, I answered Ted's offer with an objection: "I'll need an attendant to take me."

"Just leave it to me," Ted said. "I'll take care of everything."

My attendant couldn't work the morning of the game, so Ivy got me up, glad that I was doing something so extroverted and normal as going to a football game. Ted had somehow persuaded Bartlett, a pre-law student, to push my wheelchair to the stadium, so Ted, Bartlett, some other disabled students, and I left Davidson Hall together. It was a warm day, close to ninety degrees, and the sky was piercingly blue. The streets north of Haste had been closed off to traffic and were crowded with festive people.

Along the route, mostly uphill, we saw pretty girls in shorts selling programs, and posters on telephone poles informing us that "Mao Tse-Tung was the Greatest Revolutionary of his Time" and urging us to attend a Mao Tse-Tung memorial. There was much more visual stimulation than I was used to.

As Bartlett pushed me up the steep pathway that led to the north entrance of California Memorial Stadium, I asked Bartlett whether I should pay him.

"Pay me? What for?"

"For pushing me up this hill in the heat."

"Hell, this isn't work," he said. "It's a ball game."

My confidence in Ted's bullshitting skills soared.

As we entered the stadium, I saw these words engraved in stone: DEDICATED TO THOSE ALUMNI OF THE UNIVERSITY OF CALIFORNIA WHO GAVE THEIR LIVES FOR THEIR COUNTRY IN THE WORLD WAR. Apparently the stadium had been built in those calm, optimistic days when people had seen only one world war and did not expect another.

Inside the long, simmering stadium, I was parked on the east side, near the thirty-yard line, with the other wheelchairs. On televised football games, I had often seen people in chairs. They seemed like fixtures of the games, required to add a touch of reality to the proceedings. Now I was one of them, sitting at the bottom of the shadeless bowl.

I recognized Claude, whom I had met on an early trip to Berkeley. He watched the game from his power recliner wheelchair. Andi, my Fairmont OT, had declared such a device impossible to build, but I saw them all over Berkeley. My own wheelchair had been taken to the SAs' office when I moved in, and I never used it again.

Members of the Cal marching band sat by the sidelines, sweating through their blue woolen uniforms. Bartlett asked them how they could stand to wear such heavy clothing on such a hot day.

"Oh, that's easy, man," one of the musicians said. "We just cover ourselves with plastic wrap and run around the track field. After you get used to that, you can get used to anything."

Then it was kickoff. Cal was playing the University of the Pacific, which hadn't experienced football glory since the days of Amos Alonzo Stagg. Cal was expected to win easily, and Ted was boiling with optimism. He said, "All we gotta do is beat USC and UCLA, and we'll be in the Rose Bowl."

I found Ted's identification with the team, the "we," charming. It reminded me of Red Sox fans who said, year after defeated year, "All we gotta do is sweep the Yanks in their own ball park, and we'll have a shot at it."

The game was exciting. I was always fascinated by people who tried something difficult (like throwing a forward pass against the determined opposition of eleven men) and succeeded. Success has always astonished me, and when it occurred on the field, the crowd responded with whoops and cheers. Bartlett kept turning my wheelchair to try to minimize my exposure to the sun, but because I was lying flat, the changes of position had little effect. The spectacle of the athletes, the cheerleaders, and the pseudomilitary bands was all very splendid, I thought, all very Teutonic (still thinking of *The Magic Mountain*), but my brains were baking.

During halftime, Bartlett took me into the shade of the north entrance, where we heard the Cal marching band play "Sing, Sing, Sing," and "Fanfare for the Common Man," climaxing in a volley fired from several cannons. Boy, was it Teutonic.

Sunburnt, hot, and tired, I said I wanted to go home. I was so weak that I had to say it four times before Bartlett understood me. So Bartlett pushed me through the deserted streets of Berkeley, back to the dorm.

It was after three o'clock when we got back to my noticeably cooler room. I called the SA office to see whether someone could put me down, into the lung, but I got a recording. "Hi, this is Ivy. I'm on my break now, but if you want anything, just leave a message at the beep."

I said that I wanted to go to bed. Nothing happened until four o'clock, when Artie came; he put me in the tank quietly and briskly. I had heard that Artie had been in the Marine Corps. He must have been a medic, because he certainly knew his stuff. I figured that my own stuff was staying in my room and reading, and I decided to avoid football games in the future.

School didn't start until three weeks after I arrived in Berkeley, but I quickly adapted to a daily routine. Mickey would get me in my wheelchair by ten and set me up with a book. Tess would feed me lunch, and then I would read some more. Melissa would arrive a little after 4 P.M. and ask me whether I wanted to go to the cafeteria, which opened at 4:30. I always wanted to go, because it gave me a chance to get outside.

Melissa would take me down the hall, past the rooms of the normal students, leading their normal students' lives, and into the elevator. When we reached the cafeteria, Melissa would park me in front and go off to check the mail, which was underneath the building, stored in curious little safes. After she'd gone off, long arms swinging, I admired the joggers and soccer players running about on the AstroTurf roof of the parking garage. Above them, stadium lights glowed fiercely, and, in the background, dormitories reflected the orange sunlight. The fall early evenings were cool and glorious.

Melissa would then come back with the mail and take me inside, where we rolled along a metal table covered with food. She took whatever I wanted, got a meal for herself, put it on a tray on my lap, and took me to a table. It was always the same table, in the northeastern comer of the dining hall. Easily bored, she could not abide sitting still for long. She would give me a bite and then go off to get tea. Then, as I chewed the next bite, she would go off to get bread.

I was not much at conversation, particularly while eating, but, if I was lucky, Artie or Kaye would be down there, and they would join us and talk. If they were not there, Melissa got fidgety and fed me too fast.

We tried to finish by five-thirty to avoid the hordes of able-bodied students, which Melissa called "the madding crowd." Before leaving, however, she would fill another tray with food and set it on my legs. This was for Denny, the man who lived next door to me and who seldom got up. After supper, Melissa took me back to my room, put me in the iron lung, and went next door to feed Denny. Those times, the ends of my days, were the best part, filled as they were with movement and conversation. I fell asleep by seven. Thus, the days proceeded uneventfully until school started at the end of September.

On the first day of the semester, I got up early for my accounting class, my first step in acquiring an M.B.A. Although English literature had always fascinated me, I doubted that studying it would get me a job. Having depended on other people all my life, I longed for independence. I wanted to make enough money that I could live without the help of the government. With an M.B.A., I hoped I could find a high-paying executive job or run my own business. And I figured I wouldn't need to use my hands.

I arranged my course schedule in consultation with Tess, the attendant who would take me to my classes. She was the oldest attendant I had, about thirty-two, with a calmness about her that came either from age or from having been a nurse's aide for years. Plain and very tall, she had strong, round shoulders and not very good posture. I always felt comfortable around her.

Tess pushed me to the middle of the campus, where she stopped to consult a map and figure out how to get to Latimer Hall. The classroom held about five hundred seats, most of them filled. The brown-and-orange walls were done in bas-relief, and behind the lecterns there was an impressive array of blackboards, which slid up and down and sideways, revealing new layers of blackboards.

The professor came in, a big man with thin blond hair, trailed by six teaching assistants. His direct, no-nonsense way of speaking made him seem more like a businessman than a professor. He took roll call, urged everyone to subscribe to the *Wall Street Journal*, and told us that we should all invest a thousand imaginary dollars in one of ten banks he had listed on the blackboard and another imaginary thousand in one of five "gambling" stocks also listed on the board. I had thought that all stocks, aside from AT&T and the like, were gambling stocks, but the professor explained that a gambling stock was stock in a company that owned casinos. Oh.

So began my higher education.

That first semester, I was up in my wheelchair nearly every day, and I loved it. It was fall, and the air was cooling. Weekdays, I went to class. Weekends, I relaxed and read. Just going to class was exciting, seeing the sky and feeling the gentle breeze from the bay.

Most days, I would be pushed downhill on Haste Street to the little Buddhist church on the corner, then right on Bowditch (pronounced BO′-dish, for mysterious Berkeley reasons), past a white building called Casa Bonita, then up past the student housing office and KALX, the campus radio station. Turning left at Bancroft, I saw the ivy on the wall of Hearst gym, waving greenly in the breeze. At Telegraph and Bancroft, students were always standing at the corners, waiting for the lights to change so that they could cross to the main entrance. Above us, flapping against the bright sky, flew the flags of the United States, the State of California, and the University of California.

Going in the main gate, always mobbed with students, I could feel the steep incline of the ramp that had been cut into the brick pavement. And then, passing the rickety wooden stands that sold falafels, milkshakes, and noodles, I often wanted to stop and eat, though I never did. Around me swirled the horde of students—women in long, absurdly formal-looking skirts, men in jeans lugging backpacks the size of suitcases, disabled students buzzing by in high-powered wheelchairs. I loved it all.

Although I was happy that first quarter, it felt odd to have no companions except my attendants. A student who lived on my floor always got in the elevator with Tess and me and went to the same morning English class three days a week, but he never spoke to me, nor I to him. I was terribly shy. Other than when the rent was collected, fire drills were virtually the only times that nonattendants entered my room. During fire drills, a student would run into my room and throw a red banner out my window to indicate to firefighters the presence of a disabled person.

I was lonely in the dorms. Every evening, the sounds of laughter, shrieking, and hollering wafted to my room. "Every night is party night," I'd grump to myself. I felt worse than lonely: I felt shunned.

One Sunday, I was up in my wheelchair reading *Time*, when Jessie burst into my room, wearing an embroidered sheepskin jacket and looking upset. I was so happy to see her that I got an erection. I was astonished: the sight of a woman had never done that to me before.

"Hi," she said. "Have you seen Artie? He's not in the SA office. I don't have the keys. Shit. He's not anywhere around, and he must have the keys on him."

I wanted to help her find the keys. I also wanted to tell her she was the most lovable thing on earth, but I was unable to do either. "No," I said. "I'm sorry."

She left in search of the keys. I returned to reading as my erection died.

It wasn't only the other students' fault that I felt shunned. Once Jessie invited me to a party downstairs in the big dance hall. I had asked Melissa to come at 7:30 on the night of the party to take me there, but I fell asleep at 6. A little later, embarrassed and groggy, I called Jessie to apologize for deciding to stay in bed. Five minutes later, I was asleep again.

Having spent my entire life in my parents' home or in hospitals, I had no social training, no idea of how to start a conversation with someone I didn't know. Apart from my natural shyness, my body just could not stand the double strain of studying and socializing. So, I got into the wheelchair every day that first semester in order to read and go to class, telling myself that I had come to Berkeley to study, not to go to parties.

Early in the semester, I had been affected by hearing a disabled woman talk about her classwork. She'd had a paper to write, but, instead of writing it, the night before it was due she had gone to a party, where she'd had a great time drinking beer and smoking pot. When she woke up in the morning, she couldn't even remember the subject of the paper. She laughed as she told the story, but, later that quarter, she dropped out. I was determined not to let that happen to me, and that attitude protected me from social risks. Talking with strangers scared me to death, but I certainly knew how to study.

Ivy criticized me for being so solitary, for not "participating." To appease her and try to meet people, I went to a few of the SA meetings. At the first one I attended, Jesse and I talked a little more about possible Christmas housing for me, but, in general, these meetings were dull. I never met anyone, and I had nothing to contribute, so I soon stopped going.

My English composition class proceeded smoothly. The professor assigned a paper a week, and I cranked them out, dictating each one to Tess. However, my problem class was Accounting. There was a lot of homework, all of which was difficult to dictate. I had to draw up balance sheets, statements of fiscal positions, and so forth, and all the numbers had to go into exactly the right rows and columns.

During the third week of school, I attended my second accounting section, after spending a good part of the day dictating homework. All that talking had tired me. Just before the section began, I asked Tess to take me to an unused classroom so that I could use the urinal. It spilled, making me grumpy and uncomfortable. She tried to dry me off with a copy of the *Daily Californian* that she found in a wastebasket, but it didn't help much.

In the section meeting, the TA was enthusiastic as usual. He was an evangelist of accounting. But I learned that the balance sheet I had drawn up had been thrown out of kilter because I considered worn-out equipment to be a liability—apparently, accountants rate useless old machinery as an asset. A hefty, bearded student asked why this was so. The TA tried to explain it, but the student didn't buy it. "They count all that junk as assets," the student said, "only because it serves the interests of the capitalists. It has nothing to do with logic."

Undaunted, the TA pressed on, jumping around in front of the blackboard with his piece of chalk. He was so active that Tess whispered, "Boy, he must have had two double espressos today." Eager to answer his questions and pose their own, most of the students seemed totally engaged. Not me. My pants were wet, and my head was spinning with all the words, concepts, and numbers that the TA kept throwing out. I decided that I couldn't take seven more weeks. After class, I cornered the TA in the hall and said, "I want to quit this course."

Pleading with me to change my mind, the TA said that it was difficult at first but that I would get the hang of it. I replied that he and the professor were good instructors but that I just could not do the homework. I did not add that accounting bored me.

"All right," the TA said, relenting, "I guess accounting is a hands-on profession and always will be."

It was the first class I had ever quit, and I was angry about the whole thing. The class had had too much homework, and I couldn't dictate balance sheets to my attendants. But what angered me most was that if I'd been able-bodied, I could have handled it.

While feeding me supper one evening, Melissa said, "Listen, there's this friend of mine, D.K., who works at the Center for Independent Living . . ."

"Oh, I know D.K.," I said. "He drove me to Berkeley from the hospital a few times."

"Well, now he's working at CIL, and they've got these hot-shit wheelchairs that you control with your chin. He wanted me to ask you whether you would like to try one." Of course I did, so we set up an appointment.

When Melissa and I got to the CIL office, on Telegraph Avenue, we found a woman in a wheelchair behind a desk, apparently in charge. Behind her was a wheelchair repair shop, filled with orderless clutter. In it, D.K., a tall black man with dreadlocks, was bending over a chair, working on a brake and chatting with the woman in charge. A radio turned on low played KJAZ. The upbeat, casual atmosphere reminded me of the OT shop at Fairmont.

In the back of the shop were large green wheelchairs. It took D.K. and Melissa a while to find one for me. They were trying to find one that had the controls on the right side of the chair, since I can't turn my head to the left. There were none, so they decided that I should sit in one of the left-controlled chairs. Melissa transferred me from my little blue push chair to the big green power chair. It was much more comfortable than the push chair, but what impressed me most was its height.

D.K. fiddled with the puff controls. By blowing into one of three holes, I could turn the power off or on, swing the controls away, or raise and lower the back of the chair. Accentuating her twang, Melissa said, "Hot damn!" And I agreed. This marvelous chair, made by Ima-Sen, a Japanese company, was being tested by the Veterans Administration. The VA had contracted with CIL to test these chairs by "loaning" them for an indefinite period to disabled people. Only eight were left. If I could get one, it would mean a dream chair at no cost to either me or the state.

D.K. blew into the controls to raise me to an angle that I was not accustomed to. I could talk to people at eye level if they were sitting down and view the room as others saw it.

"This is the highest up I've ever seen you sit," Melissa remarked. Several times she had tried to raise me higher in the push chair, but it never lasted long. I tired quickly, and my thighs ached whenever I was positioned above my usual thirty degrees. But, in this chair, forty degrees was quite comfortable. It made me giddy. D.K. called over Jean, the woman in the wheelchair.

"This is Mark O'Brien. Mark's a student at the big U" (I was pleased at this identification), "and he's been trying to get a decent power chair for some time now. This one would be perfect for him; all I have to do is take the controls off the left side and weld them to the right side."

Sighing, Jean looked away. "You know what our contract with the VA says: 'no welding or other substantial modification of the structure of the chair is permitted.'"

D.K. stroked his beard and thought about that for a while. "Well, how's about if I take the controls off of this side and bolt them onto the right side?"

"That sounds like 'substantial modification' to me," she said. I got the sense that she was struggling with herself. She wanted me to have the chair, but she needed to honor the contract. I waited, the quality of my life depending on her decision.

A compromise was reached: D.K. would do what he thought necessary, but he would not inform Jean. The agreement was delicate and not explicit, but it suited me.

That settled, Melissa transferred me back to my blue push chair. Instantly I felt small and childlike again. I was dependent on Melissa, who now pushed me down Telegraph, looking for a place to eat.

"There's a little Chinese place on Channing you might like," she said, and she took me there through the busy, four o'clock city. The sun was setting, making the brick buildings even redder. Suddenly I found myself inside a store facing a counter filled with cookies and candies. Melissa was buying Parliaments.

"Do you want anything, Mark?" she asked.

Apparently, the store had no front, just a ramp. "Uh, yes," I said, getting into the spirit of it. "I'd like to get a pack of Lorna Doones."

She bought them, and we went to the restaurant, a small, crowded place that was difficult to enter with my wheelchair. Once seated, Melissa looked through the menu, holding it for me to see. We ordered kung pao chicken and vegetable chow mein. As we waited, Melissa talked about the Ima-Sen chair. With mirrors added, I'd be able to see behind my head, to the sides, and in front of me.

When the meals came, they were too hot, so we continued to talk and listen to the radio that bathed the place with music. "You know," I said, "I've never been to a restaurant before."

"No shit?" she exclaimed. Then she said nothing, wordless at such cultural deprivation. I was amazed by how busy and noisy the place was. Almost everyone in the restaurant was speaking Chinese and eating voraciously. The chow mein was good and the portions huge—seventy-five cents for an enormous bowl. I quit early, as usual, but was surprised when even Melissa stopped eating. She usually ate like an overworked horse, but that day she thumped her stomach, saying, "Oh! I've had enough. That stuff is really filling."

In December, the dorms closed for Christmas vacation. Some of the disabled students went home, but DSP arranged for me and another student to stay in my friend Ted's place, on Blake Street.

The apartment was in a three-story brown building with a stone chimney in the front. My first day there, Artie and Kay took me on a tour. I would sleep in the large living room, which had a kitchen in a nook. The floor was covered with a maroon shag carpet that went up the walls. The vertical carpeting, the landlord's idea, protected the white walls from the nicks and bruises caused by errant wheelchairs.

I needed to use the urinal, but I was afraid to ask for it: Artie and Kay were busy unpacking my stuff. Besides, they always told me to use a condom catheter, but I didn't want to. A condom and tube attached to me seemed intrusive, awkward, and embarrassing. Besides, Ivy championed the use of catheters, which solidified my dislike of them.

However, that day, I wished I had one. I needed to pee nearly as soon as we arrived. For a while I was able to ignore the feeling, because I thought we were nearly finished. I hadn't realized how much unpacking was entailed. Then we found out that the iron lung in the apartment had a stiff, old-fashioned collar, the kind that hurt my neck. Artie put me in the lung and tried adjusting the leather straps that buckled around the collar—"It looks kinky," he said—but it didn't fit well. Melissa volunteered to go back to my room for my usual collar, but the dorms were locked, and it took her an hour to get in.

All in all, I held my urine for eight hours that day, which was unpleasant at the time and had nasty consequences: I got a urinary tract infection. That evening, my first as a guest in that home, I had blood in my urine, and I began vomiting.

The next morning, when Mickey took me out of the iron lung for a wash, I had difficulty breathing. Dizzy and feeling suffocated, I asked Mickey to put me back in as fast as possible. The feelings were, I thought, just a reaction to the infection and exhaustion from the move.

I planned to stay in the "tank" for a couple of days and then do my Christmas shopping. Jessie was eager to take me and the others on a shopping expedition, and I was anxious to go.

Later that day, Melissa brought the mail from the dorm: a package and some envelopes. I got a check from Social Security for three hundred and twenty dollars, as well as three checks from the County of Alameda, retroactive to when I had moved into the dorms. It was the first time that I had received money to pay my attendants. The four checks totaled more than two thousand dollars. I had never had so much money in my life, but I tried to look nonchalant.

My only expenses were rent and attendant pay. I didn't really want anything for myself, so I decided to spend the cash on presents. I owed my friends and family so much, and I was looking forward to being generous.

The package contained Spiratwist collars from Life-Care. Made of stretched nylon, they were the color of pumpkin pie. "Oh, these are so soft," Melissa said, stroking them. "They won't bite your neck like those plastic ones."

She wanted to put one of the new ones on right away. I was out of the lung for only a minute, but, by the time I got back in, I was almost unconscious from lack of oxygen.

I had finished reading a Joan Didion novel, *Play It as It Lays,* and noticed that my host and housemate Ted had many interesting books. *The History of Spain,* by Bertrand and Petrie, had a beautiful cover, with a ferocious-looking orange and yellow eagle holding a banner in its beak that said something about "gran liberdad." It was partly just out of boredom, but partly from a desire to know more of Ted's Spanish background that I read it. My doing so pleased my host.

"In what year did the Moors come over from Africa and take Spain?" Ted asked me one day, while I read the book.

"Seven hundred eleven A.D."

"And what was the name of the last Arab kingdom in Spain?"

"Grenada."

"And on what glorious day did that kingdom surrender to the armies of King Ferdinand and Queen Isabella?"

I had just read about that, so I knew the answer. "January 2, 1492."

"Very good!" Ted thumped the arms of his chair. I had passed my Spanish history exam.

Just after midnight one Sunday, as I was sleeping, the collar fell off the tank. The vacuum seal was lost, so the lung had no pressure: it could no longer pull my chest and lungs outward. Melissa had to pull me through to the bed part of the tank while she put the collar back in place. As she did so, it became extremely difficult for me to breathe. I whispered as loud as I could, asking her to finish the job as quickly as possible and to put me back in. She did, swearing up a storm, knowing that the repair that she had done on the collar was temporary and that it would break loose again. She wanted to call another SA, Artie. She said, "Maybe he can do something."

"No, no, he doesn't know any more about these things than you do. I don't want to wake him up. It can wait till the morning."

"No, this is serious. I mean, it's your breathing. I know where I can get him."

Later, Frances complimented Melissa on the wisdom she had displayed in calling Artie at "a local drinking palace." Artie arrived around two in the morning, perfectly alert. He examined the collar and said he might be able to fasten it with duct tape. But Artie was more worried about my UT infection than about the collar, and he insisted on calling my doctor. There was a room in the back where the SAs slept; Artie and Melissa went back there for about a half an hour. When they came back, Artie was folding a piece of paper, over and over.

"I couldn't get your doctor, but Doctor Randolph was on duty. He said that you should go to Herrick Hospital. They'll give you an IV and run some tests on you."

"I don't think I need an IV. And do they have any iron lungs at Herrick?"

"That's what I wanted to find out, so I called Herrick. They said that they didn't have any. I also called Alta Bates, and they said that they didn't have any, either. But I'm sure that they do, they both do, because that's where people who need iron lungs go when they're sick."

"Well, what should I do?"

"I don't know; that's up to you. Maybe you should go back to Fairmont. I know they have iron lungs."

Never, I thought. "I don't need an IV, and I don't have to go into a hospital just so they can run tests on my urine. Tell Doctor Randolph I'm not going."

"Okay, I'll tell him."

For the next hour or so I fumed, thinking of the choice things I would have told Randolph if I had had a telephone. It seemed like a racket, making people check into hospitals for a urinalysis. Artie came back and said that Dr. Randolph was surprised by my refusal to enter a hospital and that there was nothing more he could do for me. After a while, I fell asleep, mentally condemning the entire medical profession.

Luckily, I had more cheerful things to think about, such as gift shopping. For Christmas, I bought two copies of *The Annotated Shakespeare*, edited by A. L. Rowse—one for my brother, Ken, who had introduced me to Shakespeare, and one for myself. I wanted to get Carol, my former tutor from Hayward, a black purse to go with her long black hair. And inside it I would tuck a pair of earrings. After all the shopping had been done, I decided to get a present for Jessie. She had, after all, given me a tape of her Lily Tomlin album that fall, so I asked Mickey to buy her a book by Joyce Carol Oates.

Carol visited me a few days before Christmas. The Arizona climate had made her tanned and healthy, and she liked her presents. While we gossiped about Fairmont and I felt my old infatuation returning, Jessie arrived, wearing a green dress that came to her knees. Sitting at the kitchen table, talking with another SA, Jessie looked unusually attractive, reminiscent of some movie star from the forties. Lauren Bacall?

Carol asked me whether I wanted some dessert.

"Yeah," I replied, "my morning attendant baked a pumpkin pie, his first pie. I'd like to have some of that."

Carol went over to the kitchen, talked to the SAs, and returned with a slice of the pie and something else.

"That girl in the green dress baked some apricot cake, she said with you in mind."

She had baked with me in mind? Just for a crummy, cheap paperback? Flattered, I ate the pie and the thin slice of cake that was on the plate. Carol went back to Ted's room to make a phone call, and, while she was gone, Jessie came over and asked whether there was anything that I wanted.

"Yeah, that apricot cake was good. Would you get me another piece?"

Pleased, she went off to the kitchen. She came back to me with a plate just as Carol returned from her phone call. There was a clumsy silence.

"Well, I think I'll go now," Carol said. It was the first time that I had been glad to see Carol leave, but it gave me time to moon over Jessie. I was embarrassed that my crush was switching over from one woman to the other right in front of both of them. That afternoon, I ate three pieces of apricot cake, on top of the pie, mostly so that Jessie would stay nearby to feed me. Her silver bracelets jingled as she moved. We didn't talk much, but she paid a lot of attention to me, and I was happy.

One woozy afternoon, as I drifted between sleep and my textbook, *¡Espanol!*, Ted showed me a circular about Strawberry Creek College. An experimental part of the university, Strawberry offered interdisciplinary seminars for freshmen and sophomores, with an impressive ten units per course. I was reluctant to sign up, fearing the twenty-page paper that all the courses required, but Ted talked me into it easily, saying, "Ten units is ten units."

As Christmas vacation was ending, Artie told me I had better start getting up soon or my diaphragm would weaken. So I got up the last couple of days that I spent in Ted's apartment. It was hellish, but I managed to stay up the five hours that would be required for the move back to the dorms. I began feeling better: the doctor had prescribed some tetracycline, which had cleaned out my urinary tract, and my lungs were strengthening with use.

After returning to the dorm that winter, I went to school four days a week, trying to earn fourteen units, and the courses I took that quarter demonstrated the range of classes available at the University of California. Each school day, Tess would take me downhill on Haste and then turn up Bowditch, going west on Bancroft until we were just outside the Hot Feet shoe store across from the main entrance to campus. If it was raining, I would be covered, head to toe, with my orange plastic poncho. If it was also windy, the poncho would blow away, and Tess would have to chase it and tape it back onto my wheelchair.

On the days of the Strawberry classes, she would push me through Sproul Plaza and under Sather Gate (I had seen so many pictures of Sather Gate that I always marveled at the real thing), past Wheeler Hall, and up the steep hill by the enormous Doe library. After that, it was downhill until we came to the stop for the campus bus service, Humphrey Go-Bart. Then uphill again, often rushing, until we arrived at the sign that said "CCEW Women's Center," where she parked me and propped open the door. From that vantage, I could see the green campus below me, with cars and umbrellaed people meandering along the pathways.

We entered through a small, hot office filled with women and posters: it always seemed at least eighty degrees in there. Complaining of the stuffiness, Tess would take me down the hallway to the red door that opened into the classroom where Social Policy and the Darwinian Synthesis met. It was a curious room, large and unsettled, with bookshelves off to one side and a large table dominating the space. The room, in fact the whole building, looked temporary.

The course was taught by a history professor and a graduate student in zoology, both instructors who opted to be called by their first names. The first few weeks, the history professor, Josie, a learned young woman with a wide, pale forehead, did not say much, but the TA, Hassan, held forth on biology, particularly genetics and evolutionary theory.

In those first class meetings, it was unclear what the course was about, but after the initial reading assignments, I saw a pattern. Repeatedly, we were given articles about racist scientists of the nineteenth and twentieth centuries, together with *The Manifesto of the Communist League*, by Marx and Engels. After each assignment, Josie talked about the dialectic of history and the quack science of earlier times, concluding with this lesson: (1) the scientists of the past had brought forth theories that were not true; (2) the ruling class would use any method to retain power; (3) it would employ the authoritative voice of Science to maintain its positions; and (4) Q.E.D., we should not believe any scientific idea that tended to buttress capitalism.

I didn't accept this, but I was reluctant to argue with a historian who had read every work of Karl Marx. I liked the class, small enough to permit a great deal of discussion, and I liked the instructors. On a day when I arrived in class soaked with rain, the professor went to the women's room to get paper towels to dry me off. I was touched that she would help with such a mundane task. All the students seemed fairly bright, although we were perhaps not up to the expectations of independent study that the instructors had for us.

Wednesdays were designated "student-led sessions" in the Strawberry Creek course. No instructors came that day, but the students really didn't lead anything. Much of the homework assigned was photocopied articles and chapters, and on most Wednesdays, we just sat and read as much as we could, with one of the students holding an article up so that I could read it. On days when there was not much homework, we would just sit and talk, trapped in the building.

One such student-led session session disintegrated after half an hour. As Tess pushed me home, I said, "You know, some people think that college students are a bunch of goof-offs."

"You know," she said, "I think some people are right."

After the Strawberry class, Tess would take me across the creek and through the woods to the music department. There we would eat lunch, and I would take a nap.

One day, we heard music from far away. "It sounds like classical music to me, a Baroque trumpet concerto or something," I said, proud of my cultured ear.

"Nah, it sounds like Dixieland to me," Tess replied.

"Classical."

"Dixieland," she insisted. "How much you want to bet? It sounds like it's coming from around Sather Gate. We could go there and find out."

"All right. I bet fifty cents," I said.

As we approached the Gate, we could hear the band playing "Ain't Misbehavin'." Losing the bet was worth it to hear that band. They were called Jazzmen Tea, and I saw them as often as I could that winter.

In January, D.K. called from his workshop. His plan to move the controls on the power chair had been abandoned, but Casey, my counselor from the Department of Rehabilitation, had asked the Rehabilitation Engineering Unit at Stanford Children's Hospital to modify the Ima-Sen puff chair. D.K. also said that the VA had canceled its contract with CIL, so CIL was no longer restricted by VA rules. "Me and Casey thought that maybe the three of us could go down to Stanford someday with the chair and see what they can do," he said.

D.K. set a date for an appointment, and I reserved a DSP van. Melissa, D.K., and I made the long journey to Palo Alto one day in February. We talked with the engineers about my mobility problems, but nothing happened.

March came, and the dreaded twenty-page paper had to be written for the Darwin-Marx course. I told Jessie I had never written anything that long and that I wasn't sure that I could do it. But she told me that I could, and her assurance made me serenely confident.

Early in the quarter, I had said I would write a paper about William James, showing that his ideas were not influenced by class struggle. I proposed this topic because I was bored and intimidated by economic determinism, the staple of the seminar. I read two or three books by James before I realized that one couldn't prove a negative, that I couldn't prove that William James's thought was totally unaffected by economic interests.

The week before the papers were due, I changed my topic. I decided to write on the roles that chance and determinism had played in nineteenth-century thought. One of my attendants had lent me *Essays in Radical Empiricism*, in which Henry James expresses his horror at the idea of the "block universe" as postulated by the German philosopher Hegel. I shared this horror, knowing that Hegel had described history as a purely predictable process. He had left no room for freedom, which was bad enough. And then Marx postulated a purely material universe governed by Hegel's "iron laws."

As I saw it, this marriage of determinism and materialism had produced the brat of utilitarian ethics, which meant that I, as a disabled person, was cooked. In a purely deterministic universe, there could be no room for the unexpected, such as a respirator-dependent quadriplegic studying at a major university. In my argument, I used the writings of Charles Sanders Peirce, a nineteenth-century scientist and philosopher who did not believe that the universe was governed by iron laws; he said that chance played an important part in its workings. After Josie suggested that I read something by Marx before writing the paper, I read *The Eighteenth Brumaire of Louis Napoleon*, one of Marx's slimmer volumes.

I had already been dictating the paper to Tess for about an hour before I plunged into *The Eighteenth Brumaire of Louis Napoleon*. It was tough going, and I asked Tess to turn on the radio before she left, to help keep me awake. Listening to a broadcast of the Oakland Symphony, I read until I reached page eighty-three. It was 10:30, and my eyes were tired and sore. I called up the SA desk to ask for the light to be turned off. The SA on duty was Ivy, who came to my room, suggested that I should get some kind of a switch to control my lights, flicked off the lamp, and left.

I decided that eighty-three pages of Marx was enough for my purposes, and, for the next three afternoons, I dictated the paper. On Sunday, Tess brought two bottles of Michelob and offered me one. I declined, so she drank them both. I dictated all afternoon, occasionally asking Tess to look up something in one of the books piled on the table. We had to finish by 5 P.M. so that her friend could type it all up. I was dictating the conclusion when Tess turned a page and said, "Page nineteen." I would fulfill the demands for quantity, if not for quality.

The next Tuesday, Tess took me to the Strawberry classroom so that I could get the grade on my paper. We sat a long time waiting for Josie and Hassan to make their report. Our meeting had been scheduled for 1 P.M., and as it neared 1:30, I resolved that if they didn't show up within fifteen minutes, I would leave. As this private deadline approached, Josie and Hassan entered.

"Sorry we're late," Hassan said. Calm and relaxed, they looked to me like a couple. Josie, Hassan, and I made small talk until I couldn't take it any more. Finally I asked, "How did I do?"

"First of all," Josie said, "we'd like to know how you think you did."

"Well, I talked about it with Tess, and I told her that I thought it was good for a B, but she said a C." In fact, I felt terrible about the paper, thinking that my arguments were not tightly reasoned.

"We think it's much better than that," Josie said. "We're giving it an A minus." She handed me a critique in the form of a letter saying the paper was well written but that Marxism was not as deterministic as I had said it was. Surprised, I thanked them. The grade pleased me, but, as usual, I was tired, so I asked Tess to take me back to the dorms.

All I had to worry about then was the music final, on which I had to get a good grade to make up for a disastrous midterm. In order to stay up for the exam, held between 5 and 8 P.M., I stayed in the lung all day.

In the late afternoon, Melissa dressed me and pushed me toward Hertz Hall. She seemed more nervous than I was. I had given her my midterm so that she could learn the spellings of all the jargon, but that hadn't lessened her anxiety. "I haven't taken one of these god-awful exams in fifteen years," she said. "I hope I don't ruin it for you."

As we entered the building, my TA approached, saying. "Look, the auditorium is going to be filled tonight, everybody will be here for the final. We were wondering if maybe you and your attendant would go up on the stage so that there would be more room in the hall."

I agreed, although the request seemed rather strange. I had never blocked the flow of traffic in that hall before. The TA let us into the auditorium early, while it was still empty.

Some buttons were pushed, and the whole front of the fifty-foot wide stage lowered, steadily and silently. Then it was raised again, with us on it. On stage, there was no seat for Melissa, so she sat on the floor, her head as near to mine as possible so I could dictate answers.

The students filed in, all four hundred of them. My chair was turned so that I could see the screen upon which instructions would be flashed, but Melissa could see the crowd, which made her still more nervous. The professor bounded on stage and told the class that the final would be on Verdi's *Requiem Mass.* He would hand out the test, play the piece three times, and take no questions.

The thunderous sound of the Mass made it nearly impossible for Melissa to hear my answers, even though I shouted the dictation. It seemed the longest exam I had ever taken. I wasn't finished until 7 P.M.

"Is it over?" Melissa asked.

"Yeah."

"Well, thank God. My butt's getting sore." She rose and went to hand in my final.

The TA came over to me, raised his arm in some kind of signal, and the stage lowered to the floor. For the first time, I saw all those people, hundreds of them, all looking at me. No wonder Melissa had been tense.

That spring I took three classes, the most I had ever taken. Because my adviser recommended it, I took a rhetoric course. Also, I took an undergraduate course in journalism because it fulfilled a requirement and because it was taught by Ben Bagdikian. I knew of Ben as the husband of Betty Medsger, a journalist who had interviewed me for a book on disabled people. Last, I picked a philosophy course, Introduction to the Theory of Knowledge, but not for any rational reason. I liked philosophy, and theory of knowledge seemed especially gnarly and mind-bending. It looked as if it would be an interesting, if strenuous, quarter.

Tess had to stop working for me at the end of the spring quarter, so to get to classes I hired Emily, a stout Chinese American lady. A jazz pianist, Emily supplemented her income by working as an attendant. Emily was gentle and soft-spoken, but she never hesitated to express her opinions.

The first class of the semester was philosophy, scheduled for nine-thirty in Dwinelle Hall, a building I didn't know. The first day, Emily found an accessible entrance, but we had to search for an elevator. She finally found one, pushed me in, and pressed the "2" button. When we got to the second floor, a back door opened, and a man in dirty green coveralls helped Emily take me out of the tight space. We found ourselves in a great, dark room festooned with thick pipes and filled with mysterious machines. There wasn't a classroom in sight.

"Why don't I just park you here and go see if I can find the way to the class," Emily said. She was gone for what seemed the longest time, although it was only ten minutes. What would happen, I thought, if she got lost and I was stranded in this noisy, industrial room? I was going through my desertion fantasy ("Sir, would you do me a favor and phone DSP at 642-0518? Tell them I'm at school and my attendant has disappeared.") when she suddenly materialized from the gloom.

"There's no way to get directly from here to your class. The only way out is back through that damn elevator."

The overalled man came back, to summon the elevator on my behalf. He pressed the button. There was no response. He pressed it again, several more times. I looked at the pocket watch pinned to my wheelchair. It was ten o'clock; we were already half an hour late. As I was hoping that there was another way out of the damned place, the elevator opened. Amid much thanking, Emily and I got aboard.

We moved up a hallway with clean, painted walls and busy students, a complete contrast to the factorylike room we had just left. "Well, we'll be late," Emily said, "but we'll get there."

But we found an empty classroom with a message on the blackboard, "Intro to Theory of Knowledge has been moved to Room 2506 Life Sciences Building."

"Shit!" Emily, now perspiring, pushed her hair from her eyes, and we went in search of the Life Sciences Building. Behind Dwinelle, Emily parked me and ran down the path to get directions. Again, I felt afraid at being left alone.

The correct building was long and white, with imitation Greek pillars and engravings of snails, goats, and other creatures along the side. Along the top of the building ran the names of various life sciences: Bacteriology, Botany, and Zoology. With its immense length and engraved griffins, the whole place seemed Babylonian and sinister. Emily took me up the ramp and through the doors—massive slabs of wood. Inside it was dark and overheated, and, when we tried to get into an elevator, it was too small to fit the wheelchair, which was more than five feet long.

Emily blew out her breath in exasperation. "Is there any way that I can make this thing shorter?"

"Well, you can raise the back of the chair up, but only so far, just to forty-five degrees."

The chair had always been set at thirty degrees: sitting up higher was one of my many failed projects. As Emily raised the back of the chair, I felt sharp pain in my thighs, but I would have to endure it only briefly. She pressed the button, and we waited while the elevator slowly rose. When the door opened, she pulled me out into the hallway and lowered the back of the chair. She trotted down the hallway, reading directions painted on the walls. We went down three corridors before she found Room 2506 at the end of a long, sloped hallway. It was 10:30; I was an hour late, frustrated, and embarrassed.

Just before we entered, I asked her to pull me up in my chair; all the moving around had caused me to slip down low. She pulled me with such force that she nearly pulled me out of my pants. Just then, people started to flow out of Room 2506.

"He must have let class out early," Emily said. "They usually don't do much on the first day. I'll go ask the professor what they did."

She returned with a syllabus, saying, "He said you didn't miss much. It was just organizational stuff, no lecture. Where do you want to go now?"

I wanted to go back to Davidson Hall to get my pants adjusted in privacy. We started that way, but, en route, Emily said, "You know, you don't have to go all the way back there for this. I could take you to a men's room." She was not put out, just offering advice.

"But they wouldn't let you into a men's room," I replied.

"People don't get uptight about that kind of thing. It doesn't make any difference."

I agreed, and she took me to the nearest building, where the first men's room we found was a tiny, antique, wooden horror. We had to squeeze through two separate doors, and, once we got inside, the smell was overpowering. Still, it was private, and she pulled my pants back up to waist level. We decided to avoid that room in the future, but at least I had been introduced into men's rooms, places I had never seen before. It gave me a certain freedom; after that I didn't have to, in the manner of Clark Kent, seek out an unoccupied classroom in the middle of a crisis.

The time was coming for me to move out of the dorm. One evening, my attendant Melissa showed me the housing listings. I wanted something on the ground floor, south of campus, and cheap, but all the listings were in upstairs apartments, on the north side, or too expensive. I'd heard nightmare tales of disabled people who lived upstairs: when an elevator broke, these people would wait days for the elevator to be repaired, or else they had to crawl downstairs, which I would not be able to do. I spent more than a month looking through these listings without success and was about to give up on a ground-floor apartment when Mickey told me about a vacancy.

It was in the building of another person he worked for, Mickey explained, on the ground floor. "His neighbor is moving out, but he hasn't told the company that runs the building. If it's like Chub's place, it's really nice, and it's only four blocks south of campus."

I said it sounded good, so Mickey phoned the company before anyone knew the unit would be vacated. He asked what the move-in costs were, said thank you, and hung up. "Well," he said, "it looks like you've got yourself an apartment!"

The semester went well after the horrible first day. Ben Bagdikian showed the journalism class a videotape of Richard Nixon's "Checkers" speech. It was, as Ben said, a masterpiece of television rhetoric. The young Nixon had known to appeal to the conservative heart of the Republican Party, and the speech salvaged Nixon's career. I was interested, and angry that the other students ignored Ben's comments and laughed at the film. They just saw the speech as a fine specimen of fifties camp.

In another class, Ben talked about the book he was writing, *The Media Monopoly*. He said that, when he started writing the book, twenty-seven companies controlled more than 50 percent of all American media outlets: newspapers, magazines, television and radio stations, and publishers. By the time the book had gone to the print, the number of controlling companies was down to twenty-three. He said it would be down to twenty by the time his book came out. This was before the merger mania of the 1980s; I wonder how low the number is now.

For my philosophy midterm, I dictated to Emily out in the hallway so that the other students wouldn't hear my answers. The test was easy, and I concluded it in forty minutes. After Emily handed in my exam, she asked, "Do you want to go see your new apartment?"

Of course I did, so she took me. About fifteen feet wide and thirty feet long, it had a kitchen in back and a bedroom and bathroom off to one side. There was brown wall-to-wall carpeting and electric heat. The bedroom looked too small for the iron lung, so I decided I would sleep in the living room.

As Emily took me around the place, noting the dirty curtains and the lights that didn't work, a man from the realty company came in. Emily mentioned the defects in the apartment, and he said he would get them straightened out, as well as lay new tiles in the bathroom. It seemed my best hope for housing, so I agreed to take it.

One day, as Emily pushed my chair through Sproul Plaza, a woman approached me from my left side, where I couldn't see her, saying, "Isn't it a wonderful day?"

"Yes, it is," Emily said pleasantly.

"So you're disabled," the woman said, grabbing my left hand and shaking it violently. "Congratulations!"

It felt as if she were trying to yank my arm out of its socket. "Let go, goddamn it," I howled. "Let go!"

She kept pumping until Emily coolly said, "Hey, lady, cut it out."

She cut it out and walked off. Emily asked me how I felt.

"Oh, it hurts," I said. "But I don't think she injured me."

We went to Dwinelle, where a note informed us that my class was canceled. I definitely felt like going home, to go back to bed and rest. But as we were leaving, I saw all the people in front of Dwinelle, and I thought of the community of disabled people. I seldom thought in such political terms, but I thought that that woman might harass other disabled people, so I asked Emily to take me to the police station in the basement of Sproul Hall.

Emily gave a description of the woman, whom I had not seen.

"Oh, her," a policemen said. "We had another complaint on her this morning, and we told her that if she gave us any more trouble, she'd be banned from campus."

A paunchy, middle-aged cop bent over my wheelchair and asked me not to press charges. The cop said that the woman was mentally ill and that a jail sentence wouldn't help her at all. I agreed not to press charges, even though my arm was hurting.

A week later, I was sitting near the Campanile eating the lunch that Emily fed me while she sat on a bench. Also on the bench were a man and a young woman with a dog in her lap. My arm was still sore, and I felt tired as I looked through the catalog of summer courses.

"What's the dog's name?" the man asked.

"Beethoven."

"I bet you have a unique whistle for him," said the man, whistling the first four notes of Beethoven's Fifth.

She did not reply. The dog was becoming restless, so she let him go.

I pondered the problem of my major and my class schedule. Having read *Psychology Today* for years, I thought I wanted to be a therapist. It was a job where I could think and feel, but I wouldn't need to use my hands. A woman in the psychology department had told me I did not have all the prerequisite courses needed to declare a major so, reluctantly, I chose introductory courses in sociology and anthropology. However, I was still undecided about a major, so I also picked an English course.

"That's fourteen units," Emily said.

Good, I thought. I wanted to immerse myself in school, because studying was the only thing I did well. Meanwhile, my arm was killing me.

Somewhere a dog was barking. "Beethoven's barking at his own reflection," Emily told me.

I thought, *Aren't we all?*

The journalism final was brought to my room by Professor Bagdikian himself. "I've never had a professor deliver the final to me personally," I said, thanking him. Emily opened the envelope that contained the test, which required us to watch an evening of network television and then write a report to the president outlining recommendations for governmental actions in regard to the media. We had to pick one channel and stick with it from 8 till 11 P.M.

Emily came to watch a Friday evening of CBS with me and to take notes. She brought beer, crackers, and clam dip, and we wisecracked our way through three shows: *The Incredible Hulk, The Dukes of Hazzard,* and *Dallas.*

I hadn't watched TV since Fairmont, and I hadn't missed it. Although I feared that the TV would hurt my eyes, I was willing to risk them for the cause of Scholarly Research. I also liked spending the evening with Emily.

Emily watched *Dallas* every Friday, unless she had a piano gig. She told me she especially enjoyed the character J.R., but I was disappointed by him. J.R. was just an egomaniacal, alcoholic oil tycoon, and, in the final scene, he raped his wife.

Indignant, I said, "Why do you like this guy?"

"It's not that I like him. It's just that he's really out there, a total scumball, and there really are people like that, especially rich people."

Although I still didn't understand, I didn't press her. After all, she was smarter than I was. Her explanations of music, Buddhism, and politics had convinced me of that.

Over the weekend, I remembered Bagdikian's remark that, if you watch a lot of television, your memories of the programs blended together until they all seemed like one long show. My exposure to the CBS Friday line-up confirmed this, so I dictated a paper titled "The Amazing Dukes of Dallas." Emily disagreed with much of what I wrote, saying that *Dallas* was much better than the other shows, but she typed the paper the way I wanted it, and it got an A.

When time came for me to move out of the dorm, I had attendants move most of my belongings to my new apartment several days beforehand, so there was little left to pack on moving day. Mickey put what was left in my backpack, then put me in my wheelchair and pushed me out into the hall. As Mickey closed the red door to my room, I felt no sentiment whatsoever. A borrowed room, it had been Ted's the year before, and it would be someone else's the next year.

Frances came by and leaned in the doorway. "Well, Mark, are you going to go outside now and watch the big show?" she asked, referring to the crane removing the iron lung from my room.

"No, I don't think so," I said in my usual, apathetic manner. "I just want to go to my new apartment and get to bed as soon as I can."

"Well, I'm going to watch. The guy at Lifecare called up all the TV stations and told them about it. I got calls last night from Channel 5 and Channel 7. They'll probably want to interview you."

Flattered, I changed my mind and told Mickey to take me out on the sidewalk of College Avenue so that I could watch the circus. As we left the dorm, I saw a man holding a film camera. "Hi, Ma!" I yelled at the camera. The show was on.

The truck that supported the crane was parked on College Avenue, blocking half the street. The crane reached up to my window, which was open, the curtains fluttering. Marty, a neighbor, was there, too. A graduate student in journalism, he had interviewed me the previous November for one of his classes. Since then, he had dropped by occasionally to talk, the only student ever to do so.

A reporter for Channel 7 stood next to the truck. Thrice he delivered the same line: "If you think moving is a hassle, consider the case of twenty-nine-year-old Mark O'Brien of Berkeley." There was no power to record the first recital of this speech; during his second attempt a fire engine passed, and so he did it a third time, with exactly the same expression and inflection.

The hooks on the crane had been put in place. The lung came out of the window, while above it students leaned out of their windows, cheering as the crane lowered its burden to the sidewalk. The bright yellow lung, which always dominated any room, looked tiny against the vertical expanse of Davidson Hall. As four men loaded the tank aboard a pickup truck, the television reporters interviewed me. They asked many questions, all variations of "Isn't this terrible what they're doing to you?" Knowing that film clips of angry people were standard on local news, I responded honestly, if dully, that the university had been very kind to me, that dormitories were only temporary housing, and that disabled people had to scramble for housing in Berkeley, just like everyone else.

At my new apartment, Mickey opened the door, and we saw Melissa setting books on the shelf that my parents had brought down. "Hello there," she said. "Welcome home."

She had all the furniture arranged and had discovered some rolled marijuana in the refrigerator, left over from the previous tenant. I wondered whether my parents had seen it when they had inspected the place. Mickey and Melissa smoked the frigid dope, while I waited for the lung to arrive.

It was inexplicably late. When it did arrive, it took the efforts of several men to push it up the driveway and into my apartment. Once inside it, I relaxed, trying to feel at home.

That evening, Mickey and I watched ourselves on the TV news. The SAs had told me I would need a live-in attendant, so Mickey offered to spend nights in my apartment. Everything was fine the first two nights, but, on the third night, he said he wanted to sleep with his girlfriend. He wanted to be with her the fourth night, too, and after that, we agreed that I didn't need a live-in attendant.

Denny, my next-door neighbor from the dorm, was going to rent the apartment next door to my new one, but his would not be available until early in July, so he stayed in the bedroom of my apartment for three weeks. He was out in his power chair most of the day, roving around Berkeley, coming home only to eat supper with Melissa and me. I liked hearing him chat with Melissa, thinking him a much better conversationalist than I was. But when apartment number two opened up and Denny moved out, I had the whole apartment to myself, and I decided to keep it that way.

9

English Major

(June 1979–December 1980)

H aving decided for academic reasons to take classes in anthropology and sociology, I had to ask my morning attendant,
Mickey, for permission. Usually Mickey began my morning
routine at 8:30, but my proposed anthro class started at 9 A.M. Reluctantly, he agreed to come a little before 8. Most days, I was up in the
wheelchair, with Mickey applying sunblock to my face or putting on
my glasses, when I heard the clicking sound of Emily locking up her
bicycle. She and Mickey would say hello and goodbye, and then Emily
and I would set off.

On a typical day, with the morning air cool and the streets nearly
deserted, Emily took me up Telegraph, right on Channing, and onto
College. The first class was Introduction to Physical Anthropology. The
students would be yawning, rubbing their eyes, and drinking coffee,
trying to wake up. I liked the professor, who was about twenty-nine,
not much older than I.

After that class, Emily rushed me to Introduction to Sociology, for
which we had two books: *The Spirit of Protestantism and the Rise of
Capitalism,* by Max Weber, and *The Godfather,* by Mario Puzo. My
mother had given me a paperback copy of the novel years before, but
I had never been able to get past page 30, because I had been so annoyed
by the constant references to Sonny Corleone's "enormous pole." Now
I had to read the whole book.

On Tuesday and Thursday afternoons, I took a class in Shakespeare,
taught by a professor named Jackson Burgess. While the reading for
the other courses was light, it took me all weekend to get through one

of Shakespeare's plays. We had to read ten of them. I was using the Rowse edition I had bought the previous Christmas, which had many pictures but few footnotes. Burgess recommended the Riverside edition, and, when I finally bought it, years later, I realized its superiority.

Raised on a chicken farm in North Carolina, Burgess had been a journalist before earning his M.F.A. The only member of the English faculty without a Ph.D., he was the greatest professor I ever had.

The class met in a ground floor room that had been designed to accommodate forty students. One hot summer afternoon, it held about fifty-five of us, and the roar of a huge lawnmower came through the windows. Burgess sat on the front of his desk, his jacket off and his skinny legs crossed, talking at the top of his voice about *I Henry IV,* which he deemed a nearly perfect play. He pointed out the antithesis between the foolhardy Hotspur and the cowardly Falstaff. Prince Hal, Burgess said, was a synthesis of these two characters: brave, but intelligent enough to pick his fights.

According to Burgess, many celebrations in Shakespeare signified real joy because the harvest had come in. "If the harvest didn't come in, you starved! There were no food stamps, no welfare: you starved." In explanation, he referred to the anxiety he, as a child, and his family had felt after a hurricane had knocked down their chicken coops.

Later that day, Emily ran into Burgess at a campus sandwich shop. Chomping into an extra-thick BLT, he told her, "I need this. That last lecture nearly killed me."

Years later, after he died, I saw a graffito on the outside of a Berkeley *taqueria* that said, "Michael Jackson Burgess." Jackson Burgess was as important to me—and at least one other person—as Michael Jackson was to many Americans. Shakespeare and Burgess changed my mind about my career direction: I became an English major for life.

Near the end of summer session, Emily parked me near a tree and sat on the bench around the trunk, saying she had something to tell me. "This is the hardest job I've ever had," she sighed. She took out the rubber band that held her hair in a ponytail. "The chair's really heavy and hard to push up all these hills. I don't know if I'll be able to do it next quarter."

I hoped she would, because I enjoyed talking with her; she was fun and generous. Mickey always packed a lunch for me in the mornings, but, when Emily noticed that the lunches did not include desserts, she shared her sunflower cookies. Like all of my attendants, Emily was paid an hourly wage by the State of California. Once, on the way home, she asked me whether I wanted to stop at Bud's Ice Cream, but I said no, because I couldn't justify having the state pay for her time while we ate treats. A week later, when she said, "How about an ice cream on the state?" I was unable to resist her wit. Bud's Ice Cream's doorway was too small for my wheelchair, so we stayed outside in the shade, she feeding me a vanilla cone while she had strawberry yogurt. It was a wicked abuse of state funds.

Once, while talking about art and Buddhism, she said there was no such thing as beauty or ugliness; things just were. I disagreed, and, to prove my point, I asked her whether UC–Berkeley's Dwinnelle Hall was beautiful or ugly. Dwinnelle looked to me as if it had been designed by a maniac. (One of my attendants had corrected me: "Two maniacs.") But Emily said Dwinnelle Hall just *was*, like the squirrels and Sather Gate.

After a hard day of classes, I would wait for Melissa to come and put me in the iron lung. Tall and strong, she could settle me in about five minutes, but she often didn't come on time. When she was late, I would call her but usually got no answer. If she hadn't come by about five o'clock, I would call Mickey and ask him to put me to bed.

When I first got to Berkeley, I was told that, sooner or later, everyone had to spend the night in a wheelchair because of a no-show attendant. I dreaded this possibility, knowing that a night in the wheelchair would kill me—at that time, I could stay out of the iron lung for a maximum of seven or eight hours, using a portable respirator.

When Melissa came, she prepared supper for me and for Denny, who lived next door. If Denny was up in his wheelchair, he would come over, and Melissa would feed the two of us. He loved to make dumb jokes at Melissa's expense: "Hey, Melissa, you don't dry the dishes on the curtains." Melissa would curse back at him with complete good cheer. He and Melissa watched a lot of TV, and they often talked about what they had seen on the Carson show the night before. Sometimes Melissa sent Denny out to buy her Parliaments and a beer. I envied Denny's freedom to go into a store and buy things, to do Melissa a favor.

One day Denny announced that we would be having Nude Attendant Day next week. "Shit, I'll do Nude Attendant Day," Melissa said, "if you pay me fifty dollars an hour."

I began going to Stanford Children's Hospital, where engineers were modifying the Ima-Sen wheelchair that I had obtained from Center for Independent Living. To get to Stanford, I hired Melissa to drive me in a Disabled Students' Program van. As we went through Palo Alto, I was amazed by the mansions set far back from the streets: they were as big as apartment houses, but each was a private residence.

After entering the Stanford campus, we drove on for several minutes through a eucalyptus wasteland before reaching the quadrangle. It was so different from the crowded, urban Berkeley campus. At the hospital, the engineers and I discussed what sort of control I should use for the chair; some favored a chin mechanism, but I pointed out that if I slipped down in the wheelchair, I would lose control. A disabled engineer had the idea of putting one lever under my left knee and one under my left foot to take advantage of the movement I have in those limbs. The foot lever would control the direction of the wheelchair, and with the knee panel I could moderate the speed.

To see whether I could operate this combination, the engineers hooked up the controls to a computer. It was the first one I'd ever seen in real life, and it looked nothing like the ones on TV. Instead of taking up a whole wall, this machine looked like a typewriter with a small TV on top, and it was programmed to play Pong, a game that required me to bounce a spot of light back and forth between moving panels. Using my new controls, I excelled at Pong. While playing, I asked the engineers what kind of computer this was.

"Apple," one of them told me. "It's a local company from Cupertino."

I thought "Apple" was a funny name for a computer.

Eventually the controls were attached to the chair, and I was able to putter around the parking lot outside Stanford Children's Hospital. Moving inside was much easier, because the floors were smooth and the distances shorter.

Moving myself—for the first time since Fairmont—was new and eerie, as well as thrilling, and I recognized something that I'd been missing. When I talked about it to my neighbor, Denny, he said, "Yeah, it's really neat; when you're talking with people you can change the position." I wasn't used to being able to move closer or further away from people, and I found that small movements could offer great psychological differences. A few inches one way or another made me much more comfortable.

The wheelchair wasn't delivered until the spring of 1980. In the meantime, Emily continued to push me to class and take notes for me.

In September 1979, a year after my arrival, I began taking the first of three classes about British writers. The first, covering literature of the thirteenth to the sixteenth century, was taught by Professor Ackroyd, a big, bearded, graceful man who reminded me of the young Orson Welles. When he lectured, standing with one foot up on the desk, leaning forward, I feared he would rip his pants. He was the only person I ever heard read Chaucer aloud, so whenever I recite the "General Prologue," I rely on my memory of his pronunciation.

Later, when we got to Edmund Spenser, I became bored. An attendant who had been an English major saw me reading *The Faerie Queene* and asked my opinion. I said I wasn't likely to become a Spenser freak. But Ackroyd loved him and championed a complicated theory about the visual aspects of the half-finished epic. Visual aspects notwithstanding, I could understand why it was unfinished.

That fall, I tried to sign up for Jackson Burgess's class in creative writing. Eighty students jammed into a basement classroom built for thirty-five. Burgess said all seniors were automatically admitted and, then after asking the juniors to raise their hands, he let them in, too. The rest of us were told to write a sonnet and deliver it to his office; after reading them, he'd announce whom he would allow into the class.

Leaving the classroom, I asked Emily what a sonnet was. She suggested we go to the undergraduate library to look it up. The encyclopedia told us there were Petrarchan sonnets, with rhyme schemes ABBA CDDC EFGGFE, and Shakespearian sonnets, ABAB CDCD EFEF GG. We went back to my dorm room, and I dictated one of the worst sonnets in the history of the English language. When we checked Burgess's door a few days later, I wasn't surprised that my name wasn't on the list.

My other class was the beginning of a two-part rhetoric course called The Craft of Writing. Our textbook said that any piece of writing could be seen as an argument, and any argument could be composed of two interlocking syllogisms. This theory influenced my writing and thinking for many years. Before I took that class, I had had trouble filling up a five-page paper, but after it, words came easily.

Melissa told me she wanted to cut back from five to three evenings a week, so I got a list of attendants from the Disabled Students'

Program and began calling people. The first one I hired was a man with a thick but understandable accent. Joao, a tall graduate student with both Brazilian and Israeli citizenship, had been in the Israeli army and had been a guard in the Knesset when Egyptian president Anwar Sadat addressed it. He and his girlfriend, Naomi, had driven across the Sahara in a VW bug: surely he could handle me and my iron lung.

Aside from studying for a Ph.D. in mathematics, Joao played Bach and samba on his guitar. He cooked well, his specialties being vegetarian lasagna and cheese melted on rice. He got up at 5 A.M. every day to practice Kundalini Yoga and to read Krishnamurti, and he told me about spiritual experiences he'd had while dropping acid. Some days he would arrive with a bag of fresh-baked gingersnaps. Before starting dinner, we would, as he said, "boolsheet" while we ate all the cookies. "We killed the bag," he would announce happily, crumpling it up. But even half stuffed with gingersnaps, I still felt I had to eat dinner.

After Naomi, his Uruguayan girlfriend, came to Berkeley, they invited me to their apartment in married students' housing. Naomi wore flowing, filmy white dresses that set off her deep tan and black hair. Their apartment was decorated with a large, gold-foil camel she had ripped off a cigarette billboard and a revolving Timex watch stand, which they used to store cassettes. I spent one fascinating afternoon at their place, discussing religion with them and with Michael Klass, a disabled math professor. I was glad to have made a new friend or two.

Occasionally I'd see my friend Jessie, the SA, on the streets. She always ran up to me and hugged me—the only person to do so. I still had a crush on her, and her hugs made me ecstatic.

My bad experience with the accounting class had convinced me that I could never get an M.B.A. and thus would never have an M.B.A.'s financial and professional opportunities. As an English major, I began to wonder what sort of future lay ahead for me, what careers I might have. I thought of going into special education, and I considered journalism and graduate work in English. I didn't think I had the imagination to make up stories or the skills to create a new writing style. So I thought my only chance to write professionally would be as a journalist.

While taking the last part of the British writers course, I'd become entranced by the gentle rhythms of Wordsworth's poetry. Reading it encouraged me to write some of my own, and I began to write verse for myself and for friends. I typed my first poetry on the Possum type-writer I'd brought from the Fairmont.

The new power wheelchair was finally ready and delivered at the end of the spring quarter of 1979. Emily agreed to teach me how to drive it but said that she would stop working for me when summer session began, so she could devote all her time to playing and teaching jazz. That meant I had about six weeks to master the intricacies of driving the chair on the hilly campus and in Berkeley traffic.

   At first I just drove safely in the bumpy parking lot behind my build-ing, Emily walking close by. Then I decided to venture to the Center for Independent Living, one and a half blocks from home. This was quite a different journey; as we started out on the sidewalk, I was glad that Emily told me what to do. When I reached the end of my driveway and peered into the mirrors, the end of the chair looked as

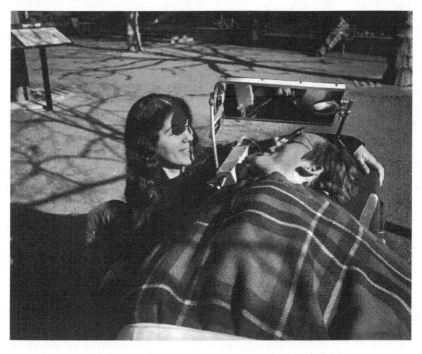

Mark with a friend on the UC–Berkeley campus, 1980.
Note the mirrors he uses to steer the chair.

Photo courtesy of Betty Medsger.

though it was hanging over in the street. But Emily told me to drive a little further to get onto the sidewalk. I trusted her. She said to turn right. I did, and sure enough I was in the sidewalk, just as she'd said I would be. Once we had gone around the corner, driving was easier; I just had to stay going in one, predictable direction until I came to the Blake Street ramp. Emily told me to park in front of the ramp and then head down the middle of it at full speed.

As I crossed Telegraph Avenue, it seemed as wide as the Amazon, and more dangerous. We had a breather at the median strip, then continued between the white lines. California law requires cars to stop for pedestrians, but I wasn't confident that they would do so. Finally, in the CIL parking lot, we practiced doing figure eights, circles, and tight curves.

Returning to my apartment, I let myself in by blowing into a straw that controlled the door opener. I drove inside, being careful not to bump into the furniture in my crowded apartment. Inside, I blew into the straw again to close the door.

As I got more skillful, Emily took me further along new streets and onto campus. She advised me to drive as if all car drivers were crazy, something she had learned while bicycling through town.

Careful but increasingly confident, I began to imagine going to class by myself and running errands independently. That meant greater self-reliance and higher self-esteem. Having a power chair was a status symbol, whereas being pushed around embarrassed me. It also meant more money saved for the state, which was why the state was investing in the wheelchair. I was grateful to one of the first disabled students at UC who talked state bureaucrats into buying him a power chair; after that it had become state policy to provide them.

Emily wanted me to drive alone to Shattuck Avenue, three and a half blocks from home, which seemed terrifying. But, to please her, I tried. I drove one block west, then came to a hole in the sidewalk covered with wooden boards. For several minutes I tried to decide whether to risk going over the boards or to return without completing my trip. Scared that the weight of the chair would break through the boards, I turned around and went home.

When I told Emily the next day that I had failed her assignment, she shrugged, forgiving me. "Okay, let's try something else."

She had me drive up to campus and back, while she walked on the opposite side of the street. When I completed the trip, she smiled one of her infrequent smiles and said, "It looks like you won't be needing me anymore. Congratulations."

The Monday after my first solo expedition, I used my new confidence to drive to the drugstore on Telegraph. Once inside, I told the clerk that I wanted to buy a cheap wristwatch. He took some from the display case, and I picked a Timex with a metallic wristband. I had him attach it to the wheelchair's mirror, then told him my money was in the backpack hanging from the back of the chair. He took out the money, made change, placed the wallet back in the backpack, and zipped it up. I thanked him and left, feeling like a real American adult.

The clerk was nonchalant about the transaction, having seen other disabled customers. One good thing about Berkeley is that people don't freak out about wheelchair users, even a severely disabled person.

Two days later, I decided to go window shopping on Telegraph Avenue. I drove to the corner and crossed to the traffic triangle. Emily had always told me to look for red, because ramps were painted red. At one corner of the triangle, I saw some red paint and, heading for it, drove right off the curb. Seeing the windows of Moe's bookstore fly up in the air, I thought I was about to die, that the wheelchair would roll on top of me and crush me.

I fell sideways on the asphalt, my left leg still strapped to the wheelchair, which lay on its side, wheels spinning madly. A small crowd gathered, and I asked someone to unstrap my leg. Within a minute, an ambulance arrived. Once inside it, I realized my left knee was swollen and that I had a bump on the back of my head. A paramedic asked me three times whether I wanted to go to the hospital. I kept saying no, that I just wanted to go home. More scared than hurt, I needed to go back in the iron lung to rest.

When they took me out of the ambulance, the door to my apartment was ajar. Apparently the door opener had been set off by the fall, and the door had remained open since then. I told the firefighters how to open the lung and put me inside. Then I called Joao, asking him to come over early to do my evening routine.

When Joao started taking my pants off, I yelled in pain. My left knee was so swollen he could hardly remove my clothes, even though he was slow and gentle. After I told Joao what had happened, I began crying, ashamed of myself for having wasted Emily's time. Later on, I cried for myself as well as for the shock and pain, but at the time I just chastised myself for letting Emily down.

The next day, with great reluctance, I called Emily and told her about my fall. Although she wasn't angry with me, she sounded frustrated. She wanted to concentrate on her music that summer, but she offered to train me more on driving the wheelchair.

The next Wednesday, I got in the wheelchair, but my knee was still so swollen I couldn't lift it enough to operate the speed control. I was crawling along at half a mile per hour when Emily got impatient, switched off the motor, and took over pushing the chair. It was faster that way, but the electric chair was very heavy, and afterward she said she would never do that again.

For the next two weeks, until my knee completely healed, she pushed me in the regular wheelchair. Then I once again began driving the power chair to my history class, with Emily accompanying me to take notes.

I admired the history professor because, even though he stuttered, he had entered a profession that required public speaking. Then I realized, much to my embarrassment, that I was admiring someone for being brave about a disability, an attitude that has always disgusted me because it is so condescending.

By the end of summer session, I again felt confident enough to use the power chair unaccompanied. I had two classes that fall, one in rhetoric and the other in political novels. Driving to the rhetoric class was easy, but the political novels class met in a building on the far side of campus, across a difficult route. To get there I had to drive to Wheeler Hall, trundle slowly up the long hill, turn north at the top of the hill, then go east past cubelike Evans Hall. Behind Evans was a great asphalt valley that I had to roll down and then up again to reach the door of Cory Hall. At that point I had to wait till someone came along and then ask the person to open the door for me.

Fortunately, another disabled student, Jenny, also attended the political novels class. She sat in a reclining wheelchair, able to use her hands enough to operate a joystick. During break in the first class meeting, she asked one of the able-bodied students to feed her lunch. I would never have thought of doing that, being so afraid to ask people for favors. I had hired an attendant to meet me during the class break, feed me lunch, and take me into the men's room. But Jenny had an outgoing personality and charmed people, which made them eager to help her.

After class, I would drive to the elevator and wait for someone to ask whether I needed help. Sometimes I waited ten or fifteen minutes while people walked by. One day Jenny buzzed up and asked me, "Do you need help with the elevator? Let me go get someone." Despite my protests, she got someone not only to open the elevator but also to ride down with me and to open the door at the bottom.

Mickey got a job and wanted to quit working for me. I didn't think I could live without Mickey, who did everything so well and efficiently, but I had no choice. I started looking for another morning attendant.

I hired Kate, who said that, even though she had no experience as an attendant, she was a mother and that should qualify her. If anything, Kate was overqualified for most jobs. She had grown up in Brazil, had a master's in anthropology, and spoke five languages. She'd been accepted to work as an administrator for the Peace Corps starting the following January, but she would work for me until then.

Close to six feet tall, she had short, swingy, shining hair and big glasses. Often she entered my room in the morning saying, "¡Lección numero uno! ¿Cree usted que va a llover hoy?" (Lesson one! Do you think it will rain today?) Once she came in soaking wet, asking me the same question and whether she could change. She put on my big red shirt, wrapped a striped sheet around her waist, and proceeded with the routine.

Some mornings, she would greet me from outdoors by beeping the horn of her red-and-white Volkswagen bus, its spare tire in front painted like a yin-yang symbol. Actually, the yin and yang were two whales, white and black, swimming endlessly around. Kate had once been known as the Whale Lady, because she gave whale puppet shows at primary and secondary schools.

Kate liked Mickey and Joao but loudly disliked other attendants. On days that I didn't get up, she called me a "slug-a-bed." Other days, when I tried to get up despite feeling weak, she would inform me that I had a case of "the punies" and ought to stay in the tank. She easily lifted me into and out of the power chair, which she christened The Great Unwieldy. By the time I had rolled onto the sidewalk, Kate would have driven her bus to the end of the driveway. To say goodbye, she opened the window, raised a fist, and encouraged me by singing a few bars of the Italian version of the "Internationale." "Avanti, il pololo di mundi ...!"

Even though it was the fall of 1980, the traffic lights still bore Carter-Mondale stickers from the 1976 election. Near Sather Gate, a man in a green shirt (the official Carter color) could be seen shouting, "Support the ERA! Support President Carter! Support SALT II! Support President Carter!" But that year, for the first time, the Campus Republicans had a table in Sproul Plaza, along with all the other tables. The evening before the election, I saw people dressed in black, covered with ashes, pulling a cart through campus and shouting, "Repent! Repent! The end is near." Their cart bore a poster for Reagan-Bush.

On the evening of Election Day, as Melissa fed Denny and me, I asked her to turn on my radio. The NPR newscaster said, "The networks project that Governor Reagan will carry Massachusetts, New York, New Jersey, Pennsylvania, Ohio . . ." It was horrifying. Denny threw his head back and droned, "Oh, Ga-a-awd."

The morning Reagan was inaugurated, Kate was washing me when she burst out, "I can't believe they elected that dumb actor to be president!"

At Christmas break, I was exhausted from driving the wheelchair. My left leg hurt all the time, and I considered dropping out of school, because I was sure the state wouldn't pay attendants to push me to school, since I had the power chair. I worried about my future. If I quit school, I would lose my last chance to get the education I needed to make a living and to create a life for myself. Berkeley was full of disabled dropouts who spent their days hanging out on street corners, and I didn't want to end up like them.

To give myself time, I asked the wheelchair mechanics at DSP to work on the power chair. It needed brakes, and I wanted it to move faster. Many wheelchairs went up to seventeen miles per hour, but I was often passed by even the slowest pedestrians. It took me half an hour to get from my place to the entrance of campus, only four blocks away. Perhaps if my wheelchair were speedier, I wouldn't be so sore and tired.

I needed a substitute to work my lunchtimes through the December break, so I called someone from a DSP list. The woman I talked to said she would come over for an interview the next day. When Kate opened the door and the woman saw the lung, she asked Kate, "Will he die if the power goes out?"

Such was my introduction to Kerry. She was a short woman with a brilliant, clear mind and California-blonde looks, offset by a dainty nose-ring. That day, and often afterward, she wore green OshKosh overalls, and, like Emily, she never failed to say what was on her mind.

I hired her to feed me lunch and to run some errands. That first day, she said she wanted to talk a while before she went out but that she would subtract that time from her pay. I told her that I was an English major and that I used the power chair to go to my classes. After we talked for quite a while, she got ready to run some errands. She put a piece of paper over the book I was reading, saying, "Wait until I'm gone before you read this."

Curious and amused, I kept my eyes averted until the door closed, then looked at her note, which said, "I love you."

Somewhat stunned, I waited with great anticipation for Kerry to return. What did it mean that she loved me? When she came back with the groceries, I hardly let her get in the door before I said, "I'm flabbergasted."

Laughing, she went into the kitchen to put the food away. When she came back out to talk, she said something about how brave I was, how she admired my writing. I had put up a brave front at her interview, I reflected, not telling her my fears about using the power chair or showing my social nervousness. Quickly Kerry switched the subject to the schedule: she couldn't work for me until the following Monday, because she had to work at the FAITH Center.

I said, "I heard the FAITH Center is a cult."

To my surprise, she didn't get angry but responded peaceably. "That's what we get called. But really we're just a bunch of Christians living in community. I don't live there, but a lot of people do." She explained that they were doing a play over the weekend; she was doing the lighting. "I don't get paid, but I love the people there. We all eat together— the organization provides the meals—and I get counseling there. The minister is wonderful; you should meet him."

I liked her so much that I was willing to believe that what I'd heard about the FAITH Center might not be true. At least I tried to keep an open mind about her religion. Excited about being able to talk with someone who seemed interested in me, I fantasized about some kind of romance. My ideas up to that time had been derived from movies that featured—twenty minutes after the opening credits—a woman confessing to the male lead, no matter how tedious or messed up he might be, that she loved him.

That weekend, I heard on the radio that John Lennon had been shot. It seemed odd and sad that a singer had been murdered, but Lennon's music had never been important to me, and I had never really felt part of the sixties—I had watched it happen on television—so I wasn't devastated.

But Kerry was. She arrived saying, "Isn't it terrible?" as she opened the door. Though I knew what she meant, I had trouble sympathizing as deeply as she wanted me to. She said the FAITH Center was having a special service to commemorate Lennon's death, and she invited me. To my relief, I couldn't go because I had plans to go to the zoo with Kate.

"I'm sorry," I lied. "Why is the church doing that? John Lennon wasn't a Christian, was he?"

"That's not the point," she said. "He was very important to a lot of us. And, besides, the minister said Lennon had a great soul. He worked for peace and justice; we want to celebrate his life."

While Kerry and her church mourned Lennon, I played at the zoo. This was the first time I'd been to a zoo, and it was delightful. I saw all kinds of animals in person, including an elephant and a macaque, a monkey with a bright red ass. I felt childlike and gleeful, eating popcorn and ice cream, enjoying myself with Kate's family. Kate and her husband had a ten-year-old girl, Jenna, who relished explaining things to me. "That's a giraffe," she said. "It's brown and yellow. The sign says 'Giraffa camelopardolis lives in the grassy savanna of east Africa.' Mom's going to West Africa with the Peace Corps. What's the name of that country, Mom?"

"Niger, sweetheart."

We rode home in the Disabled Students' Program van, singing folk songs in two-part harmony. We got through "If I Had a Hammer," and "Los Colores," Jenna leading us all. The family favorite was "Gypsy Rover," during which Jenna shrieked the chorus out the window. As we got back into Berkeley, I didn't want to end the day. They'd all been so warm—I wished they'd adopt me. Although I had only known them a few months, they felt like family.

As for my real family, at that time, my parents came to visit me about every two weeks. For Christmas, they brought down presents and a small, artificial tree that they set up in my apartment. O'Bie was in charge of the arrangements, as he was in charge of everything.

"Brand new tree," he said as he decorated it. "One hundred percent plastic, a real evergreen. No needles to step on. It'll look great with the lights."

My mother began vacuuming, as she did on nearly every visit. My father and I tried to stop her, but she ignored us. While she was busy, my father talked to me about football and politics. Having voted for Reagan, he was pleased with the election results. Having voted for Carter, I told him that Alameda County, which includes Berkeley, had voted for the loser by the same percentage that the rest of the country had elected the winner. He laughed, "Those damn Berkeley hippies."

When she and I were alone, my mother filled me in on how Rachel and Ken were doing, then asked about me. She enjoyed hearing about my social life, so I told her about a wedding I had recently attended, and the zoo. I mentioned Kerry and how much I enjoyed her company. I didn't volunteer that I was feeling fairly moony about Kerry: I was very attracted to her, I thought she was fun, and I loved our long, heartfelt conversations.

Usually Kerry arrived after my morning routine, when I was dressed, breakfasted, and ready for the day. One morning, she came in carrying a big red cloth bag. From it she pulled out two books, *A Wrinkle in Time*, by Madeleine L'Engle, and *The Drama of the Gifted Child*, by Alice Miller. She left the books on my table, but she tucked into her pockets her wallet and a small plastic bottle to bring with us.

"What's that?" I asked her.

"Show you later," she said. We got to class a few minutes early, and she took the little vial out. She opened the cap, withdrew a plastic wand, and blew several perfect bubbles.

"Oh!" I said, delighted. "I haven't seen one of those in ages."

"Well, get used to it," she said, smiling. "I do this all the time. It relieves stress." Three more luminescent spheres bobbed toward my face. I laughed and puffed air at them.

"This is excellent bubble weather," she said. "Humidity is good for them. They pop too fast if it's dry."

She held up the dripping wand, and I blew a series of small, cheerful bubbles that danced toward her. We alternated—she'd take a big breath and blow giant bubbles, then I'd do little puffs to make tiny ones. "It's my favorite vice," she said.

"Yeah, I think I'll take it up," I said. "It's not addictive, not fattening...."

"Not expensive," she added. Then she paused before her next stream of bubbles.

"Did you do this when you were a kid?"

I tried to remember. Making bubbles seemed vaguely familiar, but I couldn't recall a specific time when I'd done it. "I'm not sure—" I began.

"What do you remember best?" she asked. "I hope you don't mind if I ask questions."

I assured her that I didn't. "I remember running around the neighborhood with my brother, Ken," I said.

She nodded.

"We were always outside, snow, rain, it didn't matter."

"How did he treat you?" she asked.

That day, and in the months and years of close friendship that followed, I was drawn to Kerry because she seemed curious about me—not just my disability, which is a part of me that makes many people curious, but my heart and mind.

We talked about philosophy, history, and religion, as well as more personal topics. I had never been asked so many questions; no one had ever shown so much interest in me. She even asked follow-up questions: How did I feel about what had happened? What did I think about it? One of my journal entries called her "the question lady."

In another of my journal entries, I speculated that parts of my brain or personality had been slowed down as a result of my immobility. I had read in *Psychology Today* that children who are active with their hands develop certain parts of their brains better than those who are not active. I wondered whether such a correlation might go on into adulthood. Certainly I seemed to have zero social skills.

I could see that, when it came to my relationship with Kerry, I was as passive as I had been with my parents—by necessity, they had made all the decisions for me, and I had let them. Being a hospital patient makes children very passive, and I had had little opportunity to grow out of that. Nor had I had any opportunity to develop skills I could use in a romantic relationship. Other than what I had gleaned from movies, I had no idea what to expect. Ken introduced his girlfriends to me but never confided about his romantic attachments, the ups and downs or the emotional context. Mickey had had a girlfriend, but his comments about her were brief and superficial.

While I worried about how to behave with Kerry, Kerry worried that the old attendant would want her job back in January. After all, Kerry had been hired only as a substitute. If she weren't working for me, Kerry feared she wouldn't see me as often.

As winter quarter began early in 1981, my power chair was still in the shop at DSP. It was taking longer than I'd thought to make it go faster. Every time I called to check on its progress, I was told that I'd have it back in a week.

10

Fiat Lux

(January 1981–June 1982)

One day while Kerry and I were doing homework—and blowing the occasional wandful of bubbles—my old attendant dropped by to announce that she'd gotten a full-time job and thus would not be coming back to work for me. Relieved, because it meant Kerry could stay on, Kerry and I offered hearty congratulations.

When school began in January, my power chair was still in the Disabled Students' Program shop, being repaired. So Kerry took me to class, although she insisted that she had no sense of direction and feared getting lost. Pushing me tired her; we always had to stop halfway to campus so that she could catch her breath. After I'd guided her to Wheeler Hall, she would ask me to tell her exactly how to put the chair into the elevator, how to get it out, and which way to go to the classroom. She asked me where I wanted to sit, and she told me to remind her to set the brake. I did all these things cheerfully, feeling nervous that I was more in charge than usual, but also feeling nurturing as I protected her from making a mistake. I was taking care of her as she took care of me.

Kerry often said that she loved me, which always surprised me. I'd say, "Oh!" She found my exclamations amusing. She made cards for me, and I bought her small gifts: flowers, books, cassettes. I not only enjoyed her company, but I found her so attractive and lovable that I wanted to marry her. In the meantime, though, I was afraid even to ask her for a kiss.

Wheeler Hall, where my writing class met, had an impressive front lobby, with chandeliers shining down on light marble floors. Although the lobby was accessible, I couldn't get from there to the classrooms, because the wheelchair lift was too small for my chair. So I entered Wheeler through the back, under ugly concrete steps, with a back door buzzer that bleated loudly.

Inside, Kerry and I passed the cigarette machines, which were frequented by all the English majors nervous about writing papers or finding jobs. We traversed halls with peeling paint and flickering fluorescent lights, the old-fashioned bulbs inside what looked like Venetian blinds.

The creative writing class that term had just as many would-be students on the first day as there had been the previous time I'd tried to enroll. This year's teacher was Thom Gunn, a respected British poet who had lived in the United States for thirty years. Though I had never read any of his poetry, that didn't deter me from wanting to study with him. Apparently, many other people felt the same way. This year, Gunn, like Jackson Burgess the previous year, first let in all the seniors. Then he had the other students write their names on slips of paper, which he collected and put in a student's wool knit cap. Holding it out to pull the names, he said, "This is so dramatic—just like television." I was one of the lucky winners.

Gunn gave us a reading list and told us to choose two texts: I picked *The Fixer,* by Bernard Malamud, and *Life Studies and For the Union Dead,* by Robert Lowell. On looking up some of Gunn's poems, I found them clear and elegant.

Between classes, Kerry took me to the English department lounge and fed me lunch. This wood-paneled room, with deep carpeting and yellow couches, was a quiet place for students and faculty to sit. They read the trade journal of English professors, *Publication of the Modern Language Association,* gazed out the windows, and talked in low voices. Sunlight washed the lounge some days, while, on rainy days, it felt cozy. It was considered bad form to bug the professors in the lounge.

Around the middle of February, after I'd been told for months that my chair would be ready "next week," it finally arrived. I arranged to meet Melissa at the end of my first day of driving it, thinking it would be no problem to get myself around for a few hours. I was wrong.

The mechanics had done something that caused the power chair to pull sharply to the right every time I braked. I got out of my house all right and crossed the first street, but, as I tried to go up the curb cut,

I veered ninety degrees to the right. Horrified, I considered going back home, but I had classes to go to, so I crossed streets carefully, having to turn a complete circle every time I came to a halt. It took me about an hour to go the four blocks to campus, and the problem became more frustrating throughout the day as I got more tired.

The trip home, even though Melissa joined me, was even worse. I had terrible trouble getting my chair into the elevator—it was more than five feet long and would fit only with the back raised, which made me uncomfortable. Then, every time I touched the brakes, the chair swung to the right. Finally, Melissa grabbed the chair to keep it from turning too much.

I was furious with the mechanics—hadn't they test-driven it? Apparently they had neglected to put any brake on the left wheel. On the way home, as I was crossing Bancroft, the chair swung right. Before I could get myself straight again, the light changed. Traffic began zooming around the corner toward me, but fortunately the drivers saw me and stopped.

By the time I got home, I was exhausted and terrified. When Melissa put her arms under me to lift me off the chair and into the tank, I screamed, "No, not yet! Not yet!" Out of my mind with anxiety, I was too afraid to move. She lifted me anyway and set me in the iron lung. Once I was breathing and comfortable again, I thanked her for ignoring my protests.

The next day, I didn't go to school. I called Frances, the director of the Disabled Students' Program, and told her what had happened. I thought she should fire Ned, the chief mechanic, and give me a written apology. The chair went back to the shop, and a meeting was arranged.

Frances, Ned, a disabled professor named Sandy Muir, and I attended the meeting. After hearing both sides, Sandy Muir, acting as arbiter, ruled that Frances should keep a closer eye on the shop and that the mechanics should finish work on my chair and should keep me and other clients better informed of their progress.

I repeated that I wanted an apology. Sandy spoke quietly to me. "Look, what do you want? You want your chair back. This way you'll get it back. Forcing an apology won't accomplish anything."

Six weeks later, Ned delivered the chair to my apartment. It worked. He seemed very proud of himself for completing the job. Cocky as could be, he said, "Here it is! Call me again, if you need any help."

Though I was still furious, I didn't express my anger, because I would have to call him again if anything went wrong.

The power chair continued to change my life and improve my self-image, but it also attracted some unwelcome attention. One day I was late to class. To take a place where I wasn't blocking the door, I had to drive across the front of the classroom, right in front of the professor as she lectured. Embarrassed, I said, "I'm sorry," as I passed.

She smiled hugely. "Oh, don't apologize!" she said, all cheer. "I think you people are wonderful!"

Another day, in my rhetoric class, a man sitting in the back of the lecture hall started heckling. Every time the professor tried to say anything, the man would yell back. Everyone in the class glared at him, trying to get him to shut up, but, undaunted, he moved to the front of the room. Fed up, the professor told the guy to get out. He wasn't a student, at least not in that class—I had never seen him before. The professor was tall but aging, and I wondered whether he'd be a match for the obnoxious heckler. Finally, two of the larger male students stood up, guarding the professor, and the guy ran out.

Later, as I was driving home, the heckler appeared by my chair. "Hey, isn't that professor strange?" he said. "This is quite a rig you've got here. I hate that novel we talked about today." His movements were so aggressive and stiff, I was afraid he'd knock the chair over. I didn't have an attendant with me, so I yelled to passersby, "This guy is hassling me! Get rid of him!" A few people glanced over, but, it being Berkeley, where street arguments were not uncommon, no one did anything. When I turned off Telegraph Avenue, the guy stayed behind. I never saw him again.

I enjoyed the freedom the chair gave me, especially coming home from school, when I could breeze downhill fast—five or six miles an hour. The evening sun slanted into my eyes, turning everything into silhouettes. I liked getting myself around.

Although I loved the freedom it gave me, the chair wasn't perfect. I had to hold my left leg up to move, which tired me so much that I had to stop and rest about once a block.

Driving got to be automatic. I was thirty years old, and, for the first time since I caught polio, I could go outside without anyone knowing where I was. Gradually, I came to feel relaxed and competent in the chair, knowing that I could get myself where I had to go, getting assistance if I needed it. When I stopped to rest, people often came up and asked me whether I needed anything. Usually, if I did need help, such as with an outside door, I would only have to stop driving and look woebegone; before long, someone would offer to help. It was a good thing I lived in Berkeley, where residents were accustomed to seeing people in chairs and used to helping, because I could never stop a stranger and ask for help. I was too shy.

Once I had problems registering for my Spanish class, and, when I called the department to talk about it, the secretary said I'd have to come in. I was dressed and in the chair, so I just opened the door, went up to campus, took care of my business, and came home. I felt like an adult.

While driving through campus one afternoon, I heard the Cal marching band in the distance, playing the school's fight song. I had to stop. Tears fogged my vision as I thought of how this school had been one of the few institutions to take me seriously and to give me what I wanted, a first-rate education. I thought of my professors, people of astonishing brilliance whose erudition had been surpassed only by their kindness to me. I thought of the school's motto: *Fiat Lux*—"Let there be light." The University of California, Berkeley, had let light into my life by giving me a home and a future. I would always be grateful.

Going with Kerry to my astronomy class, we talked about how much better it was for me to drive myself. She was relieved at not having to push, and I felt more equal to her when I controlled my own movements. Also, it was easier for us to converse, since she didn't have to walk behind me. On one of the first excursions, she stopped to look down at something by her feet. A second later, she picked up a bright, wiggling snake and held it close to my face. "A water snake," she said. "Isn't it sweet?" I didn't think it was sweet, but I thought her caring for it was. Carefully pocketing the reptile, she said she would take it home. I knew that she wouldn't even have seen the creature, let alone picked it up, if she'd been pushing my chair.

Everything Kerry did endeared her more to me, but she was discovering my flaws. My childlike adoration of her—exemplified by what she called my "Lassie look"—annoyed her, as did my tendency to see her as being more powerful than I was.

When I asked her permission to see Jessie, she exploded. "My permission? Why do you need my permission to see Jessie? She's your friend; you've known her longer than you've known me. My permission?" She shook her head. "I'm sorry. I shouldn't get so upset; it's just that sometimes I forget how all of this is so new to you. When you're brave and funny and when you talk about Shakespeare or Jonathan Swift or something, I forget. You seem so capable. But you're just out of the nest, like Prince Myshkin in that book. Did you read it?"

"*The Idiot?* By Dostoevski? Sure, I read it."

"Well, you're just like him, so naive. "Naive" isn't even the word for it; it's more like . . . is that why you proposed to me?"

"I proposed to you because you're funny and pretty and kind. You like and accept me. Besides, it's hard to find hetero women in this town."

She laughed. "All those lesbian attendants, I see. When was that, that you proposed to me?"

"February." It had been a fleeting, spontaneous burst of bravery on my part, or maybe bravado. After having a glass of wine one evening, I had told Kerry she was the one woman for me. I had asked her whether she would accept an engagement ring from me, although I had had no such ring to give her had she accepted on the spot.

"February," she mused. "I still can't believe how you knew me just those two months and, whammo, you wanted to marry me."

"Well, yes," I said, embarrassed. "I didn't think that was unusual. You're neat. You're perfect."

"You're pretty neat and perfect yourself, Marko," she said, ruffling my hair. "But, right now, I think you need a friend more than you need a wife. There's so much you need to explore and understand. Now let me ask you a question. Will you be my friend?"

"Sure, of course."

"I mean for the rest of my life. Or your life."

"Yes, yes. But why do you ask?"

"I'm insecure myself, you know. My intensity bothers a lot of people. People always tell me, 'Lighten up, Kerry, don't be so life-and-death about everything.' But I can't stop it, being intense. Does that bug you?"

"No, that's one of the reasons I love you."

"Okay, Marko. We'll always be friends. And go ahead and see Jessie or any of your other friends whenever you feel like it. Remember, I'm not your mother."

At the end of spring quarter of 1981, Kerry resigned as my attendant. She wanted to work with animals, and a pet store had offered her a good position. Though I was sad about her leaving, we arranged to see each other weekly: she had a regular appointment with a therapist whose office was near my building, and she could visit me afterward.

I was curious that she, whom I considered perfect, felt the need to be in therapy. "What about the minister at the FAITH Center?" I asked. "Don't you talk to him?"

"He's okay up to a point. But I want to see a real therapist, too. You know, you might get a lot out of seeing someone, too."

Being preoccupied with Kerry and seeing Jessie so infrequently, I had mostly given up on Jessie, until she invited me to her nursing school graduation. Since she had only six tickets, I felt that the invitation was significant. I accepted partly because I wanted to see her and partly out of a sense of obligation, just as I thought she was inviting me out of a sense of obligation.

To get to the ceremony, I had to arrange for a Disabled Students' Program van and a driver. I got the blue van, and Joao agreed to drive, stopping on the way so that I could see my friend and attendant Kate. I was looking forward to a full day of socializing, but Joao had so much trouble getting me into the van that I almost canceled the trip.

The van had no wheelchair lift, but it carried a portable ramp that folded up for storage, then flattened so a chair could roll along it. Joao leaned the ramp against the van and tried to get me over it, but the ramp kept buckling under the weight of the chair. It was scary for me and difficult for him; he ended up almost lifting the chair and me into the van. I hoped that the ramp would work better at Kate's house, but it was just as awkward. We couldn't understand how anyone could design such a terrible piece of equipment.

Once I finally got out of the van, I saw that Kate had a wonderful, three-story castle of a house on an acre alive with flowers, cats, plum trees, and chickens. I enjoyed touring her home, and I loved her conversation, but the visit was marred by my fear of having to use the ramp again.

We struggled with the collapsing ramp four more times—getting back in the van at Kate's, getting out at the graduation ceremony, getting back in after the ceremony, and when I got home. The last time, Joao was folding up the ramp when he bent to look closely at the hinges. Then he stood up, flipped the ramp over, and set it up. He stepped on it and jumped up and down. The ramp held perfectly.

He looked at me, laughing and embarrassed. "I'm sorry," he said. "I was using it upside down."

During my final summer as an undergraduate, Joao and Naomi went to Mexico, where they would swim in the Gulf, live with the Indians, and take peyote. I needed a new dinnertime attendant, as well as a lunchtime replacement for Kerry after she started her new job. My morning person wasn't working out, either, so I was in terrible shape as far as attendants went.

I hired Tracy. Talkative, athletic-looking, with a delicate face, she was pleasant and strong. Her double major, Chemistry and French, impressed me. When I asked about lifting, she said she'd worked at UPS, lifting heavy boxes and crates. To demonstrate, she hefted my wheelchair about five feet into the air, then set it back down. Pointing at it solemnly, she said, "Stay." I saw that my seventy pounds wouldn't present a problem.

The first day she worked for me, I asked her to take me to an organic food market after class so that I could buy fruit. As Tracy shopped, a pale, bloodless-looking man walked up and stood too close to my head. Squatting down with his mouth close to my ear, he said, "That's a cute-looking girl you're with. She your girlfriend?"

I mumbled something, wishing I could back away. He pressed closer, saying, "Wish I had a girlfriend. Wish I had a cute girl."

Frightened, I yelled, "Tracy!" From the other end of the market, she came bounding toward me, as the man faded away. Tracy stowed the oranges and peaches in my backpack and began pushing me home.

Shaken, I didn't talk much until I was back in the tank. Then Tracy asked me why I'd been so upset. I told her I didn't like strangers who talked to me as if they knew me and that what he'd said had been weird.

Tracy interpreted my fears to mean that I didn't trust her. She'd been watching me and the man all along, she said, and if anything bad had happened, she would have protected me. She seemed annoyed. Afraid of losing her as an attendant, I apologized.

Tracy's combination of strength and gentleness attracted me. As we spent more time together, I began to have romantic feelings for her.

Despite her broad back and strong arms—she played basketball— she was very tenderhearted. Once, when she had had to remove dead mice from traps, she came over to my apartment crying. Another time, her cat had a heart attack and died. Tracy didn't cry in front of me that time, but she was quiet for days.

She had a boyfriend and wasn't interested in me romantically, but she cared about my wellbeing. One afternoon, when I was alone, I threw up. I called to ask Tracy to come clean me up, and she dropped what she was doing to rush to my place. She wiped my face, changed the collar and pillow, and brushed my teeth. It took about half an hour, maybe more. When I was clean and calm again, I thanked her and told her to take an hour's pay out of my wallet.

"Oh, no," she said, waving it off. "This was a friend thing, not an attendant thing."

I have always been afraid of being lifted. But I felt least fearful with Tracy, because, when I started to get scared, she'd calm me. She'd say things like, "I'm not going to do anything to hurt you; I won't do anything until you say to do it." After such reassurance, I would relax.

Sometime in the winter of 1980–1981, I realized that I was nearing the end of my school years. I needed only two more courses to complete my B.A. in English. I believed that getting my degree would signify my final entrance into adulthood. In the meantime, I hoped to get into an advanced poetry class, but, fearing my work would not be judged good enough, I registered for two other classes, as well.

To my surprise, I was accepted into the poetry workshop. It would be a class of only eight students, taught by Peter Dale Scott. Since I had been writing poetry for two years, I had no trouble completing the assignments of three poems a week. Because the class had so few students—usually only five or six showed up—we sat facing each other around a table. In this setting, I could speak up easily. A student would read his or her work, then the rest of us would talk about it.

Scott didn't interfere with our discussions of people's work; he wanted us to have our own dialogue, he said. He did critique our work after class; he began with me by suggesting that I rewrite one of my early poems, eliminating the generalities and beginning with action. Seeing that everything I had written was in iambic pentameter, he suggested that I try free verse. When I took his suggestions, my work came out much better. In that class I wrote "Boucher," about an orderly at Fairmont. It was my first free verse poem and the first of my poems to be published.

The first time I went to see Scott, the sloppiness of his office amazed me. He sat behind two desks, both covered with papers, magazines, pencils, and coffee mugs. When the phone rang, he had to stand on the desk to find the phone and answer it. But that didn't matter; Scott encouraged me; he told me that I could be a good poet.

The rainy season in the Bay Area lasts from December through March. That year, I worried every time it rained, because Kerry's roof was leaking.

Every Thursday, after seeing her therapist, Kerry would come over to see me. Her visit was the high point of my week. Arriving fresh from therapy, Kerry usually wanted to talk about issues like self-esteem and childhood traumas. I told her my stories, and she told me hers.

She told me that when she was seven, right after she had first seen the film *Bambi*, her father came home drunk from a hunting expedition, carrying his weapons. Walking crookedly in the door, he called to Kerry to come see what he'd got. Looking outside, she saw, strapped to the fender of the Chrysler, a dead, bloody Bambi. In tears, Kerry fled to her room, but from below she heard the sounds of her father dragging the carcass to the back yard and butchering it. For months afterward, the big freezer held lumps of venison. That event had made her into a vegetarian.

That spring, she was having terrible problems with her landlord. The cheap bastard kept telling her he would fix the roof, but all he ever did was put in pieces of plastic, which would collapse under the first rain. All her books and clothes were growing moldy.

In February, fed up with her landlord and unable to find a new apartment, she moved to the FAITH Ranch east of Santa Cruz, two or three hours' drive from Berkeley. I was distressed that her weekly visits would be no more, but she said she would still come to see me every few weeks, because she had been designated one of the FAITH members who could run errands in "the world," as they put it.

There was only one phone on the whole ranch, and it belonged to the minister, so Kerry and I could no longer chat. Instead, I began making tapes to send her—long monologues about how I missed her, how great it was when she was around, how much I looked forward to her visits. She said that they were "excessively adoring" and that she wished I would see our relationship more "realistically." She kept insisting she was not a saint. Of course, I knew she wasn't a saint, but I couldn't help being infatuated with her.

Because she had more belongings than she was allowed to take to the FAITH Ranch, she began bringing things to my house. "Don't bliss out," she said. "I'm not moving in. It's just that on the ranch I'm not allowed to have more than one suitcase of clothes," she said. "Can you imagine?" She stored many boxes of stuff in the back room.

She moved into my place the following month. The people at the ranch kept guns, she said. The place was beginning to remind her of Jonestown.

Setting up a household was new for me, but Kerry had been through it many times. We established rules: she would clean her room and the bathroom. I would hire a housecleaner to clean the rest of the apartment twice a month. No one could enter her room without knocking on her door first. We would not answer the telephone or receive guests after 7 P.M. These weren't rigid rules; we would, for example, have evening guests if they made arrangements ahead of time.

Kerry's presence improved my life in many ways. Having a regular housecleaner was an improvement over my previous nonsystem of letting attendants clean when they felt like it. She installed towel racks in the bathroom, a bamboo curtain in the hall, and Vermeer prints on the walls. The place looked better, and it felt homey. But mostly it was her companionship that so much improved my life.

Upon returning from her early morning walks, she would make coffee and ask me how I had slept. We talked about the coming day, what difficulties and pleasures it might bring. We gossiped about my attendants, discussed the nature of God, and bitched about Reagan. She read aloud from the *San Francisco Chronicle*, asking for my reactions to the columns and stories.

One morning, she pulled the curtains of the front window. "It's out there," she said.

Knowing that "it" meant the day, with all its demands and frustrations, I said, "Can't you keep it out?"

"Wish I could, Marko," she sighed. It surprised me that anyone as positive and energetic as Kerry could not want to face going out.

In 1979, Frances, the director of the Disabled Students' Program, asked me to write a book about my first year at Berkeley. DSP provided a secretary, to whom I dictated my memories. She typed it and had ten copies bound at a copy shop. Titled *A Free Man in Paris*, the memoir came to about a hundred pages.

Now, living with Kerry, who encouraged my writing, I showed the manuscript to Ben Bagdikian's wife, Betty. She said it could never be published because it didn't say anything about the way I felt.

"I didn't think people would be interested in my feelings," I said.

"That's *all* that people are interested in." She suggested I write a shorter version that could be sold to a magazine. Like the book, the article would combine the elements of an autobiography with an argument for independent living. Again, DSP provided a secretary. I called the revised piece "How I Became a Human Being" and dictated it in four days.

The *New Yorker* sent a handwritten rejection letter that I treasured as a model of courtesy. However, not all magazines were so polite, and none accepted the piece. In that year, I received six rejections before Kate suggested I send it to a friend of hers who was an assistant editor of *CoEvolution Quarterly*, a descendant of the *Whole Earth Catalog*, founded by Stewart Brand. Two weeks later, I received a postcard saying that my article had been accepted by *CoEvolution Quarterly*. It was published in the spring 1982 issue, along with pieces by writers I admired, Will Baker, Ivan Illich, and Pat Califia.

That March, I received the tear sheets from the magazine and a check for two hundred dollars. It was the first time I had ever been paid for any sort of work, and it was for writing! I was amazed as well as pleased. Writing, although seldom easy, always seemed an agreeable task, not real work. At Berkeley, I had initially entered the business administration program because it seemed like real work that would lead to even more real work in a business career. Working as a corporate executive would have meant real money, far more than enough to get off S.S.I. When I dropped out of that practical course of study, I had worried that I would never earn a living. But now writing was beginning to pay off.

I really needed that money: most of the two hundred dollars went to pay debts. Even more than the income, though, I enjoyed receiving congratulations from Kerry, Ben, and Betty.

Shortly after my debut in *CoEvolution Quarterly*, I received a phone call from Pacific News Service asking me to write a shorter version of the article for newspaper syndication. This led to a second check, a long association with PNS, and a gratifying, long-term friendship with its executive editor, Sandy Close.

In May, my poem "Boucher" was published.

Boucher

Slouching through the hospital corridors,
Tall and blond,
A former high school star athlete,
Now an orderly, his shoulders down,
Complaining that he would not empty the hampers
Filled with shitty cloth:
"It's not in my job description;
Read it."
Now on the weekend afternoon,
Things are slow,
Discussing sports with the Chicana nurse:
"D'you know how much the average salary,
The *average* salary,
Of a player in the NBA is?
A hundred and fifty thousand dollars a year.
Jesus, I'd sell my soul
For a hundred and fifty thousand
And it's a beautiful soul."

It was published by the *Berkeley Poetry Review*, a student magazine that paid me two free copies of the magazine. It felt wonderful to have a poem published.

That was my spring of success, the spring after I had finished all my classwork and was waiting to graduate. During that spring, I'd often wake up in the small hours, staring at Kerry in her bathrobe. "What?" I'd mumble, startled.

"You were screaming. I thought someone was out here murdering you. Are you okay?"

I'd tell her that I must have had a bad dream. But the screaming persisted, sometimes waking me. Kerry suggested I see a psychotherapist. I didn't think I needed one until the night I woke up screaming, "No! No! No!"

I began seeing Claude, a disabled therapist who had an office at the Center for Independent Living. Like me, Claude used a reclining power chair, but, unlike me, he could use his hands to operate the chair. He looked comfortable in it, usually leaning back and sipping tea from a long straw.

More daring than I, more confident about exploring the world, Claude impressed me. His apartment was large and more expensive than most; he had a live-in lover and a good professional job. I was encouraged by his accomplishments, but I also knew that he was less disabled than I was.

For appointments with Claude, I used to drive my power chair to the CIL parking lot, the one in which Emily had taught me how to drive. Claude's office was in a trailer parked in the lot, and, to enter it, I had to go up a ramp whose angle challenged my chair's tiny motors. I often received a push from a sympathetic CIL employee. In therapy, I told Claude about my family and about how bored I was now that I had finished school. He listened sympathetically.

After three sessions, he said my problem was that I wasn't comfortable using the power chair. He pointed out that the only places I would drive it were to campus and to CIL and that much of the world lay beyond. We began a series of wheelchair tours of Berkeley. The first one, a ramble through the west side of campus, terrified me. Neither of us could use our arms, and we were alone, unescorted by attendants. What if I fell out of the chair?

I was still in therapy when Claude stopped working at CIL, but he said I could see him at his place near the Oakland city line. It sounded easy enough, so I arranged that, every Thursday, a driver from Pronto Van Services would pick me up and help me get on the wheelchair lift on the back of the van.

I was always terrified while going up in the air on the jerky, stop-and-go lift. But once I was safely inside, the driver would rev up the van and the rhythm-and-blues station, and we'd be off. Later, at Claude's place, the lift made a purring noise going down, much more soothing than the one it made going up. Though their duties officially ended as soon as I got on the sidewalk, the drivers always helped me navigate the long ramp that led to Claude's upstairs flat.

Exhausted from the trip, I would sit in Claude's small living room, made smaller by the presence of two reclining power chairs and a pile of empty boxes. I'd talk about myself while his girlfriend came and went. Very soon, the driver would rap on the sliding glass door, and I'd go down the ramp and up into the van. I enjoyed the energy of the R & B on the drive to Claude's place, but, on the drive back home, the repetitious music would irritate me. Outside my house, the driver would take me out of the van and wave good-bye as I moved away. I'd drive the last fifty feet to my building, open the door, and go into my apartment. Feeling as independent as I ever would, I'd await Tracy, who would put me in the iron lung.

On a morning in May, pulling up one of the blue wooden chairs my parents had given me, Kerry casually said, "How long have you been in love with Tracy?"

"I'm not in love with Tracy."

"But you talk about her all the time."

I wasn't sure; maybe I wasn't admitting it to myself. "She's an interesting person," I hedged. "She's smart and funny."

"Tracy's very funny; I heard what she said about the roaches in the kitchen. But do you think I'm accusing you of something? I didn't mean it to sound like that. I was just wondering how you feel about her."

"I like her. She's neat."

"I just want you to feel free to have as many friends as you can. God knows you're isolated. And if you want to fall in love with her or anyone else, that's fine with me. She has a boyfriend, girlfriend, whatever?"

"Yeah, Warren, you met him. That tall guy with the sheepdog haircut."

"So he's her boyfriend. I couldn't understand a word he said." After we talked randomly about Tracy's boyfriend, Kerry went back to the subject. "She hasn't expressed any interest in you, then? I mean, beyond friendship?"

"No," I said. Then, summoning all my courage, I asked, "Are you relieved?"

"No, it's not a matter of me being relieved or me being angry. I told you I want you to have friends; I want you to have lovers, even. Sometimes I think you give me too much power, like I'm your mother. I don't want to go through that whole damned Jessie trip again. Remember how you asked me for permission to see Jessie?"

"Yes," I said, embarrassed. "I think I've learned a few things since then."

"I hope. Look, if her boyfriend went overseas to study, would you make a play for Tracy?"

"Oh, I'd be too scared to. Anyway, it's not going to happen." As a matter of fact, the opposite was happening: Tracy was leaving California, going to the École Polytechnique in Paris. My only comfort was that she had said she would write.

Although I completed my undergraduate studies in December of 1981, my graduation ceremony didn't take place until June 1982. It was one of the most exciting days of my life.

Graduation Day

Why is my graduation on the news?
Is it because I've done something unique?
I don't agree. I've done the work required,
Accomplished all the goals that I have set
For myself. Where were the cameras on those days
I had to drive to campus all alone?
Come back with me to such a day. A day
When I am by myself, driving quickly
Across the open space of Lower Sproul,
I sense the feelings of the student crowd.
The band is playing eighties rock. I feel
That I am out of place. The students feel
That I am out of place, disturbing things,
Their golden California childhoods,
With visions of disease, mortality.
You think you'll live forever at eighteen,
But suddenly this apparition comes.
A girl will drop some yogurt on her dress,
Pretend to be annoyed at that, ignore
The funny looking wheelchair buzzing by.

Today I hear the crowd's applause, receive
Congratulations from my friends, today
I hope I've found a place among the rest.
I hope you see a man upon this stage,
Who studied, read, wrote, and passed the test,
In cap and gown, diploma on my chair.

Tracy worked for me the morning I graduated. It would be one of the last times she did before leaving for France, and I was glad to share this day with her. After carefully shaving and dressing me, she lifted me into my wheelchair. She draped my graduation gown over me, then taped my mortarboard to the back of the wheelchair's rearview mirror, a few inches behind my head. The tassel dangled jauntily when I moved. We agreed to meet again at Zellerbach Auditorium an hour before the ceremony, and I set off solo for the campus.

As I was driving along the crowded streets, the mortarboard slipped off the mirror and fell on the ground. I stopped, panicking, afraid I'd have to graduate without the right headgear. But a stranger stopped his vehicle, jumped out, picked up the mortarboard, and set it in my lap. "I think you'll need this," he said, then trotted back to his car.

The auditorium was milling with excited students swishing in their robes. Tracy reattached the hat to the mirror, using more tape this time. "You know," she said, "I'll probably miss my own graduation. I hate ceremonies. I'll be off hiking somewhere. But this graduation is

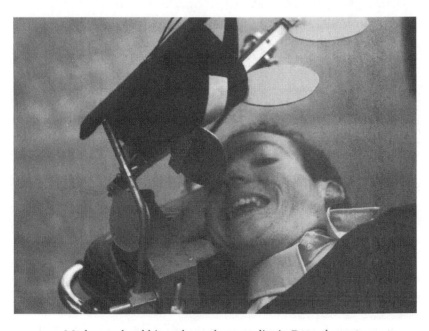

Mark completed his undergraduate studies in December 1981.
He graduated in the June 1982 ceremony.

special to me." She promised to meet me on the other side of the stage after I got my diploma, blew me a kiss, and left.

When my turn came to receive my diploma, I started across the immense wooden floor, using the mirror for direction and concentrating on not crashing into the university officials giving out the diplomas. Also, I had to avoid driving off the front of the stage; I had a fairly narrow band of floor to traverse, and it was unfamiliar territory. But I was distracted by the sight of my father running below the front of the stage with his camera, flashbulb popping. More that that, I was stunned by a loud roaring, which I suddenly realized was people clapping and cheering.

I received my diploma and made it to the other side of the stage, a graduate. There Tracy met me. She said, "I tried to see you, but it was hard—all these tall guys were standing in my way—so I jumped up and down and yelled, 'Let me see! He belongs to me!'"

My friend Jessie, from the Disabled Students' Program, was also backstage, along with my parents, my brother, his girlfriend, my sister, her boyfriend, my aunt Joan, and Tillie Olsen, the commencement speaker. Olsen gave me copies of her books and a kiss on my cheek.

My father was so wound up and excited that he offered to carry me in my wheelchair down a flight of steps. Fortunately, Tracy persuaded him not to. "It's all been arranged with the stage crew, Mr. O'Brien. Mark'll drive to the front of the stage, and they'll lower the whole thing for him."

We all moved to the stage apron, which lowered smoothly. Once at orchestra level, my father began pushing me up the red-carpeted center aisle. I offered to drive myself, but I really did need help: the aisle was steep.

Out in the vast lobby, with feudal-looking blue and gold banners hanging from its rafters, we grabbed what Brie and champagne were left, then moved into the bright daylight of Lower Sproul Plaza. My housemate, Kerry, met us there, having just returned from another building, where she had read one of my poems for Channel 5. My Hayward friends were outside, too, along with a television reporter and crew.

Later, the mob of us strolled down leafy Dana Street in the warm sun until we reached my building. Inside, we partied in my crowded apartment. My graduation brought together my family, my Hayward friends, and all my friends from Berkeley for the first and only time. My small apartment was crowded with people.

Mark is interviewed at his graduation from UC–Berkeley.

Amid all the congratulations and conversation, one anecdote stands out in my memory. My brother's girlfriend accused Cesar Chavez of being a communist. Though I wanted to defend Chavez and his organization of the farm workers, I was too timid. However, my aunt, a postal worker, took on Ken's girlfriend, arguing as I would have liked to. I was relieved and impressed. To me, that exchange symbolized the generational contrast between my father's FDR liberalism and the conservatism of my brother's generation.

A couple of days after the graduation, someone told me I'd been on the CBS news on Sunday night. Watching myself on videotape at the Disabled Students' Program office, I cried because Charles Osgood, a journalist I've always admired, was saying wonderful things about me. I felt embarrassed at the attention but happy and gratified for the recognition of my hard work. These feelings would reoccur often after Jessica Yu's documentary about me won an Oscar.

I wished that Joao and Naomi could have attended the ceremony, but they were spending the summer in Mexico. After they returned, they threw a party for me at my place, at which I read my poems until my voice gave out. On my door, Joao had taped three signs:

MARK O'BRIEN

B.A. IN ENGLISH

1982

MARK O'BRIEN

PH.D. IN JOURNALISM

1985

MARK O'BRIEN

PULITZER PRIZE FOR POETRY

1990

11

Graduate School
(July 1982–June 1983)

Whether I would ever be admitted to grad school was still undecided after I graduated. Hoping to attend the UC–Berkeley Graduate School of Journalism in the fall of 1982, I had applied the previous year, but that spring I had gotten a letter from the dean, saying that he doubted I could do the necessary "legwork" for daily journalism. I was surprised that he was so open about his prejudice, but the openness made it easier to fight. He went on to propose that I meet with a committee of three instructors from the school to discuss my application. When I showed the letter to Frances, the director of the Disabled Students' Program, she advised me against attending such a meeting because it was illegal for the dean to request it; it showed clear intent to discriminate against me because of my disability.

I wanted to get into graduate school for very rational reasons. First, I knew that the greater a person's disability, the more education that person would need to get a job. I was the most disabled person I knew of, so I felt I needed the advanced degree. With a regular job, I could get off the dole, so I would no longer have to answer to the persnickety workers at Social Security and county welfare. Also, more personally and less rationally, I wanted the master's degree because it would compare to my brother and father's doctorates, and I wanted to show that I was as smart as they were. For these reasons, I decided to go to the meeting.

To protect me from further discrimination, Frances came to the meeting, too. In the plaza in front of Dwinelle Hall, she breezily invited me to accompany her up the long, curving ramp that led to the main entrance. I had always entered through the basement door, afraid of ascending the ramp because it ended right near the top of the stairs everyone else used. I feared that I might get dizzy, lose control of the wheelchair, and topple down the hard, concrete stairs. But I didn't want to look chicken to Frances, so I drove up the ramp. Once at the top, I didn't think of the stairs. I just drove through a door that a student held open.

In a classroom, the instructors from the journalism school grilled me. When one of them suggested that my record showed I was more interested in poetry than in journalism, I said that poets and journalists both tried to convey complicated information as clearly and as succinctly as possible. I said that Lincoln Steffens and Walt Whitman had worked successfully in both forms. The committee still seemed skeptical. After the meeting, I told Frances that I didn't think I had changed their minds.

That summer, I got a letter from the admissions committee of the journalism school rejecting my application. I immediately took it to Frances, who showed it to Michael Klass, the disabled math professor I had met through Joao, and to Sandy Muir, the disabled political science professor who had mediated my wheelchair dispute with the Disabled Students' Program. Klass wrote a beautiful letter to the dean on my behalf, saying, among other things, that Immanuel Kant had explored the universe without ever leaving Koenigsberg. Frances wrote and asked that the dean meet with the three of them. In the meeting, the dean agreed to submit the question of my admission to a vote of the whole graduate school faculty. I was told by someone at the school that this was a sop, that the faculty never reversed a decision of the admissions committee, and that there was no hope because the fall 1982 quarter would begin in a few days.

Five days before classes began, I drove my wheelchair to the Disabled Students' Program office, where I saw my California Department of Rehabilitation worker, Casey. I had just heard a news item saying that DR would no longer pay for the postgraduate education of disabled people. I asked Casey whether it was true, but she said not to worry, that she would take care of the situation.

The Friday before school began, Ben Bagdikian called. Ben, who had won a Pulitzer Prize and who had worked as an assistant editor of the *Washington Post* before coming to Berkeley's Journalism School, told me that the denial of my admission had been reversed by the faculty. I was elated but confused. How could I pick classes two days before the quarter began? Ben offered to be my instructor in an independent study course that fall. I called Casey, who said that the tuition, fees, and book money had been approved by the Department of Rehabilitation. I was in!

As an instructor, Ben was fair but demanding. Coming to my apartment once a week, Ben gave me tough assignments. I had to interview people about their jobs in the places where they worked. I interviewed an astronomer, an entomologist, a basketball coach, and an electrician, taping the interviews and dictating my stories to one of my attendants. Ben gave these stories Bs or Cs, saying that I had failed to ask tough questions. I told him I was too shy or afraid that I might offend my subject. Ben said that tough questions forced people to respond with tough answers and that asking them indicated a degree of respect for the subject. At the same time, he emphasized the importance of civility in interviewing people. For example, he said that, in asking a hard follow-up question, I could start with, "Some people would say that's hooey," instead of, "I think that's hooey."

Besides reporting, I had reading assignments. I had to look at the *Wall Street Journal* once a week, as well as wade through the whole *Sunday New York Times*. Also I had to subscribe to a local newspaper; I picked the *San Francisco Chronicle*.

I had attendants hold the newspapers up for me, because there was no way I could handle them. I gained a favorable impression of the *Wall Street Journal:* it seemed thorough. But I could never get interested in all those stories about Amalgamated Federated's hostile takeover of Federated Amalgamated. I was willing to suffer the *Sunday Times* up to a point. That point was where my eyes went to red alert, usually after page seventeen. After that, I'd ask my attendant to read aloud. The *Times* offered many exhaustive reports on places seldom in the news, places like Chad. Ben told me that, every time I saw a lead that said "Special to the Sunday *New York Times*," I could be sure some poor bastard had written it knowing he could sell the story to them and to no one else. The *San Francisco Chronicle* struck me as lightweight. Ben and I would flip through it and deride all the fluff, Ben wagging his head, shaggy eyebrows pulled together over his scimitar nose.

One Monday, page one of the *Chronicle* was devoted to Sunday's

Giants game. As a fan, I was delighted. It had been a terrific game, with Joe Morgan scoring the winning run in the ninth inning for the Giants, thereby depriving the hated Dodgers of the Western Division title. But as an apprentice journalist, I was appalled by the placement of a sports story on the front page.

But Ben surprised me, saying, "Every once in a while a paper has to run a story like this on page one just to prove that the editors are human. And, besides, 'Beat L.A.!' is not an uncivilized chant."

Ben assigned me to cover Berkeley city council and school board meetings, which were the most tedious events I'd witnessed since my days at Fairmont staring at the oxygen tanks lined against the wall. The council would pass long resolutions commending some retiring city employee, who often replied with an equally long, boring speech. I asked Ben how to write an article based on these nonevents. He said, "If you don't have a story, wing it." I would remember that advice later when I interviewed Stephen Hawking.

My boredom with covering these stories made me wonder whether I was cut out for the kind of daily journalism that the school taught. When I entered J School, I'd had some vague idea of writing a weekly column on politics or disability. But I knew that the people who held cushy jobs like that first had to spend years writing obituaries or re-writing the police reports at the station, or they had to log many evenings at dreary city council meetings. I had an inkling that jour-nalism might not be for me, but I wasn't admitting it yet. Ultimately, my body decided for me.

I couldn't take independent study courses forever. In January, I would have to get to class by myself, most likely to North Gate Hall, the sprawling wood frame building that housed the journalism school. So, for practice, I asked my attendant Melissa to accompany me on a trip in my power chair to North Gate.

On a warm fall day, we made the trip. We passed Sproul Hall, crossed the bridge behind Sather Gate, and examined the dogs sunning themselves on the grass by Wheeler. I said the dogs ran the English department. She said they were the reincarnations of professors who made their students read *The Faerie Queene*. We passed the immense main library and the Quonset hut where I had struggled with Marx and Darwin.

Thereafter, it was terra incognita, a very steep terra incognita. I knew only that north was straight ahead. The power wheelchair that Kate had christened "The Great Unwieldy" crawled up the forty-degree slope at less than half its usual pokey speed. As the motor groaned, Melissa offered to push, but I refused, saying that I had to know whether I could drive to North Gate by myself. I arrived at North Gate an hour and forty-five minutes after leaving my apartment. Exhausted, I knew I'd be too wiped out to concentrate on a class. I contemplated the view and the possibility that I'd have to drop out. All I could do then was drive back home.

I called Frances to tell her I couldn't drive to North Gate and would have to leave graduate school. To my surprise, she said the Disabled Students' Program would pay an attendant to push me there.

As it turned out, I wouldn't need the "pusher money" until spring quarter. That winter, I took my last independent study class, as well as Law for Journalists, which met in Wheeler, the home of the English department. It was fairly easy for me to drive to and through Wheeler. On my way to class, I would pass Ishmael Reed's class in creative writing, the same class I'd taken with Thom Gunn. Reed always left the door open, and often I wished I could just sneak in there. But I couldn't. My English major days were over.

Law for Journalists was required: I wouldn't get the master's degree if I didn't pass the course. Morrissey, the instructor, was a brisk, brilliant woman in her thirties who had worked as the libel attorney for the *Chicago Tribune* and the *National Review*. On the first day of class, she informed us she would use the Socratic method to teach us, but it didn't seem Socratic to me. She'd lecture from notes, point at a student, and say, "Tell us about *Barnes v. Willoughby*." If, as often happened, the student hadn't read *Barnes v. Willoughby*, she'd silently direct her index finger at another victim. No, this wasn't the Socratic method; it was the I-talk-you-listen method.

One morning, a student opened the only window in the classroom before Morrissey arrived. When she arrived, she was furious. "Young man, if you ever become an instructor at this great university, you will be able to say when the windows in your classroom are to be open or shut. Right now, I'm the instructor, this is my classroom and I want that window shut, so shut it now!"

Humiliated, the student closed the window.

Morrissey seemed to respect me. I did the reading, participated in study groups, and worked like hell trying to get a big, shiny A. I remembered that my father had said that he had had to rely on what he called "brute memory" to get through law school. We had a midterm, but Morrissey put off giving us the results until the week before finals, because she thought the people who did well on the midterm would not study as hard for the final.

"I've been receiving a lot of calls from you people," she said toward the end of term, "asking for locations of bridges and towers."

We laughed the laugh of the oppressed. I escaped the class with a B. I was relieved: I would never have to take that course again.

For the spring quarter, I chose two classes, both of them in North Gate. North Gate was one of the architectural glories of campus, but for me it was a multilevel monster with only two wheelchair-accessible rooms. One of the many inaccessible ones was the J School lounge, which contained a book where students could write comments about instructors. Marty told me the book had more complaints about Morrissey than anyone else.

I hired Melissa to push me to North Gate. Usually arriving late, she would lift me out of the iron lung, put me in the wheelchair, and then push me up Telegraph Avenue. Once on campus, she'd start running, her pace determined by how late we were. We'd run through Sather Gate, past Wheeler Hall, past the main library, past the big eucalyptus tree in a valley near the center of campus. In front of Hildebrand, the social welfare building, we'd stop so that Melissa could collapse on a concrete bench to catch her breath. I always worried that I would be late for class, but I always got there on time.

David Littlejohn taught the Literature of Journalism. I had seen his novel, *The Man Who Shot Mick Jagger,* and in my Sacramento days, I had watched his PBS series, *Critic at Large.* Perhaps his fame drew me to take his class. I was surprised the first day: he walked on crutches, crutches that I had never seen on the television series or his book jacket. When I complained to him once about how inaccessible North Gate was, he said it was accessible enough. I realized that it was "accessible enough" for him, but it wasn't for me. I found his lack of empathy disappointing.

He assigned us ten books to read, and we had to write a paper on one of them. I chose *Dispatches,* by Michael Herr, one of the best books to come out of the Vietnam War.

My other class was in science and environmental writing. Rawley, the instructor and a former science reporter, explained that the word *environment* had been added to the name of the class because students had asked for it a few years prior, when the environment was a hot item. This year's hot item was AIDS: half the papers turned in by my five classmates were about AIDS.

One day, Rawley announced that Ontario's Minister of Health would be holding a press conference on campus. He told us to attend the press conference, but, when I said it was in an inaccessible building, he granted me an exemption. Then Rawley asked, "Where is Ontario, anyway?"

No one knew except me. "It's the biggest province in Canada," I said. "Goes from New York to Minnesota." I was shocked by others' ignorance of geography. Perhaps gazing at the atlases my father had given me in Children's Hospital had given me an edge.

One place where I had no edge was in researching and writing the five-hundred-word papers we had to turn in each week. When I began journalism school, I reasoned that, if I could analyze a Shakespeare sonnet, I could easily write journalism. But I had problems writing lead paragraphs ("lead grafs," in J School parlance). I found that the lead graf is as arcane and difficult as any other form of writing. Rawley had us read *The Elements of Style*, by Strunk and White, which real J School people referred to as "Strunk and White." Ben Bagdikian, one of the most graceful writers in the school, told me he read Strunk and White once a year.

The prime directive of Strunk and White is "Omit needless words!" Rawley gave me Cs and Ds, and I worried about these grades. My papers returned half covered in red-penciled comments, half of them "ONW!" Perhaps I wasn't a real J School person, after all. Although I could picture old Professor Strunk squeezing his lapels, leaning on his desk, and hissing, "Omit needless words! Omit needless words!" I could not put the advice into practice. I was too much the English major, too much in love with ironic observations, eloquent phrases, and gut-wrenching puns.

Less than a month into the term, I began getting sick. Vomiting frequently and feeling extremely tired, I dropped Literature of Journalism before I'd had a chance to write my paper on *Dispatches*. Although I preferred the literature class, I felt I had to concentrate on science writing. After all, the science writing class could lead to real work, while another class in literature would be utterly useless.

Somehow, I got through that quarter. My later papers drew Bs from Rawley, and I finished with a B.

On the last day of the quarter, Rawley, who owned a vineyard in Mendocino County, threw us a wine and cheese party. He brought wine made from the grapes on his land. I attended the party, but, when I left it, my declining health gave me a feeling that I would never see the inside of North Gate again.

12

A Berkeley Life

(June 1983–July 1991)

T he early part of my life, years of living with my parents, had accustomed me to a world of few people and little change. My time as a student was livelier, but even then I knew only a small number of friends and attendants. Only after I left school did my social world expand. During the eighties, I met many people and consequently had a bewildering variety of experiences. I acquired my first computer in 1983, which meant that, for the first time in my life, I could keep a journal. Writing in the journal, working with my therapist, Miriam, and continuing to talk deeply with my housemate, Kerry, enabled me to see myself in new ways.

Even before I got sick with what I later learned was postpolio syndrome, my Department of Rehabilitation worker, Casey, had wanted DR to buy a computer for me. She persuaded Sony to lend me one of its early attempts at a laptop, the Typecorder. But the one-line screen hurt my eyes, so Casey returned it. Shortly after that, I got my first pair of eyeglasses.

Casey knew I wanted a laptop computer because it would fit more easily into my apartment and because I feared the cathode ray tube used in big computer monitors would damage my vision. She had heard of a Radio Shack computer that might work for me, so we went to one of their stores. There, a salesperson showed me the Tandy Model 100, about as big as a textbook—and it didn't bother my eyes at all. Trying out the keyboard with my mouthstick, I found that the keys were easy to hit, and I could reach all of them. Although it had only eight kilobytes of memory, Casey and I agreed that this would be the perfect computer for me.

But getting it was more complicated than wrapping it and stuffing it into my backpack. DR regulations required that purchases that exceeded one thousand dollars had to be approved by the High Muckety-Mucks in Sacramento. I waited most of the summer for the computer. When I finally complained to Casey in August, she intervened. The paperwork, she learned, had been buried, but she said I should get my computer within the month.

Finally I got it, in October. New, shiny, and mysterious, it was the most wonderful toy I'd ever owned. Kerry asked whether I was going to learn BASIC and become a computer wizard. I said no, I just wanted it to write on. Embarrassed by computer hype, I called it "the typing device" instead of the computer. Kerry couldn't stand such inverse snobbery, thank God, so I soon reverted to calling it a computer. At first it kept falling off my little wire bookstand, so I asked a DSP mechanic to make a wooden stand to hold it. Then it took me a couple of weeks to figure out how to work with it. DR had also bought me a daisy-wheel printer, whose print reminded me of a connect-the-dots game: the lower-case gs looked like 9s. When printing, it made as much noise as a dozen typewriters.

My first journal entry is dated October 13, 1983:

"Nothing is either real or unreal."
                    —MIKE DITKA, football coach and philosopher.

I had never kept a journal before, but Kerry told me about hers and how she used it. With her encouragement, I went wild with the journal, often spending whole days at it. It gave me a privacy I had never known. Falling into it, I became more introspective and self-aware.

The computer took me many places. Participation in the WELL online service enabled me to meet people I would never have known otherwise. I've written journalism for Pacific News Service, letters to friends, and poems for myself. I've progressed beyond the Model 100 but have always used that wooden computer stand.

In the summer of 1983, I felt a pain in my right side that amazed and terrified me. I was in such agony that I found myself screaming,

"Mommy!" It felt as though someone were trying to drill through my lower ribcage. Vomiting and diarrhea quickly dehydrated me.

Kerry sat with me much of the morning, trying to comfort me. "They say kidney stones is the second worst pain there is," she said. "Only childbirth is worse."

"That's good to know," I panted, depressed and confused. Just the week before, I had been munching Brie and baguettes in Rawley's classroom. Now I had to be cleaned up all the time, and my breakfast attendant had said my cries for my mother struck her as unmanly. If I had to carry on like this, it was good to know I was being attacked by the worst pain known to men.

"Just take these," Kerry said, offering a pill and a bit of a cookie. "It's not much; you should be able to keep them down. They'll help you get some rest."

The medicine she offered was a Valium and part of a marijuana cookie. I took both with a little water and slept for fourteen hours.

The next morning, we called Dr. Falcone, who confirmed Kerry's diagnosis and ordered a visiting nurse to examine me at my apartment. He prescribed codeine, and, after I took the drug, the sudden absence of pain lifted my spirits. I ate a little. With a clearer mind, I decided—reluctantly—against taking summer classes.

While I was recovering from the kidney stone attacks, I needed someone to substitute for a supper attendant, and I got Ilse's name from an attendants' list. The first time she arrived, she asked, "Would you like me to read to you before I start cooking?"

Pleased by her friendliness, I said yes. She bent over to look in my bookshelf.

"How about *A Distant Mirror*? Have you read that?"

"No. My mother gave it to me, but I haven't read it yet."

She pulled a chair next to the iron lung, sat, and read in her lilting voice. After half the introduction, she set the book down. "Do you want me to start supper? You must be getting tired of hearing my horrible accent."

"Accent? I hadn't noticed an accent."

"I'm Danish, couldn't you tell? People in Berkeley are always teasing me about my accent."

"No, I couldn't detect one; I just thought that was the way you talked. Yeah, I'd better have supper, that's what I hired you for. Make me some mashed potatoes and peas, with some tea."

"No meat or fish? Tofu?"

"No, I've been sick lately."

Aside from cooking well and enjoying books, Ilse was entertaining. I called her whenever I needed a substitute that summer. A graduate student in architecture, she also had a degree in English literature. Like me, she wondered about the career value of an English degree. "I memorized Cordelia's lines," she said, "but that never got me a job."

When a lunch attendant quit, I hired Ilse to replace her. Soon she was fixing me two meals daily. Most of the time, lunches consisted of canned tomato soup. She also tried to get me to eat crackers, which I usually refused. But when she bought a soup bowl with an attached snack tray for my birthday, my cracker consumption shot up.

That July, I didn't get my check from In-Home Support Services, a state program that provides money to pay attendants. I called my IHSS worker, Mr. Druzhinsky, who explained in heavily accented English that I had not received my check because I hadn't mailed in the timesheets my attendants were required to fill in. I knew I had mailed them, but that made no difference. How would I pay people? I phoned my father and brother, both lawyers. They lent me money and advised me to photocopy the timesheets in the future and to send them by certified mail.

Although I began keeping the proof of mailings, I didn't get the missing checks. I didn't like having to borrow money, and the stress of dealing with IHSS and worrying about paying attendants wasn't helping my health. Finally, in October, Druzhinsky's superior phoned to tell me that Druzhinsky had lost my timesheets. Rather than admit his mistake, Druzhinsky had lied to me and put me through hell all summer. As calmly as I could, I asked that another worker be assigned to my case. He agreed. That kind of stress was the reason I wanted to earn my own money, to be free of bureaucracy.

One afternoon in August, Ilse phoned me and called me "darling" as she said good-bye. I didn't know what to make of it. When I saw her later that day, she said her roommate had thrown her out in a fit of irrational anger. She asked whether I'd let her sleep on the floor in my room.

Although the idea of seeing her more often appealed to me, I worried that her presence would make my apartment too crowded. I stalled for time by telling her most people couldn't sleep with the noise of the iron lung and that I'd have to talk with Kerry before I made a decision.

When I asked Kerry, she said, "No, I don't mind. Why should I? Maybe you guys will be lovers. She seems to like you."

"She called me 'darling.'"

"Yeah, you told me."

"On the day she got kicked out of her old place."

"Yeah, you told me. Why are you so suspicious? She seems like a decent woman to me. I'd give it a go if I were you. Her sleeping bag's all ripped, though. I'll leave out one of mine. Tell her she's welcome to use it."

The next morning, I saw Ilse's blonde head and small pink left shoulder sticking out of Kerry's sleeping bag on the floor beside me. It was an odd thrill to see a sleeping woman and to watch her emerge from her sleeping bag, rubbing her face and shuffling toward the bathroom.

She usually woke at eleven, fed me soup and crackers around noon, got the mail, and then ran my errands. After that, she would be gone until evening, looking for work and reading books on architecture in the library. When she returned at 11 P.M., I'd wake up, having fallen asleep four hours earlier. I'd ask her about her day, and she'd ask me about mine. Standing behind my head, she would lightly stroke my hair as we talked. I would look up at her. When she kissed my forehead, cheeks, and lips, I would close my eyes, the outline of her face burning on my retinas.

Dr. Falcone arranged to have my kidney stones removed by a specialist, Dr. Garton, in San Francisco, who had invented a technique of implanting a water-filled tube in a patient's back. Ultrasonic waves, shot through the tube, would enter the kidneys to pulverize the stones. It sounded frightening, but I was ready to undergo it so that I could resume my old life. Ben, who had become dean of the J School, visited me and said I could return to my graduate program at any time within the next five years.

Ilse rode with me in the back of the ambulance that took me across the bay, stroking and kissing my head and face. The ambulance attendants, who had shown her how to give me oxygen, looked away. She ran her hands into my flannel shirt, which surprised me. She had never touched me with so much affection, nor had she made me so aroused. Since I had never before been out of the lung with her, she had not touched any part of me except my face. Reluctantly, I told her to stop, fearing that having an orgasm the day before surgery might be dangerous.

It took two hours to check into my room at the University of California, San Francisco Medical Center. Nurses, techs, and social workers came and went to give me their spiels and wish me good luck. I thought they would never stop.

When they did, Ilse requested privacy, closed the door, and kissed me more passionately than I'd ever been kissed. Heaven lasted nearly an hour. Then slowly, reluctantly, she left. Her kissing, tender and prolonged, made me feel as though I were a soldier departing for the front.

That evening, four doctors examined my torso as I lay in an open iron lung, my head sticking out of the collar. First, they stuck a needle into my groin. A nurse put her hand on my forehead and explained this was a blood gas test, that she had had one and knew it hurt terribly. She was right. I was even more uncomfortable because so many people were touching me. I never have liked having more than one person handle sme. If one of them hurt me, I wouldn't be able to tell the right one quickly. Now, four doctors, each apparently convinced he had sovereignty, were stretching, prodding, turning, and puncturing me. The nurse spoke to me calmly, trying to control my panic.

Then, Dr. Garton stood up and stopped touching me, saying, "We can't do it." The other doctors abruptly quit examining me. The nurse, as astonished as I was, took her hand from my forehead and closed the iron lung.

"Your scoliosis is so pronounced that your right kidney's pressed right against your lung," Dr. Garton explained. "If we went in there, we could puncture your right lung and you'd die."

What a reprieve! Although I dreaded the continued presence of the stones, my overwhelming feeling was relief that I wouldn't have to go through with the surgery. The next morning, the anesthesiologist told me he would have had to insert a central catheter to pump anesthesia directly into my lungs, and there was a 25 percent chance that that procedure alone would have killed me.

Ilse, sullen, kept her arms crossed as we rode in the back of the ambulance that took me back to Berkeley. After I got home and was back in my old, familiar iron lung, I asked her what was bothering her.

"You just seem so damned blissful," she said. "You still have those damned stones. Don't you realize that? I was looking forward to you regaining your health. I wanted to see you back in your wheelchair, go out with you, have a real life with you outside this stinking little apartment. But you're just thrilled. No big scary operation. Well, maybe I'd be thrilled, too, if it were me. I don't know. I gotta get back to the city, meet some people. I'm all—I'm sorry, I'm emotionally all strung out. I gotta go. We'll talk tonight, or tomorrow or sometime."

She slammed out the door, leaving me feeling ashamed of being such a coward.

Missing my old friend and attendant Tracy terribly, I had written her a letter every month since she had gone to France just after I graduated. She had sent me one letter and a postcard. Suddenly, one afternoon in November 1983, Tracy was standing outside my picture window, sticking out her tongue.

"Tracy!"

She entered, kissed me on the forehead, and tousled my hair. "Sacre blooey, mon sewer, good to see ya."

We talked all afternoon. I told her about how sick I'd been, about staying in bed all summer, and about Ilse.

"I saw the sleeping bag, I wondered about that. New girlfriend, huh? Look, what I wanted to ask you is, you think I could work for you again?"

"You want to work for me again?"

"Yeah, glutton for punishment. And I need money. I was thinking weekend suppers, nothing too heavy. How's that sound?"

Ilse had already asked to work Saturday lunches and suppers, but I felt no hesitation in agreeing to Tracy's request. "That sounds terrific," I said.

Tracy, who had worked for me in so many different situations, was a better attendant than Ilse. She had lifted me and cleaned up my vomit, doing intense, difficult personal care. Ilse had only fed and smooched with me. I lusted after Ilse, but I was fonder of Tracy, and I was not going to give up the chance to see more of her, even though I worried that Ilse might be jealous or put out by losing some hours of work.

Tracy wanted me to go outside more often. When I told her I couldn't afford to go outside because I was still broke from the IHSS screw-ups the previous summer, she offered to take me outside on Sunday afternoons for free. Touched by her generosity, I accepted.

"Great," she said. "And if you can stay up in the wheelchair for more than an hour, I'll take you to a movie."

Ilse was peeved when I told her I had rehired Tracy, but she accepted it. "You know, Thanksgiving's coming," she said. "I could cook up a special dinner for you. What do you think you'd like?"

I said I'd like a traditional turkey and stuffing meal. She cooked it but later complained she hadn't cooked turkey in years and hated all the work it required.

Often, Ilse went to San Francisco for two or three days at a time. When I asked her to tell me when she would be out of town, she exploded. "Hey, I'm a grown woman, I can go anywhere I damned well please," she said. "It's just that sometimes I get sick of this place, it's so morbid and weird."

"I'm just asking that you tell me when. . . ."

Kerry entered the front door. "What's morbid and weird, Ilse?"

"Mark and you are morbid and weird. I mean, you're not married, you're not lovers. I've never seen—"

"Who are you to judge Mark and me?" Kerry asked. "Mark's been very generous with you, he's given you a job, a place, he's—"

"And that's my jacket you're wearing!" I snarled.

"Here!" Ilse shouted, taking it off and throwing it to the floor.

"And who are you to judge," Kerry continued, "how Mark and I are supposed to relate to each other? Who made you queen of relationships? You don't know anything, lady! You think you're a know-it-all, but you don't know shit! And whose sleeping bag have you been using and whose underwear are you wearing? They're mine, remember? Or have you—"

"I'm leaving. You folks are nuts, totally nuts, and I'm not putting up with it another goddamned second!" Ilse slammed the door.

Kerry and I stayed up late that evening discussing friendship and ingratitude.

"I should compensate you for the loss of your clothes," I said.

"Oh, never mind, she needs them more than I do."

"She's a real operator. I bet she only pretended to love me."

"I wouldn't be so cynical, Marko, I think she really had feelings for you."

At 6:30 the next morning, Ilse entered, put her keys to my apartment on my table, and left. We didn't speak. I was mad at her and didn't want her in my place. About a week later, I began to feel the sadness, realizing that her eyes would never again burn into my mine.

That weekend, Tracy took me to my friend Ted's apartment so that I could interview him for an article I was writing about disabled people and computers. *"Bienvenidos a mi casa,"* he said, rolling ahead of us in his wheelchair down the hallway. He owned a big desktop IBM PC that beeped and showed the IBM logo when he turned it on. He said, "This baby has so much memory it has the manual right on the hard disk."

"How much memory does it have?" I asked, trying to sound casual and high-tech.

"Five hundred and twelve K. You know what a K is?"

"A thousand bytes. It has five hundred thousand bytes? My God."

Ted accepted my envy as he pecked with his index fingers at the keyboard, which lay flat on the table in front of the disk drive. Occasionally, he would pick up a tiny white bag.

"What's that?"

"This?" he said. "It's a bag of shot, the stuff they put in shotguns. Sometimes I have to hit the shift key and another key at the same time. I just lift the bag and put it on top of the shift key and hit the other key." This system allowed him to type properly even though he was able to use only two fingers.

Impressed by Ted's computer smarts, I watched and asked questions until I got tired. When I asked Tracy to take me home, she congratulated me; I had been out of the iron lung an hour and a half.

Two weeks later, Tracy took me to a movie theater to see *Never Cry Wolf.* At the end of the evening, when she put me back in the iron lung, I was exhausted but happy. I had been up for three hours: it was the longest I had stayed out of the lung since getting sick with the kidney stones.

Kerry often asked questions about my sister, Rachel. Rachel was twenty then, but Kerry wanted to know how we had gotten along when we were little. She wondered whether Rachel knew about my other sister, Karen, who had died two years before Rachel was born. She asked how long it had been since I talked with Rachel one-on-one. I said I hadn't really talked alone with her since 1976, seven years ago, and I didn't know whether she knew about Karen.

"Did you ever tell her?"

"No, I didn't."

"Maybe it's about time you talked with her," Kerry said. "Maybe you could invite her down here by herself sometime."

When Rachel came to Berkeley, I asked her to take me to the Thai restaurant around the corner. Once we had ordered, we began talking. She said she was so glad that I invited her that she drove herself all the way—a hundred miles—even though her diabetes was beginning to affect her eyes, making driving difficult.

I told Rachel that Kerry had asked me about her and that I had been unable to answer most of her questions. Mainly, I remembered Rachel as a young child running into my room and making me laugh. I asked her whether she had known that I had polio.

"No, that's the damnedest thing. When I was little, I asked Mom and Dad what was wrong with you, and they said you were tired. Or that you had broken a leg. I didn't know about the polio till, God, I was twelve or thirteen."

"They told you I had broken a leg? For ten years?"

"Yeah, it was kind of silly. I thought something was going on."

I looked out the window at the Telegraph Avenue scene: students, panhandlers, tourists, drug dealers wearing Raiders caps. I found it hard to ask the next question. "When did you find out about Karen?"

"Karen? Oh, God, that was just a couple of years ago, and that was just an accident," she said, running a pale hand through her hair. "My friend Janie's mother told me, and she thought that I already knew, but I didn't. I'd never heard of Karen, never knew I had a sister. So I went home and asked Mom, and she started crying. I didn't want her to cry. I felt awful when Mom told me, but I felt I understood everything, like why Dad wouldn't let me go out in the rain and why they didn't let me date till I was eighteen."

"They were trying to protect you," I said. "Overprotect you."

Rachel nodded and sipped her iced tea. "'Overprotect,' that's the word, all right. God, why didn't they just tell me?"

"Well, *I* didn't tell you either. I was part of it, too. I guess it sounds stupid, but I was afraid, too. I don't even know what I was afraid of— maybe of causing you some psychological trauma, or of breaking those family rules of silence. I was as afraid as they were."

After our day together, I felt closer to Rachel—she said that whenever she came down to see me with our parents, she felt like the butt of O'Bie's jokes. We liked talking to each other as adults, and I was grateful to Kerry for suggesting it. It made me put even more trust in her advice after that.

journal 1/15/84
Does anyone ever finish a poem? I'm suffering from the illusion that I've finished writing the Karen poem, but I'm nagged by the possibility that it could be better. A perfect Karen poem haunts me as the fantasy of a thirty-year-old living Karen.

journal 1/28/84
Writing DOES help, somehow. Still tired from watching *King Lear,* but wrote considerable portion of a well-written letter to Charlotte. At least, I can do that well: I derive satisfaction from knowing that. Despite my intense awareness that the Karen poem isn't perfect, I printed it. Want to write other poems; feel I can't until I think of the Karen poem as "completed." Am I running away?

June 1984 was a month of departures. Tracy was leaving again, this time for good, to take a teaching position at the École Polytechnique. That spring, I had pretended she wasn't going, but, as the day of her leaving approached, I felt sadder and sadder. I wanted to tell her I loved her, but I lacked the nerve, so I typed a letter telling her and mailed it to her Regent Street address.

journal 5/14/84
VERY anxious about how Tracy'll react to my letter. I had the feeling, while writing it, that she would like it, and at least it's honest. Still, I never know how people will react. Maybe she'll hate it (and me) and never speak or write to me again. Maybe the letter will be lost in the mail, and she'll never receive it. Maybe she'll get it, read it, and act as if she never received it. There are so many terrible things that could happen; I think I've thought of them all & dwelt on them all.

Also, I wrote Tracy a long poem about our trips through the woods by Strawberry Creek and the Christmas dinner we'd had at her parents' house. She liked the poem, but she never received my letter. I got it back in the mail; I had her address wrong, and the post office returned it to me. Terrified, I had an attendant leave it on my table, where Tracy would see it.

"This is a letter I tried to send you," I said. "You see, it has the wrong address on it."

As she started to open it, I continued, "The letter's real stupid. It says I love you and dumb shit like that."

She put the letter down. "Mark, I know you love me." She moved the table and kissed me on the forehead. "I love you, too." I cried, feeling overwhelmed.

The next Sunday, she took me to the woods on campus. We sat near Strawberry Creek under the redwoods, smelling the damp earth and the eucalyptus grove nearby. We didn't talk much; she identified some flowers for me. She pushed me home and, for the last time, put me into the iron lung. Very sad, I started crying.

"Don't worry, bunny, we'll be in touch." She leaned over and kissed my forehead. I cried quietly as she left.

journal 6/12/84
Her "willingness of the heart" may be the thing about Tracy that baffles me the most. Why does she care?

Why, in particular, does she care about an ugly, deformed, boring cripple like me? Why should she give a shit? Why, in general, does she care about the fertility of the soil in third world countries? Would it matter if everyone south of the Rio Grande, everyone between Greece and Japan, starved because the soil had been depleted? It would matter to Tracy cuz she cares. I see God shining through her. Is that why I love her? But I also love her gloriously female body (slobber, slobber), her skin so smooth, her face so sweet, her unpretentious but, nevertheless, interesting breasts, her strong, sexy legs, eminently kissable and lickable and suckable yum-yum-yum.

Lust or spiritual admiration? Being a creature, I feel both.

Later that month I attended Joao's graduation. Resplendent in a rented black tux and brown shoes, he looked happy and proud. There was a party with Joao's friends, Brazilians, Israelis, and Americans. There was more food than anyone could eat, conversation in several languages, and much music, some provided by Joao on guitar.

When the van arrived to pick me up at 9:30, I asked someone to tell Joao I was leaving. I heard Joao's voice from the next room: "Oh, no, I want to have the honor of pushing Mark to the van." I was touched that he considered the chore of pushing my wheelchair an honor. He and Naomi took me out of the house and into the van. I was trying to maintain a light farewell conversation in my limited Spanish, mainly joking about how bad my Spanish was. The last I saw of them, Naomi and Joao both kissed me before they jumped off the rear of the van. The driver closed the back doors, and I cried some more.

In the midst of all the departures, my old friend Jessie called and asked whether she could take me to a movie. I hadn't seen her in six months or a year. "I like junky movies," she said. "The new Indiana Jones movie sounds pretty junky; do you want to see that?"

"Yeah, sure, of course."

At the theater she told me she saw about a movie a week, mostly trashy ones because she didn't have to think: she just wanted time off. I imagined that working as a nurse must be stressful for her.

There was a space in the theater for wheelchairs, so she sat on the floor next to me as we watched the movie. I could see her head, and we whispered through the movie. I liked the first fifteen minutes of *Indiana Jones and the Temple of Doom* because there was lots of action, but later the film got violent and gory. Afterward, she pushed me home, and on the way we stopped at a corner under a eucalyptus tree. She pulled a leaf down and held it under my nose. "Smells good, huh?"

"Yes. Thank you."

"This was fun. You want to see another movie in two weeks?"

"Yes, sure, that would be great. What movie should we see?"

"I don't know. I don't know what will be playing then. I'll call you in a week or so, and we'll make a plan."

When she called the next week, I told her I was feeling very tired and couldn't go. I didn't hear from her then, but, accustomed to her sudden and long disappearances, I assumed she'd come back sometime.

In fact, three years would pass before I ran into her on campus. We exchanged warm greetings, and she said she would call me that night. I waited and hoped, making excuses in my mind for why she did not call that night ... or the next day, or the next. It took me several days to accept that she was not going to call. Jessie and I had a few more desultory communications, but, over time, the relationship dwindled to nothing.

When I heard that a polio specialist worked at nearby Herrick Hospital, I made an appointment to see her, in case anything had changed in the way of polio treatment or prognosis. To get to the hospital, I asked my attendant Chloe to take me. My favorite attendant during the mid-eighties, Chloe was smart, hardworking, and very funny. She once told me about her role in a college production of *Hair,* when she and two other black women had worn one big sequined dress to play the part of the Supremes.

Examining me in her office, Dr. Clements asked about my history. After she heard it, she perched on her desk and said, "I'm afraid I really can't do anything for you. You're as healthy now as you're ever likely to be, considering the scoliosis and the respiratory problems. But I should talk to Dr. Reiss."

I had heard of Reiss. One of the nation's leading polio specialists, he practiced in San Francisco. She said he was in the building, and she'd get him. When they returned, Dr. Clements introduced Dr. Reiss. Chloe, being a mere attendant, sat in a corner, flipping through a magazine. As Dr. Clements explained my condition to Dr. Reiss, he lifted up my left leg beyond its limit, hurting me. I shrieked, "Stop it!"

He dropped my leg. "You know, we could do a lot with him," Dr. Reiss said. "I work with patients with scoliosis as bad as his. We set them up in vertical wheelchairs with padding to support their spinal columns. We snip the tendons that connect the buttocks to the thighs. But, after that, the patient has to lie on his stomach for six months. I don't think he has the guts to do that."

"You just hurt my leg," I said, stunned.

"He doesn't have a realistic sense of his own body," Reiss continued. "He should get a full-length mirror on his ceiling. That way maybe he'd get more realistic."

"Maybe you can afford full-length mirrors on your salary," I said. "I'm on SSI and I can't—"

"If you had the will, you could figure out the finance part," he said. "I don't see any will here."

Dr. Clements tried to intervene, but Dr. Reiss brushed her objections aside. "I think we've done about all we can do today."

Chloe pushed me home in silence. After three blocks, we stood under a tree, waiting for the light to change. "You know," Chloe said, "I don't think any white, straight, able-bodied man knows what it's like to feel fear."

"Not unless they've seen combat," I said. "You thought he treated me bad?"

"He treated you shitty." The light changed, and Chloe pushed me across the street. "I should have slapped him."

My interest in baseball, started when I was nine years old, kept developing even after I left graduate school. At nine, in Boston, I'd supported the Red Sox, but, when my family moved to Sacramento, my baseball allegiances switched to the San Francisco Giants. In September 1986, I watched the Giants playing the Mets in Shea Stadium. The Giants had had a spectacular season, bouncing back from last place the year before to pennant contention in midsummer. By September, however, the Giants had slumped and were no longer in the pennant race. Still, the games with the Mets were so exciting that even Kerry—previously not a fan—became interested.

"Would it bother you if I sat and watched the game for a while?" she asked. "I'm just interested in the uniforms. My father used to take me to watch the Orioles when I was little. I hated it, just waiting for some big guy to come up and hit a home run."

At that moment, Robbie Thompson of the Giants laid down a perfect sacrifice bunt. "Why'd he do that?" Kerry said. "He got out—why? That doesn't seem logical."

After I explained the logic behind bunting, she nodded. "I get it. So it's not all about hitting home runs."

Kerry thought that the blue of the Mets uniforms was too bright. She liked the Giants road uniforms, gray with the SF logo on the shirts. Kerry became fascinated by the way the managers tried to outfox each other, sending in pinch hitters and relief pitchers. "It's like chess," she said. "I never knew there was all this thinking. What's that guy doing with his hands?"

"That's the third base coach. He relays signals from the manager to the batter. Those signals are really complicated. Most of them mean nothing, but some will tell the batter to swing or not swing, or to bunt."

Kerry watched the rest of the Giants-Mets series with me. She especially liked the Mets' center fielder, Mookie Wilson. "I guess I'm a Mets fan," she said. "Is that okay? You don't mind?"

"No, I'm just happy you've discovered the game."

The rest of the Giants' season was all downhill. Kerry watched fewer games, but we were both riveted by the postseason playoffs, myself by the contest between the Red Sox and the California Angels, she by the Mets-Astros series. Marty, my former neighbor and a friend from J School, dropped by to help me root on the Red Sox, who were down three games to one. He was lying on my futon when Dave Henderson hit the homer that started the Red Sox's comeback, and he cheered.

During the sixth game, though, he said, "I gotta go. The J School is holding a run, and there's a student I want to get to know better."

"I didn't know you ran," Kerry said.

"Oh, I don't, I have terrible knees. But I really want to meet this lady, Joyce."

The next year, Kerry and I would attend the wedding of Marty and Joyce.

The playoffs ended with the Red Sox and the Mets set to play each other in the World Series. "You won't be mad if I root for the Mets, will you?" Kerry asked.

"No," I said. "Baseball is about rooting for a team. Your team is the Mets."

The Mets lost the second game on an error by the second baseman, Tim Teufel. Annoyed, Kerry took to calling him Ted Tofu. The series went on, each game tense and dramatic. In the sixth inning of game six, the Red Sox led three to nothing. They were ahead in games, three to two. All they had to do to win the World Series was take that game.

"It's all over," Kerry said. "The Mets look dead. Roger Clemens is pitching for the Red Sox. Didn't you say Clemens is the best pitcher in baseball?"

"He is," I said gleefully. "But you never know with baseball."

"Well, looks like it's all over to me. I'm going in my room. Call me if anything happens."

I called her in the ninth, when the Mets tied the game. We watched the rest of the game until the Mets won it in the bottom of the tenth inning. They went on to win the World Series, but the details are too tragic to recount. Anyone curious and vicious enough to want more information should read Roger Angell's book of essays, *Season Ticket*.

The End of Summer

Tonight, Fenway Park is cold, quiet, empty,
Inhabited by pigeons, grass, and wind.

The fans have turned to important tasks.
Raising children,
Removing tumors,
Teaching mathematics,
While forgetting the children's names,
Hesitating over how to reach the tumor,
Stumbling through the equations,
Tossed from reality by a spasm of thought,
   They could've won it.
They had 'em,
   Mistrustful, dismayed, embittered
By the wild pitch,
The medley of catastrophe,
The awful, throbbing repetition of
   They could've won it,
They blew it.

Marty and his girlfriend, Joyce, started taking me to Giants games the next season, 1987. These became big, epic trips: we went to one a year, and afterward I would have to stay in bed and recover for a week or two. The first time we went, I rented a van, Joyce sat in the front seat, and Marty sat in the back with me and the portable respirator. We left at 11:30 to get to Candlestick Park by the 1:00 start. The trip across the Bay Bridge to San Francisco went fairly quickly, but in the city we were slowed by traffic. As we approached the choked streets near Candlestick Park, we hardly made any progress. We were lucky to reach the park on time.

Marty helped the driver take me out. I had already scheduled the return trip for 4 P.M., even though I didn't know when the game would end. As Marty pushed me past the statue of Saint Francis and through Gate C, I was amazed at the number of people it took to operate a big-league ballpark. There were ticket-takers, vendors, private security, and police officers everywhere, and zillions of fans. Fans crowded the narrow hallways, paraded up and down the ramps, and lined up in long, snaking lines at the concessions. I was afraid people would bump into me, but I wasn't seriously jostled as we moved through the crowd. Finally, through an open door, I glimpsed the green, shining field.

Marty, Joyce, and I settled into the wheelchair section at the back of the lower deck, right behind home plate. We had a great view: I could see everything except right field, and I could overhear the radio and TV announcers in the booth above us. The crowd noise was so constant and loud that I had to shout into Marty's ear. We ate Polish sausages and beer as we watched the game, and I watched everyone else watching the game. The crowd's attention was riveted on the game; the game was the center, the most important thing in the universe.

We had to leave before it was over, with the Giants trailing. Marty, Joyce, and I waited in the parking lot for the van to return. The van was late, and, after about twenty minutes, a roar went up from the ballpark.

"I gotta go in there," Marty said.

"But the van—" I said, watching Marty run off.

"Don't worry," Joyce said, sitting on her San Diego Padres backpack. "I'll get you in the van. Marty can take a bus home."

The roar died, and, a few minutes later, Marty emerged from the ballpark. "The Giants had the bases loaded, and Candy Maldonado was coming to bat. Everyone was going crazy, but he struck out."

That year and for the next three, Marty and Joyce helped me to see some of the great players of the game: Will Clark, Matt Williams, Eddie Murray. Seeing them with my own eyes instead of through the lens of a television camera was a real thrill.

In 1987, I had bought tickets for a Giants-Reds game. Pete Rose was still playing for the Reds, and I really wanted to see him. But, that morning, as my attendant put his arms under me to lift me, a stabbing pain in my foot made me scream.

Marty offered to help lift me, but it was no good. The least movement drove me crazy with pain. Earlier that week, someone had turned me the wrong way, and my foot had bent too far. I had hoped it would heal before the day of the ball game, but that had been wishful thinking.

"I can't go," I said. "You take the tickets and go." Though angry with myself for ruining the day for Marty and Joyce, at least I could offer them the tickets.

"We wouldn't want to go without you," Marty said. "Look, the game's on TV. It looks like it will take a while for your attendant to undress you and everything. Why don't Joyce and I go get some Polish sausage and beer, and we'll be back here at game time?"

I wrote about the day in my journal. At that time, I was using more abbreviations and nonstandard spelling as my energy waned.

journal 6/19/89

SAT. MORN was absolute horrorshow/my foot hurt so much wen my
attendant slid his arm undr my right leg and that pushed my right
ft in per usual only it HURT/! !!/MY GOD like aftr its bin rammed into
th Tank/marty&joyce were coming and we were all sposta hav a jolly
time at candlestick watchin th giants beat th reds/allovasuddin, that
was at risk/my attendant propped my right leg up so it wdnt shmoosh
into my left leg wen he lifted me/i was so HORRIFIED of makin a
decision/if i let my attendant lift me, we cd go to th ballgame, but
it might hurt evn worse, injure it more/and wut agn about gettin
back in?/i didnt think i cd prop up my leg s while i was inth chair/i
thot of doin a 2-person lift w my attendant and marty, but th thot of
me screeemin in marty's presence scared me/i was hysterical w fear/
thasswut i tol my attendant/i feared th pain of bein lifted and i
feared th anger of joyce&marty for ruinin their day/i'm always ruining somebody's life/startin w my mother/and it was all happenin
so damned quick/marty & Joyce came, th van was comin AAARGH!
!lmarty calmly tolme not to get up, we cd watch th game on tv/i tolim
they cd still go, i had th ticketds/he sd they wdnt want to go without
me so i tol my attendant not to get me up, to undress me and put me
back in the tank/then i started crying really loud anfd forcibly/before
i had bin weeping, now i was sobbing/right infruntv every1/i thot- i
gotta think of a way to kill myself/my life is all horrorshow and i cant
stand it any more/sumhow i communicated to joyce&marty that it
wd take a while to get back in th tank/they left w th promise to return
at gametime w hot dogs and beer/i had gotten back in and was cryin
w my eyes closedl i felt kerry tuch my forehead, wch surprised me/she
spoke in a low steddy voice/i lookt at her eyes/she tolme to enjoy th
game, to let it be a healing experience/i felt too lost and tired to do
anything but agree/i lookt to kerry as my link to sanity/she askt how
i felt and i toler bout wanting to kill myself/she was surprised, sd no
1 wdv gest i felt so badly toler how i always ruin evry1's life/she askt
ifi thot she was mad at me/i sd evry1's mad at me/she encuurkjd me
to ask if she was mad at me/i did and she sd no/she then encuurijd
me to ask my attendant/'o no. why wd any1 be mad?' he askt/

I was very grateful to Marty for his understanding. That afternoon,
the Giants won. "Good thing you didn't go," Marty said. "Giants have
lost every time you've gone."

In those days, my housemate, Kerry, would feed me if an attendant didn't show up, or she'd get the emesis bowl if I had to throw up, but she generally thought it was a bad idea for her to work for me, fearing that being my attendant would hurt our friendship. She did everything a friend could do.

By talking about her own therapy, she encouraged me to hire Miriam, a therapist who came to my apartment every week. The day after an appointment, Kerry and I would discuss it. Kerry noticed that I usually had forgotten much of what Miriam had said, so she suggested that I type notes on my computer after each session. This helped me remember insights that I would sometimes have preferred to forget.

journal 7/25/84
Miriam said, "I'm being real clear on this—you have to be less passive." She also said that my SAYING I'm passive has become a part of my passivity. That I mope over absent women like Tracy because it's SAFER than pursuing the women of here&now. Tracy can't hurt me (a lot), but there's the risk that someone new will hate me. That I buy into my parents' view of me as the helpless child, that I have to decide for myself that that's NOT the way I want to see myself. Is it the way I see myself. I LOVE being taken care of. I feel as if I am a kid because I'm small&helpless.

Besides suggesting therapy, Kerry lent me her psychology books. I read a lot of Alice Miller, and I liked Paul Kegan's book, *The Evolving Self*.

Kerry had a habit of reading five or six books at the same time. The range of her material amazed me, while the limits of mine amazed her. Kerry asked why I didn't read more about religion, or about psychology, or about polio. She wondered why I didn't read more poetry or more junk. The "junk" novels she lent me weren't that bad: Andrew Greeley's *Ascent to Hell*, Marge Piercy's *Woman on the Edge of Time*. I liked Kerry's science fiction books, especially the Neuromancer trilogy by William Gibson.

Kerry also taught me little things, like how to respond when someone knocked at the door at the same time that the phone rang. She taught me to eat the pickle while my mouth was still full of sandwich. My mother had always taught me to wait until my mouth was empty, but eating the pickle with the sandwich was, as Kerry said it would be, more fun. She encouraged me to buy loose-fitting sweat pants because they would be easier to don than my jeans.

On days when I had to get up, I was usually nervous. Kerry and I disagreed about what the word "brave" meant; I thought it was fearless, but she said it was doing something even though you were scared. She said it was brave of me to get up, and that comforted me. On the other hand, she said it was also okay if I didn't want to get up. She said there were some days she didn't want to leave the apartment, either. It surprised me that an able-bodied person might dread leaving the house. And, occasionally, she would postpone the day's commitments, break out the bubbles, and relax and talk with me for an hour or so in the morning.

Kerry was the first person to talk to me deeply and at length about our personalities, about things that really mattered. Also, she would get involved in intense conversations with my attendants. Afterward, she'd say, "Why didn't you say anything?" I'd reply that I hadn't thought of anything interesting or funny to say. She'd ask me what I had been thinking, I'd tell her, and she'd tell me that it was interesting, it was funny, and that keeping such thoughts to myself was a form of selfishness. She encouraged me to participate more, and I did.

An attendant's cat had a litter of kittens, one of which he gave to Kerry. The orange and white kitten squirmed in her hands as Kerry nuzzled her, saying, "Isn't she adorable?"

"She's wonderful."

"I'll have to think of a name for her, she's all kind of orangey. Can you think of a good name?"

We went through about a dozen names before Kerry settled on Pumpkin. A few days later, Kerry started calling the kitten Pumpkin-Bumpkin; later, she became just plain Bumpkin.

Then, one day, she came home in the rain, carrying a small black kitten. After feeding both cats and putting her rain gear away, she explained, "I was just sitting in the doorway on Dana Street, waiting for the rain to ease up, and this kitty jumped in my lap. He wouldn't get off; even when I came home, he trailed me. Is it okay if I adopt him? He's a male, I checked, so he should get along with Bumpkin."

Already in love with the black cat, I said, "Of course."

Again, we played with names, settling on Calloo, a nonsense word from "Jabberwocky," one of our favorite poems.

Bumpkin was quiet, very close to Kerry. Once, while Kerry was holding her close to me, Bumpkin reached down and touched my face softly, with her claws retracted. Kerry told me cats seldom did that and that it was a sign of affection.

On the other hand, Calloo was a hell-raiser. Hearing him running up and down the apartment all the time, I nicknamed him "Thunderpaws." Every morning, when Kerry left for her walk, he would meow forlornly. I would meow back at him until he relaxed, realizing that there was intelligent life in the apartment. When Kerry returned, she would feed the cats, sit down with the paper, and talk with me. She always had a cup of café mocha, which she shared with Calloo: he liked to lick off the whipped cream.

Before I got a TV to replace mine, which had been stolen, Kerry would lug hers out to the living room so that I could watch something she thought I would enjoy. One day it was the movie *Sabrina,* with Humphrey Bogart and Audrey Hepburn. At one point, Bogart grabbed Hepburn by the shoulders, pulled her to him, and kissed her. "See that?" Kerry asked. "That's how women like to be kissed."

I must have looked downcast, because she asked me what was the matter. I mumbled, "I won't be able to kiss anyone that way."

"That's true. I hadn't thought of that. But you'll find ways, I'm sure you will."

In 1986, I finally bought a new television. Whenever there was something good on in the evening, she'd encourage me to nap in the afternoon so I could stay awake later to watch the show. We especially liked *The Jewel in the Crown* and would discuss each episode the following day, pitying the unfortunate Hari Kumar and analyzing the villainous Merrick.

Kerry also turned me on to movies. I hadn't been allowed to go to movies when I lived with my parents; the fire department considered me a fire hazard because I blocked an aisle with my cot. But, after dropping out of graduate school, I began going to theaters with Kerry, Tracy, Jessie, and others. Attending a two-hour movie could wipe me out for a week, but it was worth it for the escape.

Kerry said it was nice to see the apartment lit up at night. She loved sharing a life with someone, as I did. It wasn't always just her helping me; often she asked me questions about politics, history, or English literature. She considered me an expert on all of these, even though I kept insisting I was not. It was important for her to feel that we were equals.

When I slept late, she would throw open the curtain to wake me up, eager for someone to talk with. She always apologized for waking me, but she didn't really seem sorry.

Kerry taught me that I didn't have to be the person my mother wanted me to be. In particular, she showed me it was okay to express anger. She said that people who were close could yell at each other, yet be confident that they would still love each other. It took several years for me to understand the idea that we could fight and still be friends. All this was a revelation: I had never considered being different from the good boy my parents had wanted me to be. I don't think I would ever have seen a sex surrogate without that realization, or joined writers' group, or had as many friends.

Sometimes, Kerry and I argued about abstract ideas, things we didn't have to decide. After she quit the FAITH Center, she began attending an Episcopalian church. She declared that Catholicism was sexist and hierarchical and asked why I wouldn't leave. I told her I was sticking with it.

Once a month, I went to weekday mass, where there weren't many people and the service lasted only about thirty minutes. My lunch attendant would take me to the church and leave me there for half an hour.

journal 5/18/88
i like goin to mass/th externals slough off/jew and gentile, free and slave, male and female, we are all one in christ jesus/its good to feel that, bettern readin it/th peeple in wheelcairs, th old peepl, th pritty young girls, th professors, th janitors, all become just peepl/no legends or social roles attached/our core is reveeled/at th core, we are worshippers!

Mass ended with a short sermon. In one of them, a priest denounced the pope for refusing to ordain women. He said the pope was afraid of the truth spoken in the Magnificat, Mary's prayer of gratitude after meeting her elderly cousin Elizabeth, pregnant with John the Baptist. At the end of mass, we shared the kiss of peace. People would come up to me, put their hands on my head or chest, and say, "Peace be with you." When the time came for the parishioners to line up and take communion, one of them would push my wheelchair to the altar so that I could receive the wafer and the wine. When the priest ended the mass, "The peace of the Lord be with you," and we responded, "And also with you," I always felt very peaceful. I didn't care that Kerry disliked the church. Eventually, she accepted my stubborn faith and encouraged me to read Catholic writers like Thomas Merton, Flannery O'Connor, and Matthew Fox.

Over and over, the subject that came up was my anger at myself. Kerry asked me why I would be angry with myself, and I said because I caused other people—especially my parents—misery and inconvenience. I had always blamed myself for getting polio, saying it was my body and if I wasn't responsible for it, who was? Kerry taught me that I could have different parts of my mind at the same time, and the logical part of my brain saw that blaming myself for having polio was crazy thinking.

Once Kerry asked me to picture myself as a six-year-old boy running on the beach. She had me close my eyes and describe my feelings. I told her how exhilarated I would feel, running by the Atlantic, feeling the breeze and the wet sand between my toes. I kept describing it until I cried.

"Can you picture that boy?" she asked.

"Yes, I feel like him."

"Can you picture him from the outside? As an adult looking at him with his crew cut and his little face?"

"Yes." I was still crying.

"Are you mad at him? Do you blame him for getting polio?"

"No, no. It's not his fault. It just happened."

That visualization helped, but it took her several years to get it through my thick Irish skull that my disease wasn't my fault. That concept was one of her great gifts to me.

In 1989 I was hospitalized for a week with a urinary tract infection. During this time, Kerry realized that, if something happened to me, she'd be homeless, so she began looking for another place to live. "I'm sick of that place," she said. "It's all mold and mildew. The worst thing is the attendants. I don't feel like I can wander around the apartment without bumping into someone."

However, one attendant she liked was Flann, and she looked forward to the days he worked. Having graduated from Berkeley a few years ago, Flann was trying to get into a graduate school in medieval studies. He and Kerry would keep up long, intense conversations long after Flann had finished my routine.

One thing they couldn't agree on was psychology. Kerry had been seeing therapists for years and had read a great deal on the subject. Flann did not believe in the existence of the subconscious. They argued one day, and, after he left, she told me, crying, that she liked Flann but that she was afraid this issue would come between them. But, over time, they discussed the matter more until they came to understand and respect each other's thinking.

One day, Flann said he was going to spend the night with Kerry in her room, and then sometimes she would spend nights in his apartment. I thought Flann was ideal for Kerry.

After I left the university, Shakespeare continued in my life. At a J School picnic in 1982, a professor gave me two tickets for a production of *Hamlet*, performed by the Berkeley Shakespeare Festival.

Kerry accompanied me to that first performance, the first play I'd ever seen. Kerry had been to many shows and had worked lights at some professional productions. But neither of us was prepared for Hamlet in the round, Berkeley style. I sat in my wheelchair next to Kerry, beside a ramp that led to the stage. The performance began with a man pushing a wheelbarrow on stage, dumping a mannequin through a trap door, then trundling down a ramp three feet from me. Then guards ran on stage dressed in Green Beret uniforms. I was hooked.

Too sick to go anywhere during the summers of 1983 and 1984, I gave away my tickets. But, in 1985, I began going regularly again. The festival allowed a friend in for free, so every summer I rented vans with wheelchair lifts to take a companion and me to John Hinckle Park. Season tickets cost more than a hundred dollars, expensive for someone living on SSI, but, as Kerry said, culture is what we live for, the reason we put up with bills, smog, and illness.

The stage, surrounded by tall firs, faced a natural amphitheater, covered with concrete benches. I sat right next to the stage, near one of the light standards. Occasionally, the house manager would approach my friend and me before a performance to ask us to move because actors would be running through our spot. Once he asked us to move because an actor was going to swing on stage, in the manner of Tarzan, and we were under the flight path.

One year, I bought two sets of tickets for each performance so that I could see each show twice. During the performance of *Coriolanus*, the actor in the lead, dressed like a twentieth-century admiral, tore off his epaulets and hurled them offstage, nearly hitting me.

The following week, when I came back, the actor approached me before show time. "I'm surprised you're back," he said. "I thought I might have killed you."

I was so excited to meet him that I forgot to ask for his autograph. In fact, I was thrilled by every performance, because it was live and things might go wrong. Things seldom did go wrong, but still there was always that chance, a chance that had been banished from the deadly perfect land of movies and television.

I always read the plays before I went to a performance. As an English major accustomed to the five-word sentences and flat inflection of Californians, I found Shakespeare's language intoxicating. It wasn't just the *thees* and *thous*; all the metaphors, the jokes, the rhythms of the poetry, and the jostling, bubbling prose fascinated me. Although the heavenly language could sometimes obscure the meaning, I didn't like it when the director changed a phrase. For instance, during Hamlet, instead of "milching mallecho," the actor said, "milching mischief." Clearer, but less mellifluous.

Culture aside, going to the festival was just plain fun. The house manager always welcomed me. I chatted with the other playgoers and munched the fresh cookies, brownies, and carrot cake that were sold by a wandering concessionaire dressed in Elizabethan costume.

Then, one year, the festival announced that it had to leave Berkeley and was looking for a new home.

"Why are they leaving?" I asked Flann.

"It's the neighbors," he said. "They don't like the noise."

"I didn't think Bard freaks made that much noise."

"They don't. Thing is," Flann made a face, "people up here think the sound of a bus is too much noise. They're rich, they've got clout with the city council, so the festival has to move."

13

The Sex Surrogate

(1985)

A t thirty-seven, I was still a virgin. I was getting angry at Kerry often, and I figured it was because she was the nearest woman available for yelling at. I knew I had to do something about my anger and frustration, so I began to talk with Miriam, my psychotherapist, about the possibility of seeing a surrogate. Kerry had once suggested the idea of seeing a sex surrogate, but I had been extremely reluctant. Miriam told me that surrogates would see people only on the recommendation of a registered therapist. After six months of agonized indecision, I suddenly wanted to do it.

Even though I was in my thirties, I still felt embarrassed by my sexuality. It seemed utterly without purpose in my life, except to mortify me when I became aroused during bed baths. I would not talk to my attendants about the orgasms I had then, or about the profound shame I felt. I imagined they, too, hated me for becoming so excited.

I wanted to be loved. I wanted to be held, caressed, and valued. But my self-hatred and fear were too intense. I doubted I deserved to be loved. My frustrated sexual feelings seemed to be just another curse inflicted upon me by a cruel God. I had fallen in love with several people, female and male, and had waited for them to ask me out or seduce me. Most of the disabled people I knew in Berkeley were sexually active, including people as deformed as I. But nothing had ever happened. Nothing was working for me in the passive way that I wanted it to, or the way it worked in the movies.

In 1985, when I began talking with Miriam about the possibility of seeing a sex surrogate, she explained that a sexual therapist worked

213

with a client's emotional problems concerning sex, while a surrogate worked with a client's body. Miriam never pushed me one way or another; she told me the choice was mine.

My initial fear was that someone who was not an attendant, nurse, or doctor would be horrified at seeing my pale, thin body, with its bent spine, bent neck, washboard ribcage, and hipbones protruding like outriggers. I had also dismissed the idea of a surrogate because of the expense.

But now I was earning extra money writing articles and book reviews. My rationalizations began to strike me as flimsy. Still, it was not an easy decision. What would my parents think? What would God think? I suspected that my father and mother would somehow know even before God did if I saw a surrogate. The prospect of offending three such omniscient beings made me nervous.

On the other hand, what if one day I did meet someone who wanted to make love with me? Wouldn't I feel more secure if I had already had some sexual experience? I knew I could change my perception of myself as a bumbling, indecisive clod, not just by having sex with someone but by taking charge of my life and trusting myself enough to make decisions. One day, I finally said to Miriam I was ready to see a surrogate.

About a week later, my phone rang during my morning bed bath. It was the voice of a woman I had never heard before.

"Hello, Mark! This is Cheryl."

I knew that it was the surrogate.

"I could see you March 17 at 1 P.M.," she said. "Would that be good for you?"

"Yeah, it would be. But I'm busy right now. Could you call me back this afternoon when I'll be by myself?"

Now that I had decided when to actually see a surrogate, I faced another problem: where would I meet her? I didn't have a bed, just an iron lung with a mattress barely wide enough for me. When Cheryl called back, she asked whether I could come to her office, which is up a flight of stairs. I told her that would be difficult. Finally, we agreed to meet at the home of one of my friends.

When March 17 arrived, I felt unbearably nervous. I had to remind myself repeatedly that we were just going to talk about sex; in the second hour, we would do those "body awareness exercises," whatever they were, but only if I wanted to do them.

My attendant Chloe dressed me, put me in my wheelchair, and pushed me to my friend Marie's cottage. Chloe tried to reassure me, but it didn't help. I felt as though I were going to my own execution.

We arrived at Marie's place at 10:45, but the door was locked, and no one was home. Chloe sat on a bench in the yard, lit a cigarette, and chatted amiably as I sweated out the wait. An eternity passed: seven or eight minutes. Then I heard the buzzing sound of Marie's electric wheelchair.

Once inside, Chloe put a sheet I had brought onto the double bed. Then she lowered me onto it. The bed was close to the floor, unlike my iron lung. Since I can't turn my head to the left, Chloe pushed me over to the left side of the bed so that Cheryl could lie next to me and I could see her. Then Chloe put the hose of my portable respirator near my mouth, in case I needed air. In those days, I always used a respirator if I was out of the lung for more than an hour, and I expected to need it for whatever happened with Cheryl. All set, I glanced at the noncommittal green numerals flashing on the nearby digital clock. 11:04:30. Cheryl was late.

Marie talked with Chloe as I waited. 11:07:43. 11:11:09. Oh God, would she ever come? Perhaps she had found out what an ugly, deformed creep I am and was breaking the appointment. 11:14:55. Oh God.

A knock on the door. Cheryl had arrived.

I turned my head as far to my left as I could to see her. She greeted me, smiling, and walked to where I could see her better. *She doesn't hate me yet*, I thought. She pulled a chair up to the bedside and apologized for being late, explaining how everything had gone wrong for her that morning. Marie went out the door with Chloe, saying that she would return at 1 P.M. Cheryl and I were alone.

"Your fee's on top of the dresser," I said, unable to think of anything else to say. Putting the cash into her wallet, she thanked me.

She wore a black pantsuit, and her dark brown hair was tied behind her head. She had clear skin and large brown eyes and she seemed tall and strong—but then I was four feet seven inches and weighed seventy pounds. As we talked, I decided that she was definitely attractive. Was she checking out my looks? I was too scared to want to know.

Talking helped me to relax. She told me that she was forty-one, descended from French-Canadians who had settled in Boston.

"Boston?" I said. "That's where I was born."

After talking about Boston for a while, I asked whether she was

Catholic, like me. She told me she had left the Catholic Church during her adolescence, when her priest condemned her sexual behavior.

I began to tell her about my life, my family, my fear of sexuality. I could see that she was accepting me and treating me with respect. I liked her, so when she asked me if I would feel comfortable letting her undress me, I said, "Sure." I was bluffing, attempting to hide my fear.

My heart pounded—not with lust, but with pure terror—as she kneeled on the bed and started to unbutton my red shirt. She had trouble undressing me; I felt awkward and wondered whether she would change her mind and leave once she saw me naked. She didn't.

After she took my clothes off, she got out of bed and undressed quickly. I looked at her full, pale breasts but was too shy to gaze between her legs.

Whenever I had been naked before—in front of nurses, doctors, and attendants—I'd pretended I wasn't naked. Now that I was in bed with another naked person, I didn't need to pretend: I was undressed, she was undressed, and it seemed normal. How startling! I had half-expected God—or my parents—to keep this moment from happening.

She stroked my hair and told me how good it felt. This surprised me; I had never thought of my hair, or any other part of me, as feeling or looking good. Having at least one attractive feature helped me to feel more confident. She explained about the body awareness exercises: first, she would run her hand over me, and I could kiss her wherever I wanted. I told her I wished that I could caress her, too, but she assured me I could excite her with my mouth and tongue. She rubbed scented oil on her hands, then slowly moved her palms in circles over my chest and arms. She was complimenting me in a soft, steady voice, while I chattered nervously about everything that came to mind. I asked her whether I could kiss one of her breasts. She sidled up to me so that I could kiss her left breast. So soft.

"Now if you kiss one, you have to kiss the other," she said. "That's the rule."

Amused, I moved to her right breast. She told me to lick around the nipple, saying she liked that. I knew she was saying things to help me feel more relaxed, but that didn't make her encouragements seem less true.

I was getting aroused. Her hand moved in its slow circles lower and lower as she continued to talk in her reassuring way, and I continued my chattering. She lightly touched my cock—as though she liked it, as though it was fine that I was aroused. No one had ever touched me that way or praised me for my sexuality. Too soon, I came.

After that, we talked a while. I told her about the Guatemalan bracelet Kerry had given me for this occasion. She asked me whether I had any cologne; I said I did but that I never wore it. That we could be talking about such mundane matters right after an intense sexual experience seemed strange at first. Another lesson learned: sex is a part of ordinary human living, not an activity reserved for gods, goddesses, and rock stars. I realized that it could become a part of my life if I fought against my self-hatred and pessimism.

I asked Cheryl whether she thought I deserved to be loved sexually. She said she was sure of it. I nearly cried. She didn't hate me. She didn't consider me repulsive.

It was getting toward 1 P.M., so she got out of bed, went into the bathroom, and dressed. Taking an appointment book out of her purse, she told me that next time she wanted us to work on having intercourse. She asked me whether I had been afraid to see her that day, and I admitted that I had felt deep terror. She said it had been brave of me to go through with the session despite my fear.

Two weeks later, I saw Cheryl for the second time, feeling more relaxed and confident. We chatted briefly, but there was no formal interview. After pulling down the shades, she undressed me with more ease than before. I felt less afraid and embarrassed. As I watched her undress, I anticipated the sight of her breasts. There they were, full and rounded. Before she could even get into the bed, I had climaxed. I felt angry at myself for being unable to control the timing of my orgasms, but Cheryl said she would try to stimulate me to another orgasm. I didn't believe that she could, but I trusted her more now and let her try.

She lightly scratched my arms, which, to my surprise, I liked. I spent a lot of time kissing and licking her breasts. I asked her to rub the eternally itchy place behind my balls, which she said was called the perineum. The use of such a dignified Latin word to name a place that didn't even have a name, as far as I had known, struck me as funny. I screamed with delight as she rubbed me, surprised that my body could feel so much pleasure. Then, I felt a warmth around my cock. I realized that Cheryl wasn't beside me anymore.

"Know what I was doing?" she asked a few seconds later.

"No."

"I was sucking you."

Quickly I had another erection. Aroused and more confident, I said I wanted to try to have intercourse, so she scrambled into place on top, her knees straddling me. Filled with anticipation, I breathed more rapidly, but she nearly stepped on my feet, which rattled me. Reassuring me, she held my cock and rubbed it against her, but when she tried to place it inside her, I panicked. For reasons I still don't understand, I felt that I couldn't fit. Perhaps I feared success. Perhaps intercourse would prove I was an adult, something I had never been willing to acknowledge.

I insisted to Cheryl that I couldn't fit into her vagina. She said that couldn't be. Then suddenly I came again—outside her.

I felt humiliated. Cheryl asked me whether I had enjoyed myself. I said, "Oh, yes, up to the anticlimax." She assured me that she had enjoyed it, which cheered me somewhat. And it was still pleasant for me, lying beside her, the two of us naked. I told her I wanted to recite a poem I'd memorized for this occasion, Shakespeare's eighteenth sonnet:

> Shall I compare thee to a Summer's day?
> Thou art more lovely and more temperate.
> Rough winds do shake the darling buds of May,
> And Summer's lease hath all too short a date ...

I stumbled through it, forgetting phrases, stopping and starting again, but I made it to the end:

> As long as men can breathe or eyes can see,
> So long lives this, and this gives life to thee.

Cheryl said that she was touched, that it was sweet of me to recite the poem. I felt glad that I was now a giver of pleasure, not merely a passive recipient.

The next day I worried: why had I panicked? Would I ever be able to have intercourse with Cheryl? With any woman?

Our third appointment ended without my being able to have intercourse. Knowing how angry I was at myself, she got off the mattress and took a large mirror out of her tote bag. Holding it so that I could see myself, Cheryl asked what I thought of the man in the mirror. I said that I was surprised I looked so normal, that I wasn't the horribly twisted and cadaverous figure I had always imagined myself to be. I hadn't seen my genitals since I was six years old. That was when polio struck, shriveling me below my diaphragm in such a way that my view of my lower body had been blocked by my chest. Since then, that part of me had seemed unreal. But seeing my genitals made it easier to accept the reality of my manhood.

My having failed twice to have intercourse worried me. I became obsessed with this failure during the three weeks between appointments. What was wrong with me? Was I afraid that having intercourse represented aggression against women? Was it my lack of experience, or was it something deeper than that, something I could never figure out?

Before my next appointment, I was visited by my former attendant and friend, Tracy. She understood me thoroughly and was still the wittiest person I'd ever known. Tracy was involved with someone; she maintained a warm friendship with me, but she made it clear that she was not interested in a romantic relationship. I felt awkward. I remembered how, in a state of terrified, embarrassed passion a few years earlier, I had told her that I loved her.

I was waiting for Tracy in my wheelchair when she entered my apartment. She leaned over so that I could kiss her cheek. Then she kissed mine.

"I love you," I said.

"I love you," she replied cheerfully.

We went to a café and talked about her boyfriend and my experiences with Cheryl. She said that she felt proud of me for having the courage to see a surrogate. I felt terrific talking with her and tried to prolong the conversation by asking her everything I could think of about her graduate studies, her boyfriend, and so forth. Eventually, though, we both ran out of words. She wanted to see other friends in Berkeley, so she took me back to my apartment.

After Tracy left, I was saddened by the undeniable knowledge that she felt no sexual attraction for me. Who could blame her? I was seldom attracted to disabled women. Many young, healthy, good-looking men had been drawn to Tracy, who was in a position to pick and choose. My only hope seemed to be in trusting that working with

Cheryl would help me in the event that I should meet someone else as splendid as Tracy.

The next time I saw Cheryl, she said that, this time, she would minimize the foreplay and get on top of me as soon as I told her I was becoming aroused. She had the mirror with her again and held it up to me before she got into the bed. This time, I climaxed at seeing myself erect in the mirror. Cheryl got into the bed and positioned herself so that I could give her cunnilingus. I had to stop it after a minute or so because I began to feel as though I were suffocating. But I had wanted to do something to give her pleasure, so I asked her whether I could put my tongue in her ear.

She said no, she disliked that, but it was good that I asked. "Some women like it. I just happen to hate it. Different women react differently to the same stimulus. That's why you should always ask."

When she started stroking my cock, I told her to get on top, quickly. I was feeling the onset of an erection. She got over me, and with one hand she guided me into her.

"Is it in?"

"Yes, it's in."

I couldn't believe it. Here I was having intercourse, and it didn't feel like the greatest thing in the world. Intercourse was certainly pleasant, but I had enjoyed the foreplay more. Again too soon, I came. She kept holding me inside her. Then a look of pleasure brushed lightly over her face, as though an all-day itch were finally being scratched. Letting me go, she put her hands down on the bed by my shoulders and kissed my chest.

This act of affection moved me deeply. I hadn't expected it; it seemed like a gift from her heart. My chest is unmuscular, pale, and hairless, the opposite of what a sexy man's chest is supposed to be. It has always felt like a very vulnerable part of me. Now it was being kissed by a caring, understanding woman, and I almost wept.

"Did you come?" I asked her.

"Yes."

I was exultant. She got out of the bed and went into the bathroom. Hearing her pee made me feel as though we were longtime lovers, familiar and comfortable with each other's bodily functions. When she came out of the bathroom and began dressing herself, I asked her whether she thought I should buy a futon so that I could have sex in my apartment. I said, "I don't know if I should get a futon now or wait ... till something comes up."

"You may want to get one now because you never know when something will come up. And, if you wait till then, by the time you get the futon, it might be all over."

I asked her whether she thought we should have another session. She said she would do whatever I thought best.

"Do you think there's anything to be gained from another time?" she asked.

"No," I said, relieved that I would not have to spend any more money. I had just enough to buy a futon. And, besides, I'd had intercourse. What was there left to do? Later that year, I bought the futon, dark blue with an austere pattern of flowers and rushes.

After a year passed, I felt depressed. I realized that seeing the surrogate hadn't changed my life, that no one was attracted me. For years afterward, I felt angry at myself for wasting my time and money on the surrogate. But seeing the surrogate had changed me in ways that I couldn't see then. I found that I was more confident about my sexuality when, years later, I was drawn to a woman as splendid as Tracy.

14

Poet and Journalist

(circa 1983–1995)

*C*oEvolution Quarterly received a good deal of favorable mail about my article, "How I Became a Human Being." I was pleased that my writing had moved so many readers. Apparently, the response pleased Art Kleiner, the editor, too: he sent me books on disability to review, invited me to parties, and enrolled me in the Electronic Information Exchange Service, the first civilian computer network.

One day, he accompanied me as I went to buy a new printer. As we were leaving the electronics store, he asked whether I'd be willing to edit the disability section of the *Essential Whole Earth Catalog*. I accepted, knowing it would be good to be published in a book and thrilled to help with a successor to Stewart Brand's legendary catalog.

Still, it was hard work going through the huge packages of books, magazines, and press releases that Brand's staff sent me. My attendants helped me sort through it all, and they held up crinkled pieces of email that the magazine had received for me to read. It took hours each day, but it felt wonderful to be doing real work, work that would help disabled people all over the country. Months later, seeing the results in the published catalog, I felt I had arrived.

In that same year, 1983, POINT Foundation, which owned *CoEvolution Quarterly*, began publishing *Whole Earth Software Review* and appointed me as disability editor. The third issue's cover featured me pecking with my mouthstick at my Tandy Model 100, which Art had upgraded to an astonishing twenty-four kilobytes. That third issue was the last one. Crushed in the computer magazine shakeout of 1983, *WESR* folded. My career as a model was shot.

CoEvolution Quarterly changed its name to *Whole Earth Review* in 1984, partly because of the *WESR* fiasco. In the back of the new *Review*, I saw an ad for a book about polio. Everything I'd ever seen about the disease had been dry and medical, but this book had been written by someone who had had polio, someone named Lorenzo Milam. Charmed by the title, *The Cripple Liberation Front Marching Band Blues*, I sent in my order to the publisher, Mho & Mho Works, a company I had never heard of.

It turned out to be the best book on disability I've ever read. Overwhelmed by the book's wit, honesty, and style, I wrote a rave review for *Whole Earth Review*. Lorenzo Milam sent me a thank-you letter and a catalog of Mho & Mho's books. He also sent a poster advertising the book, which showed a man walking on crutches across a desolate plain. Around the lonely figure were quotes from reviews, mine among them.

Kerry, too, liked the book, and she encouraged me to write back to Milam. "What am I supposed to say?" I asked cynically. "Thank you for your thank you?"

"Well, sure, you can say something like that," she replied. "But you can also ask him things; that's the best way to start up a conversation. Haven't you noticed how I always ask people questions?"

So I wrote him a letter filled with questions, which instigated a voluminous and rewarding correspondence. I mailed Lorenzo some of my poems, and he sent them to his friend Sy Safransky, editor of *The Sun,* a North Carolina magazine. Safransky published three of my poems in the March 1985 issue. I was amazed and delighted. My poems were in a national magazine—a small magazine, to be sure, but one that was beautifully produced and featured writers like Ram Dass, Robert Bly, and Allen Ginsberg.

Joao was teaching at the University of Texas at El Paso, where he met a poet and English professor named Judith Root. He showed her my poems, and she liked them. In 1989, Judith collected the best poems in a short manuscript, thinking it could be published as a chapbook. In the same month, Pat LittleDog, who had seen my work in *The Sun*, wrote a letter, saying that she could put out a chapbook of my poems. I mailed her the manuscript edited by Judith; and Pat borrowed a Macintosh, set up the pages, ran off copies at a copy shop, and thereby invented LittleDog Press.

My chapbook, *Breathing,* was nineteen pages long. When it arrived in the mail, I read it in five minutes flat. Kerry was disappointed that it wasn't a big hardcover, but I was impressed. My own book! Pat, herself a brilliant writer, promoted *Breathing* at readings throughout Texas. It sold more than three hundred copies, which was, she told me, quite a lot for a chapbook. I earned thirty dollars in royalties.

After I sold a rewrite of "How I Became a Human Being" to Pacific News Service in 1982, Sandy Close, the executive editor, asked me to write more for them. I wanted to do so, since PNS sold stories to more than a hundred newspapers around the country. I considered this quite a platform, especially for someone considered too disabled for a journalism career by the dean of the University of California Journalism School.

So, in 1984, I phoned Sandy to tell her I could write for PNS again, now that I was no longer in school. We discussed story ideas, one of which was a piece on disabled people and the presidential election. Equipped with my mouthstick, cassette recorder, and speakerphone, I began my hunt for interviews.

First I called Sandy Muir, the disabled political science professor, who said he remembered fighting for my admission to J School in 1982. I asked about his writing speeches for Vice President Bush. He said he was doing so and was also pitching in for President Reagan's campaign that year. I told him about my story idea, and he gave me the telephone number of a media-relations person on Bush's staff. I gulped. She worked in the White House.

I was nervous about calling the White House, especially when I gave the extension I wanted and the operator couldn't hear me. I reminded myself to lower the pitch of my voice and to speak slowly. "Low and slow" became my mantra.

Bush's aide was helpful. She gave me the numbers of disabled people who supported Reagan, two of whom I later interviewed. Also, the aide told me that Reagan had improved conditions for disabled people by improving the economy. I didn't believe it, knowing that Reagan's Justice Department opposed strict enforcement of laws that protected disability rights. I asked a few critical questions, but I told myself it wasn't my job to antagonize her through an aggressive approach. My job was to get as much information as I could from my interview subjects. Looking back, though, I think I was just afraid to ask her the tough questions.

After four more interviews came the hard part: transcribing. I'd listen to about ten seconds of a taped interview, push the stop button, and type whatever I could remember into the Model 100. My biggest problem was other people's speech. Sometimes I had to listen five or six times to a stretch of tape. People slurred their speech, interrupted themselves, and went off on pointless asides. I'd paraphrase some of the responses, but I needed exact quotes for important or dramatic statements. Ben Bagdikian had always emphasized the necessity of getting the quotes right, so, whenever there was a pointless aside in the middle of a dramatic statement, I inserted an ellipsis.

Sandy cut the ellipses, saying they weren't used in newspapers, but she praised my veracity. "We have fact checkers go through all our stories, and usually they have mistakes, but your stories haven't had any."

I was stunned. Of course they hadn't had mistakes! I had worked damned hard to get the facts and to write about them clearly, assuming that that was the least a journalist could do. Perhaps I was being naive, and carelessness was common among journalists.

I was paid one hundred and fifty dollars for each article, money I needed to pay my bills. Sometimes a stranger who had read my piece would call to congratulate me, which was always gratifying.

As a freelancer, I wanted to write long articles, stories that would exceed the thousand-word limit set by PNS and that would, I hoped, pay more. I interviewed Ed Roberts, one of the founders of the independent living movement and the son of Zona Roberts, who had denied my admission to Berkeley in 1977. By phone, I interviewed the disabled cartoonist and writer John Callahan. But these interviews never turned into articles, because I always put off the chore of transcribing the tapes. My difficulty with transcription frustrated me and took much of the fun out of journalism.

One day, a disabled writer friend asked me whether I'd be interested in reviewing a book for the *San Francisco Chronicle*. The paper had asked her to write the review, but she was too busy. I reviewed *The Wheelchair Child* and was later asked to review more books on disability.

I liked doing the work, but I was even more pleased when the *Chronicle* asked me to review *OED: The Strange Theory of Light and Matter*, by Richard Feynmann and Ralph Leighton. At last, I had a chance to write about something beside disability. Earlier I'd reviewed a biography of Stephen Hawking; perhaps that review had persuaded the book editor that I could write about science. *OED* was difficult for me, but I managed to write an intelligible review.

While the *Chronicle* sent me one book at a time, Lorenzo mailed me fat packages: new novels in hardcover, self-published philosophical tracts, and slender paperbacks by obscure and terrible poets. I couldn't read them all. Selling them to Moe's, the big used bookstore on Telegraph Avenue, brought me needed cash. After choosing a book, I would read about twenty pages. If I stayed interested, I'd try to remember the page numbers where the most quotable passages occurred. Upon completing a book, I'd have an attendant photocopy these pages and tape the copies to the iron lung where I could read them.

Another book Lorenzo sent was *And Other Voyages*, a collection of travel essays and one of the most beautifully written books I had ever read. I wrote a favorable review of it for the *Chronicle*, where it would reach a relatively large readership.

A few months later, the book's author, Robin Magowan, visited me. "My mother wouldn't buy it until she saw your review," he said. "Then she went out and bought ten copies." Robin, a thin, soft-spoken man, gave me a book of his poems. An American who lived in London, he would soon be returning to Britain to edit *Margin*, a new literary magazine. Having read some of my work that Lorenzo had sent him, Robin asked me to submit some of my work to *Margin*. "You need to go deeper, though. Can't you write poetry about what it's like to be inside this thing?" He thumped the iron lung.

I decided to try. The result was poems such as "Breathing" and "The Man in the Iron Lung."

Breathing

Grasping for straws is easier;
You can see the straws.
"This most excellent canopy, the air, look you,"
Presses down upon me
At fifteen pounds per square inch,
A dense, heavy, blue-glowing ocean,
Supporting the weight of condors
That swim its churning currents.
All I get is a thin stream of it,
A finger's width of the rope that ties me to life

As I labor like a stevedore to keep the connection.
Water wouldn't be so circumspect;
Water would crash in like a drunken sailor,
But air is prissy and genteel,
Teasing me with its nearness and pervading immensity.
The vast, circumambient atmosphere
Allows me but ninety cubic centimeters
Of its billions of gallons and miles of sky.
I inhale it anyway,
Knowing that it will hurt
In the weary ends of my crumpled paper bag lungs.

In the spring of 1988, Frances, the director of the Disabled Students'
Program, asked whether I would attend Stephen Hawking's lectures on
campus. I hadn't even known Hawking was in Berkeley, so I told her
that I would look for more information. First, I called the university's
public information office, which told me when and where Hawking
would appear. I then phoned an editor of the *Fessenden Review* to ask
whether he wanted me to interview Hawking for the magazine. He
gave a quick, enthusiastic yes.

However, my interview with the physicist was short and disappointing. He gave brief, trite answers to the tough questions I posed on love,
disability, and raising a family. I didn't know how to write an article
based on this laconic interview until I remembered what Ben Bagdikian
had said after one of those dreary Berkeley City Council meetings:
"When you don't have a story, wing it." So I did, concentrating on my
arduous efforts to get the interview. Here are the results:

When the morning of the Hawking press conference came, I
worried that I would not get the interview. Armed only with a
cassette tape recorder and a manila envelope stuffed with a
formal letter requesting an interview, my disability poems, my
science poems, my autobiographical essay, my reviews of Stephen
Hawking's *Universe*, and Hawking's new book, I hoped to persuade
him to grant me an interview.

I had asked Miguel, my lunch attendant, to come at 10:30 to
get me into my wheelchair and push me to the press conference.
I worried that he might be late, as he often is, but this time he
wasn't. When he lifted me, I screamed much less than usual,

because my chief concern was to get to the press conference on time. Miguel took me out into the warm March day while I fretted about my lack of press credentials.

Gentle reader, all of those reporters you see on TV talking about their press credentials are working for some corporation, usually a huge one such as *Time*, ABC, or *Rolling Stone*. I, being a freelancer, which is to say an unemployed poet and novelist who occasionally deigns to work at journalism when prompted by a desire for thrills or money, had no press credentials at all. When I was a student in the UC–Berkeley journalism school, I had been issued a little white card that shrilly insisted I was a bona fide, honest-to-pete reporter for something called the California News Service, a dummy organization invented by the journalism school for the sole purpose of issuing press credentials to its students. But it had been years since I dropped out of J School and tossed out my CNS cards. I had asked the editor of the *Fessenden Review* to send me press credentials, but they were delayed in the mail. Now I approached the greatest story of my journalistic career with no more press credentials than a hyena. More reason for me to be anxious. What if they demanded proof that I was a reporter? I would sputter, "Oh, yeah?" like Tommy Smothers. No, a better idea struck me. I would tell them to phone the editor of the *Fessenden Review*. But what if he weren't in? What if he was in his office, but the person checking my credentials had never heard of the *Fessenden Review?*

Such trepidations tumbled in my mind like dice as Miguel pushed me into the student union building, where the press conference was to be held in Heller Lounge. Acting as the navigator, for I knew the campus better than Miguel did, I confidently told him that it was on the top floor.

"I remember because it's where I rented my cap and gown for my graduation."

But there was nothing called Heller Lounge up there. When Miguel told a man emerging from a room that we were looking for Dr. Hawking's press conference, the man said he was also going to it and led the way. Downstairs, we entered a long, vaguely defined area which I had always thought of as the student lounge. Miguel pushed me by students lounging, reading, or sprawling across the bright blue sofas in complete exhaustion. Near the end of the lounge, folding chairs had been set up in an open, glass-walled area, presumably as a special accommodation to the able-bodied journalists. On a long table in front of us all were press handouts and a vase of flowers in the university's colors, yellow and blue. No one asked me to produce anything to prove that I was a reporter. I concluded that if you look sufficiently disabled, people will judge you to be harmless.

We were early, so I asked Miguel to grab some handouts and get my cassette recorder out of the red backpack that hangs from the back of my wheelchair. Then we waited. The inquisitive reporters looked at each other, at the handouts, at the flowers, and at the view through the tinted glass walls of Lower Sproul Plaza. In the stark silence, I heard the low buzzing of an electric wheelchair.

"Is that him?" I asked Miguel, who can look around more easily than I can.

"No, it's someone else."

Finally, a tall bearded man started talking into the microphone.

"... Will you please welcome to the university Doctor Stephen W. Hawking."

Applause spattered the room like a sudden rainstorm. Then I saw him to my left, a slight figure moving slowly across the room in a brown, padded wheelchair. Wearing a crumpled hound's-tooth suit, he looked very English and very academic, happily fulfilling our preconceptions. His face, middle-aged and knobbly, reminded me of a pensive Alfred E. Neuman. Suddenly, he blessed us with a smile as dazzling and casual as Jack Kennedy's. A Beatle haircut, graying, remained from his student days. After he parked his wheelchair by the table, the microphone was lowered and placed next to his voice synthesizer, a plastic and metal device that sits on the wheelchair's lap tray like a large, propped-up book.

"Doctor Hawking," began the first questioner, who proceeded to ask about a recently discovered supernova.

I wanted to ask my question early to get through my anxiety. I had decided to ask him what he would say to disabled people who were stuck in nursing homes or in a room in their parents' house. I wanted to ask him this because I had spent too many years of

my life stuck in such frustrating, life-stopping places. That I have
come to live in such a jazzy, juicy place as Berkeley astonishes me
so much that I inspect the mailing labels on magazines to make
sure that my name is two lines above BERKELEY, CA.

It took Dr. Hawking a couple of minutes to type his first
answer, which came abruptly from the speech synthesizer in a
deep, American-sounding voice, impressively human though
somewhat robotic around the edges.

I wanted to get my question in, but Dr. Hawking possesses no
body language to indicate "Next?" The other reporters beat me
to it several times. During the long pauses occasioned by Dr.
Hawking's voice synthesizer, photographers scuttled about like
hyperactive lobsters, standing, kneeling, leaning, trying to get
every angle on Dr. Hawking, whose movements were limited to
his cool blue eyes and that smile. Although his answers were slow
in coming, everyone present had their attention devoted to him.
I wondered what the passersby on the walkway outside the glass
wall would make of the scene—thirty or forty able-bodied people
expectantly looking at a small, thin man in a wheelchair who
never moved his lips to speak.

A photographer knelt on the floor, blocking my view of
Hawking. I asked her in a whisper to move, but my whisper was
too soft, and I feared that if I asked her in my normal tone of
voice, I would break the eerie silence between questions and
answers. I seemed unable to croak out a medium-sized request,
so I asked Miguel to ask her to move, which she did. Now that I
could see Hawking again, I decided I should ask my question
before someone else came along to block my view. Shimmering
with anxiety, I pondered the puniness of my question. Would
Hawking be annoyed that my question would pull him away from
the pristine glory of physics and into the sad, ancient swamp of
disability? Looking steadily into his halcyon eyes, I pretended to
have the courage to ask him my question.

"Doctor Hawking, what can you say to all the disabled people
who are stuck in nursing homes or living with their parents or in
some other untenable situation and who feel that their life is over,
that they have no future?"

As I heard this long question unravel like an unruly ball of
yarn, Hawking continued to look at me and typed his answer into

the voice synthesizer. I couldn't see his right hand, the one he used to type. I waited. All of us waited. Then the silence was cracked by the voice synthesizer's crisp, booming voice.

"It can be very difficult. I know that I was very fortunate. All I can say is that one must do the best one can in the situation in which one finds oneself."

He continued to look at me as his answer was spoken, as though he missed the simultaneity of speech and eye contact. I thanked him, then the other reporters asked questions which veered away from physics, a subject few of us understood, and toward God, a subject on which we considered ourselves experts.

The final question asked whether Dr. Hawking really wanted the riddle of the universe to be solved. Wouldn't discovering The Answer have the distressing effect of ending a grand quest?

"I hope that we will find it, but not quite yet."

We laughed, even though we half-expected such a sly answer.

The press conference over, the able-bodied people got out of their folding chairs to cluster into knots of conversation, which is what able-bodied people do when they are not sure of what they should be doing. Miguel picked up my tape recorder and put it in my backpack. I asked him to give my envelope to someone in Hawking's entourage, but Miguel asked whether I wouldn't rather have him give it directly to Hawking. Suspended in indecision, I thought of how little space there was on the lap tray of Dr. Hawking's wheelchair, the possibility that he might be offended by such naked American chutzpah, and how unlikely it was that I would ever get this close to him again. After a long internal debate of a second and a half, I felt the cold, sharp gust of What the Hell blast away my irresolution.

Miguel gave the envelope to Hawking, who then approached me.

"Hello," said Hawking in his calm electronic voice.

"It's such an honor to meet you," I burbled in my tremulous, meeting-a-celebrity voice. I explained the contents of the envelope, including the letter asking him for an interview. Rather than wait for him to read my letter, I asked him for an interview right there and then, while the able-bodied reporters towered around us like a circle of curious trees.

"Yes. The week of April fourth."

"Good, good. That'll give me time to … I have my phone
number on the letter, so you … you or one of your people can
call me to set a time and place."

"Yes."

Your people, my people. I sounded like a CEO. He left to talk
with others amidst the milling, mumbling crowd.

After a week had passed without any word from Hawking, I grew
anxious. He was a busy man in a foreign country and could easily
have forgotten about me and my proposed interview. So, when
I heard that the university's Disabled Students' Program was
honoring Dr. Hawking with a barbecue, I decided to attend it in
the hope of reminding him of the interview.

Miguel took me to the barbecue, which was held in the parking
lot behind the old pinkish-red mansion that houses DSP. It was a
hot Thursday, the day of Dr. Hawking's third and final lecture on
the Berkeley campus. The parking lot was crowded with people in
all kinds of wheelchairs, blind people, attendants, deaf people
signing at feverish speed, the DSP staff, and reporters from
KQED-TV and *National Geographic*. Heat bounced off of the three
white buildings that surround the parking lot on three sides. The
last thing I wanted was to have a hard, mean, crunchy hamburger
pushed into my mouth. This being Berkeley, there was pasta salad,
but the good vegetarians of Berkeley had devoured the pasta
salad, confident that the pasta salad had never said moo, never
blinked large brown eyes, and never given birth to mewling,
puking baby pasta salads.

Where was Hawking?

God knew, having a vantage point better than mine, which was
in my new and unsteady reclining wheelchair, reclined to almost
flat, which put my head about three feet above the hot asphalt.

A man in a tall psychedelic wheelchair bumped into my
recliner, causing it to tip backward maybe an eighth of an inch.
Convinced that my skull would be cracked open like an egg and
that my brains would fry sunny-side-up on the asphalt, I screamed
in falsetto panic. As my wheelchair steadied itself, everyone looked
at me.

"Are you all right?" they asked me.

"Yeah."

Now certain in the knowledge that I was having a thoroughly terrible time, I told Miguel I wanted to leave.

"Can you see Hawking? Over there?"

He pointed, and I saw him, surrounded by people. He was eating something and looking as though he were enjoying himself in spite of wearing a tweed suit in the Fourth of July heat.

"I'll try to get you over there to see him," Miguel said.

As Miguel knifed my wheelchair through the densely packed crowd, I could see the circle around Hawking break. A DSP official tested the microphone, then said what a privilege it was to have Dr. Hawking present. She then presented the famous disabled physicist tokens of admiration, one of them a T-shirt that proclaimed: I SURVIVED THE BARBECUE AT THE UC BERKELEY DISABLED STUDENTS' PROGRAM, APRIL 7TH, 1988.

Thinking that I deserved such a T-shirt more than Hawking did, even though he wore that tweed suit, I observed the brief ceremony, which concluded with the announcement that Dr. Hawking would autograph copies of his book at the other end of the parking lot.

A DSP staffer began singing into the microphone as Hawking zoomed by me, two feet to my right. I recognized his wife from her photo in Boslough's book. I had enough cash to buy the book, so Miguel and I waited in line, the sun glaring in my face and raising a bumper crop of skin cancer cells on my potato-pale Irish face. While we waited, Miguel brought one of Hawking's attendants, a tall Englishwoman with curly reddish hair, over to talk with me. When I told her that I wanted to interview Dr. Hawking that Saturday, she said she was terribly sorry, but they were leaving Berkeley the next day.

Was all this for nothing? I asked myself.

"But I can't speak for him," she said. "You should ask him yourself." With this slight encouragement in mind, I asked Dr. Hawking whether he could still give me an interview. Close up, he looked uncomfortable. Was it the heat, or was it that I was bugging him? I was rehearsing my yes-I-understand speech when he said, "Yes. Half eleven in the lobby of my hotel."

Once again, I was startled by his willingness to talk with me.

The red-haired attendant pressed Hawking's right thumb into an inkpad, then into the inside cover of his book. I had his autograph.

Lorenzo loved my article, even though the interview with Hawking added little. It was published in one of the last issues of the *Fessenden Review*. It attracted the attention of the *Village Voice*, which featured the *Fessenden Review* in a column about fun-to-read, obscure publications, mentioning the Hawking piece specifically. Kerry was very proud of me, saying it was the best thing I'd ever written. Lorenzo then asked me to write an article for the *Fessenden Review* about my experience with the sex surrogate. Lorenzo didn't like the draft I sent him, so when the *Fessenden Review* went out of business in 1989, I sent the piece to Sy Safransky at *The Sun*, who accepted it immediately.

Lorenzo wrote me a letter suggesting that I write Robin Magowan in London to ask him to help me apply for a grant from the Ingram Merrill Foundation. Having already published two of my poems in *Margin*, Robin seemed willing to help me. But I didn't realize how eager he was until I received his reply: he sent grant application forms along with a letter saying that "Uncle Jimmy" sat on the committee that chose the recipients of Ingram Merrill Foundation grants and that Uncle Jimmy liked my poetry. Uncle Jimmy was the poet James Merrill, son of Charles Merrill, the man who had established both the foundation and Merrill Lynch.

Years later, I read two books of poetry by James Merrill and discovered he was one of the great poets of the twentieth century. Had I known that then, I would have been twice as nervous about applying for a grant. I had been nervous enough after learning from Robin that many prominent artists and writers sat on the committee.

As it was, plenty nervous, I submitted copies of my work, worried that my friendship with Robin would not matter, that my application would be rejected because my work didn't meet the committee's standards. I felt I didn't have much of a chance.

But my worries were groundless. I won the grant, amazed that I was awarded the $17,250 I requested. Although Social Security took away half of it, I still received enough money between 1988 and 1993 so that I didn't have to work as a journalist. This gave me the time I needed to write enough poems for Judith Root to edit into another book-length manuscript, *The Man in the Iron Lung*.

I was also able to complete my novel, *Ceilings*. I'd begun writing this thinly veiled autobiographical novel in 1984, and I'd shared part of it with a writer's group in Berkeley ten years later. I had joined the group, which met at the home of one of my attendants, in hopes of finding other people to talk to about writing. As in some of my smaller college classes, I liked both getting and giving help. I enjoyed the small, spirited group of people who met in the living room of the house on Virginia Street. People floated in and out, but the core members, Gillian and Scott, Sarah and Bill, heard most of *Ceilings* and encouraged me to continue rewriting it. Kerry read it and offered suggestions, too.

I completed a draft of twenty chapters by 1992, but people had told me all along I should rewrite it in first person. Shortly after finishing the novel, I suddenly saw they were right. I put it away, having never sent it to an agent or editor, because I didn't want to spend the next eight years rewriting. But producing so many pages had helped me learn how to write.

James Merrill sent postcards that bore his photographs on the front. On the backs, he wrote words of encouragement. When I saw his obituary in the "In Memoriam" section of *Poets & Writers*, I felt sad and bitter. Why hadn't I heard of his death earlier? Why didn't the media consider the death of a great poet as important as the death of an actor or athlete? I saw that this country cares little for its poets, and, knowing this, I admired him even more. Although we never met, James Merrill changed my life, and I will always be grateful to him.

15

The Blue Terror

(July–August 1991)

In 1991, the renamed California Shakespeare Festival moved to Orinda, twenty miles northeast of Berkeley. I still wanted to go, even though in previous years going to the festival right in Berkeley had pushed me to my limits. I had stopped eating when I was at the festival, because chewing and swallowing made it hard for me to breathe. By 4 P.M. on performance days, I would be more interested in returning to the tank than in seeing the play. All the way home, my heart would pound like a bongo.

For the 1991 season, I asked Flann to go with me, knowing he loved Shakespeare as much as I did. The ride in the van went by surprisingly quickly, but we encountered problems at the entrance. The man at the gate refused to let the van past and told us we had go on foot to the amphitheater. That meant that Flann had to push me half a mile up a steep, narrow path through dense woods. Afraid my wheelchair would topple over, I kept yelling, "Careful! Careful!"

In the amphitheater, an usher led us to our seats. I could see well, but the sun was directly in my face. It was 3:30 P.M., the temperature had soared over ninety, and the performance wouldn't begin for another half hour. Flann complained to the usher, who took us to the other side. It was still just as hot, but the sun was at the back of my head. The usher gave us plastic visors, but mine soon slid off, as all hats do.

Soon, *A Midsummer Night's Dream* materialized on the stage below us. Feeling sorry for the actors, who were wearing heavy makeup and heavier leather costumes, I wished it were dark and misty, the kind of weather I associated with the play. I was determined to stay and have a good time, but, after the first act, I felt so hot and weary that I decided to ask Flann to take me home when intermission came. I worried that he would resent having to miss the rest of the performance, but he seemed perfectly willing to leave.

The trip down the long, narrow path through the woods went faster on the way out, since we were heading downhill, but it still frightened me. Fortunately, I was too tired to scream much.

Flann went to the pay phone in the parking lot and called the van company to pick us up immediately. I thought they would; a few years earlier, the van company had retrieved a disabled man from the festival after he became disgusted with the first fifteen minutes of a politically correct production of *The Taming of the Shrew*. However, Flann told me the van company said it wouldn't pick me up early because I was in another county. I was hot, thirsty, and furious. Flann took me under the shade of the trees and tried to get me to drink Calistoga water, but I was too tired to take more than a few sips. For the next two hours, we waited, staring at every vehicle that entered the parking lot.

Finally, around 6:30 P.M., the big white van pulled up. Flann helped the driver get me in, and we returned to Berkeley. As Flann got me in the iron lung, I sighed, "Made it." All I would have to do now was drink a lot of water and rest for a few days.

Trying to recover, I drank so much water that my bladder became distended. It became difficult to pass water, and my urine was red. Dr. Falcone prescribed antibiotics, but I kept throwing them up. On Wednesday evening, Kerry called Dr. Falcone, who ordered an ambulance to come and get me.

As the ambulance attendants pushed my stretcher past the big window, I looked back inside, thinking that it might be the last time I would ever see my cluttered, grungy, dear apartment.

The hospital's iron lung was set diagonally across a small, white room in the intensive care unit. Flann and I were out in the hallway, considering the approach.

"I'm going to have to lift you from your left side," Flann said. "Will that be okay?"

I had always been lifted from the right side, but I could see there was no way that Flann could lift me that way and get me into the iron lung. "I trust you," I said. "Go ahead."

Flann moved me with ease, but we were horrified to see that the lung had the old-style, hard, plastic collar, the kind that digs into my neck and leaves red welts. Also, the collar was hard to adjust, and several parts were stuck or missing.

I didn't have the collar on for long, though. Nurses, doctors, and respiratory technicians kept taking me out of the lung to do things: take blood, attach monitors, put in an IV and a catheter. I was tired and wanted to sleep, but they wouldn't leave me alone. The respiratory tech kept trying to jab needles into my groin for blood gas tests and kept failing. Finally he called the chief respiratory tech, who got it the first time. All the good sites for an IV had been used during my numerous childhood hospitalizations, so they had to put the IV in my jugular vein, on the left side of my neck, which further complicated the collar. Neither Flann nor the nurses could get the collar tight enough because the IV line was in the way, so I couldn't breathe well. Though I longed to sleep, I couldn't. In addition to the constant interruptions and fuss, the catheter was driving me nuts. Every time I started to fall asleep, I would have an erection, and the catheter would hurt me. As long as I had the internal catheter, I couldn't sleep unless I was beyond tired. The last thing I remember that night was that the clock in my room said 2 A.M.

Flann came in the next day to do my morning routine. I had asked him to do so, because I didn't trust the nurses to handle me properly. The tank was open, and Flann was washing me when I suddenly lost control of my bowels and shit in the bed. I passed out for what seemed a minute, and then I woke up back in the tank. A nurse was holding an oxygen mask over my face, and Flann was peering over her shoulder, looking concerned. I shook the mask off.

"Clean me up!" I ordered.

"We can't," the nurse said. "You turned blue and passed out for forty-five minutes. We have to keep the mask on until your blood has enough oxygen."

The oxygen level in my blood was monitored by a clip on my left thumb. The clip was attached to a wire that was fed through the hole in the iron lung, which also accommodated the IV tube and the wires to the heart monitors stuck to my chest. The oxygen and heart monitors had to be disconnected every time the tank was opened, or they would pull loose. Whenever we forgot, the monitors would be yanked off my chest and thumb, setting off alarms that beeped merrily.

I had to wait twenty minutes more before Flann could open the iron lung, clean me, and change the half-sheet with the nurse's help. One of them checked my face every few seconds to make sure I wasn't turning blue. They got the messy job done in two minutes. I didn't turn blue, but I was exhausted. I had a metallic taste in my mouth, and it took me a minute to be able to talk again. Very sick, I slept most of the next two days.

One night, I felt an overpowering need use the bedpan, so I called a nurse. In attempting to put me on the pan, she grabbed me by the left knee and left arm to turn me. My limbs aren't flexible, so the way she moved me hurt and frightened me. I wasn't injured, though. In fact, I realized that perhaps I was more flexible than I thought. The next night I went through the same ordeal.

I worked out a schedule with Flann and two of my other attendants, Joseph and Doris. Either Doris or Flann came the mornings to feed and wash me, and Joseph or Flann worked early evenings to give me a preventive bedpan and to fix the collar, which always needed rearranging.

In the first two days, a nurse noticed how much air was leaking through the collar, which explained why I never felt I was getting enough oxygen. She adjusted the wheels that raised and lowered the bed inside the iron lung, but every change left me feeling more uncomfortable. More cold air whooshed in through the opening, which I thought probably led to my contracting pneumonia. Flann later discovered that the bed was out of whack, and he returned it to the normal position.

Doris fed me my first solid meal Saturday morning: cherry Jell-O and cranberry juice. A strange meal, but I was glad I could eat. Later, when the tank was open, Doris rushed around the small room to get the washcloth, soap, and towel to bathe me. It seemed comical to see the hefty Doris move so fast, but, despite her haste, I turned blue before she could close the machine.

Somehow, it was determined I had inhaled the Jell-O or juice, and that's why I had run out of breath. A respiratory doctor pushed a fiber-optic tube up my nose, down my left bronchia, and into my lung. He was kind enough to give me a local anesthetic, so I felt none of this. Shining a flashlight through the fiber-optic tube, he looked inside my lung before vacuuming out the juice and Jell-O with a suction machine. Afterward, feeling and breathing better, I thanked him.

I slept most of that afternoon but then awoke at night. I realized that I'd never been so sick before, and I feared I would die.

Mister Death

He comes at you as though he's known you
from the wet and unexpected moment
of your conception.
Irresistible as gravity,
he calls your name.
You've avoided him for years,
but that doesn't help
now that he's got you
snared by his good buddy, dumb luck.
Gripping your shoulders,
he pushes his long, metallic, stinking tongue
down the back of your quivering throat.

I wrote this poem much later, reflecting my feelings from that time. I feared being helpless in the face of death. This, I suppose, mirrors my fear of being helpless in life. I feared an eternity of nonexistence, but, more than that, I feared the wrath of God.

Around midnight of that long Saturday, I heard a voice saying, "You will not die, not of this." It was Jesus talking to me. It wasn't that I detected sound waves from outside my head; the voice was internal but unmistakable. I felt great relief and terror. Why would the Lord of Creation address me? And there was that phrase, "not of this." That implied I would die eventually: my death didn't seem theoretical anymore. I felt my mortality more certainly than I ever had, and I knew that dying would be a terrifying experience. I was afraid, and I could only hope that Jesus would see me through my dying.

I couldn't sleep the next night. Every time I dozed off, I had a terrifying nightmare of trying to move something around a diamond-shaped path. Moving it seemed impossible but crucial. I repeatedly called the night nurse, the same nurse who had frightened me so much while putting me on the bedpan. Each time, she listened patiently to my incoherent accounts of the nightmare. Though she didn't say anything special, her listening got me through the night. I saw that she cared, and I liked her for that.

The mornings exhausted me. There was always my usual morning routine, followed by respiratory techs demanding my breath and blood. Some days, technicians would wheel a portable X-ray machine into my room and, with the help of my attendant, slip a hard, cold photo-graphic plate under my back to photograph my lungs and kidneys.

In the afternoons, after Flann brought my bookstand, I could read one of my books—*The Healing Notebooks*, poems by Kenny Fries; Adrienne Rich's *Your Native Land, Your Life; The Valis Trilogy*, sci-fi by Philip K. Dick; and Gore Vidal's novel *1876*. Literature relieved the routine of hospital life.

The pages of black-on-white of print provided contrast to the white-on-white monotony of hospital decor. My room was white. The hallway was white. Some nurses did wear pastel tops over their white uniforms, and sometimes a paisley necktie would blaze above Dr. Falcone's white lab coat. But mostly the hospital was a blizzard of white. It was as if science, in its determination to eliminate all vari-ables, had painted everything white. Literature, with its mess, blood, and passion, saved me from white, that scientific superstition. I am grateful to all the writers for giving me the colors of life, especially to Adrienne Rich for her hospital poems.

One afternoon after my condition had stabilized, Kerry came to visit. I was so glad to see her, I said, "Kerry-kerry, very-merry!"

"Hi there," she said, touching my forehead. "Good to see you. You sure had me scared. Let me get a chair." She crossed the hall to the nurses' station and returned dragging a big, wooden captain's chair. "Sure is a tiny room they gave you. Why don't they turn you so you can look out the window?"

"Cause then I wouldn't be able to see the nurses' station."

"Oh, that's a good reason. You want them to hear you if there's a problem."

"How've you been?"

She frowned. "Not so merry. Very-merry's the last word you'd use about me. I've been worried about you, been having to do all this work about you, and talking with your parents and Dr. Falcone. This is the first afternoon I've had any time to visit; Flann told me they're poking and X-raying you all morning. Now your parents and Dr. Falcone and the hospital social worker all act like I'm your de facto wife. It's been rough."

"You called my parents?"

She scooted up closer to me. "I saw them the morning after you came here," she said. "They drove down from Sacramento. You were out of it. Dr. Falcone was saying he thought you'd die, and your parents were terribly upset, of course. I hadn't slept for a day and a half. O'Bie, your father—funny, I'm calling him O'Bie now—was mad at me, like it was my fault, but after a while he calmed down. He just wasn't used to dealing with me, and I can see that. I mean, for all these years I've just been The Weird Girl in the Back Room; now, all of a sudden, I'm, like I said, your de facto wife."

"Dr. Falcone thought I'd die?" I was both horrified and relieved that my imminent death hadn't been merely fantasy.

"Yeah. All your vitals were shitty; he didn't think you'd pull through. You really scared me. I wish you'd take better care of yourself. I mean, I know this isn't real logical, but I've been mad at you for getting sick. I depend on you so much, and then you go park yourself in the ninety-degree sun. Flann said it was like Sacramento out there. Like it's not going to have any consequences." Kerry was talking fast, showing how nervous and stressed she had been. After so many years together, we had developed a deep understanding, a kind of secret language, and I knew that what she was saying was not blame.

"I thought about that in 1989, when I was in the hospital," I said. "I thought, I can't die; Kerry and the kitties'll be out on the street. If I don't pay the rent, you'll have no place to live."

"That's right, that's just what I was thinking. That's one of the things that scared me. So I moved into Flann's place last week."

I was stunned. "But you told me a few months ago Flann's landlord wouldn't let you move in there because of the kitties."

"I had a long talk with the landlord. I really laid it on the line; I told him that, if you died, I couldn't rent your place because the rent subsidy's in your name and that if you died, the kitties and I would be out on the street. . . . I suppose you're mad at me."

"Well, yes, it is a bad time." I hated the idea of her not living with me.

"But, remember, I've been trying to find a place for two years now. Between the mildew and the attendants coming and going and the street people fighting and shitting right outside my window—and now, with all this," she gestured toward my IV, "it's like the universe is telling me, screaming at me to get out now."

"Yes. I know it's been rough," I began, "it's a lousy apartment and—"

"I wouldn't blame you for being mad." She opened her bag and pulled out a bottle of Coke.

I said, "There's so much going on now. I suppose I am mad—it'll just take me a while to feel it."

"Well, I'm sure you'll be mad sooner or later. I want you to tell me when you are. Want a swig?" She offered me her soda.

"No, thanks. But what about the kitties? I thought Flann's landlord was anticat."

"He was, until I introduced him to Bumpkin and Calloo."

"Well, how could he resist?"

"He couldn't, they're such darlings. And they're quiet and clean and, well, I made him feel like he'd be turning down two Nobel Prize winners if he didn't accept them." We were both quiet for a while. She continued, "So, really, I haven't moved yet, just my bed and TV and some cat stuff. It'll take a while."

I changed the subject. "How was it with my parents?"

She took a big swallow of her drink. "It took a while, but, when I finally convinced O'Bie that I was on your side, he opened up. He's really very protective, you know."

"I know. But I wasn't going to die," I said. "I heard a voice, well, the voice of Jesus, telling me I wouldn't die, not of this, not now, anyway." I paused, gauging her reaction. "You look like you don't believe me."

"I believe you heard what you call Jesus. I don't know, Jesus, Krishna, Atman, they're all different brand names for the same stuff. We can talk God some other time, but I want to tell you about your parents." She took a deep breath and leaned back in the chair. "O'Bie's been really worried. He's always been afraid he would outlive you. We talked about how unnatural that is, I mean for fathers to bury their sons. And he was prepared, well, not prepared, but trying to accept that it would happen. And your mother loves you very much. I could tell that."

A respiratory tech interrupted. Kerry opened a paperback while I breathed into the tech's machine.

"They're always barging in like that, aren't they?" she said after he left. "I hate hospitals. Anyway, we got into the thing about the polio vaccine. Remember how you told me you got polio in September 1955, and I said I thought the Salk vaccine had come out in '54 or '55? You put two and two together and realized that they hadn't vaccinated you? Well, here's the story. It was hard to talk to them about this, they were both crying, but what happened was that the vaccine had been out in the summer of '55, and then some people in southern California caught polio from the vaccine. Can you believe that? They actually took the vaccine and then ended up with polio!"

She finished the Coke, aimed, and tossed the bottle into the trash. "So after that happened, the Massachusetts Medical Association told the governor he should declare an emergency, and so the governor ordered a suspension in distribution of the Salk vaccine. They stopped distributing it in September."

"Just when I got polio."

She nodded. "That's right, you and a few thousand other people in Massachusetts got polio that month, way more than the month before, so the governor lifted the ban at the end of September."

"Jesus."

"'Jesus' is right. It was just bad luck. Your folks were very upset about it, and, when the vaccine became available, they got themselves and Ken and Karen vaccinated."

"Bad luck. Maybe I've used up my lifetime's supply of bad luck."

"I don't know, honey. Seems like there's always more bad luck to come."

"I was looking forward to going home, seeing you, the kitties. I keep thinking, home is paradise."

"I'm sure it is, compared to the hospital. But just think, it'll be more paradisiacal without me around."

"Oh, no, you're the most important part. You made home paradise."

"I thought you thought of me as being a hell raiser, a bringer of bad tidings, someone who told you that you were full of shit all the time."

"Well, there was a lot of that. Remember the night we stayed up past nine, fighting about the housecleaner?"

"You still hate me for that?"

"No, no, not at all. I don't hate you at all. I'm just saying ... well, it's like that Bob Hope song, 'Thanks for the Memories.' 'You may have been a headache, but you never were a bore.'"

She laughed. "Thanks. That's high praise. Now don't worry about me moving out. I'll visit you like in the old days, remember? I used to come see you every week after therapy."

"So how are the kitties liking the new place?"

"They send their love—they hope you'll be out of here real soon. Now could you do me a favor?"

"Sure. What?"

"You know how I've been feeding that outdoor kitty?"

"That scroungy one with his ear bitten off? Yeah, I've seen you feed him outside my window. What's his name?"

"I call him Cosmo. He's sure had a rough life, I think. Anyway, I want to ask you to feed him once a day. I'm not asking you to take him in; just have one of your attendants leave a bowl of dry cat food out by the door."

"Of course, sounds easy enough. I've had so much fun with your cats. See that black, rectangular thing on the wall? When I'm falling asleep, I think it's Calloo. I really miss him."

We didn't say anything for a long moment. We were both tired, and she left soon, to go to Flann's place. Before she did, she said, "Take care. I love you."

"I love you, Kerry."

Having escaped death so narrowly made me realize how important, how precious everyone was. I kept remembering seeing the actor Godfrey Cambridge on TV saying, "All we have is each other."

When I saw my parents the following day, I told them I loved them. I'd never told them that before. I was afraid I would be embarrassed and they would be embarrassed, but it seemed important: I thought I might never have another chance. My father said he loved me, my mother cried, and I saw that I had been right: I was embarrassed. But it had been worth it to discover that embarrassment isn't the worst thing in the world; it wasn't as bad as fear and silence. Then my father talked about how good I looked, but I couldn't believe him. I still felt weak, and we kept the visit short.

After two weeks, Dr. Falcone ordered the removal of my IV. Flann opened my collar, and the nurse took out the IV without any problems. Flann closed the collar up again before I hit the three-minute mark, the point at which I usually started to turn blue. After I caught my breath, which took a while, I had Flann open the collar and the tank so that he could pull me through and give me a shave. He and Doris had been shaving my face above the chin, but the collar blocked access to my neck and lower jaw, and that part had been getting itchy. The shaving lather felt cool, and even better were the feel of the air and the absence of the sharp whiskers that had been porcupining my neck. Best of all, being able to tolerate the shave was a sign of my progress. But, before I could go home, I had to increase the amount of time I could stay out of the tank, and I needed to have the catheter removed to see whether I could urinate without it.

One evening, I had Joseph show a nurse named Lana how to fix my collar. An hour later, when I asked Lana to fix the collar, she had no memory of what Joseph had shown her. I never had liked Lana. She always forgot to disconnect the monitors from my chest and thumb before opening the tank. My thumb would be yanked, and alarm bells would shriek.

One day, it occurred to me that Lana was one of those people Jesus would like me to love. I wondered whether I could. I wondered whether I could even begin a conversation with her. Lana was black, but I couldn't place her accent. She wasn't from the South or the Caribbean. One afternoon, I worked up the nerve to ask her where she was from.

"Nigeria," she said. "It's in Africa."

"I know it's in Africa," I said. "What part of Nigeria are you from?"

"My family is from the southeastern part."

"You mean like Biafra?"

"We are Ibo. I don't remember the war. I was too young." She shook her head. "Many people in my family died."

"God, that was a horrible war."

"It was, but things are better now. I went back there a couple of years ago. My brother owns a brick house and a motor scooter."

I quit hating Lana.

Four times a day, respiratory techs came into my room to have me blow into a machine. This was supposed to improve my breathing, but I didn't see any effect at all. My massage therapist came to the hospital and worked on my chest through the portholes in the sides of the iron lung, and I felt that the relaxing, invigorating touch helped more than the respiratory techs and their machine. But one of the techs did help me by suggesting that I listen to music.

Flann brought in my portable stereo along with a few cassettes, but I played only two of them, Stan Getz's "Voyages" and Beethoven's Sixth Symphony. I usually played one in the early afternoons, after lunch. Nurses and techs would drift into my room, saying how soothing the music sounded. I'd fall asleep after listening to it.

Dr. Falcone told me that a state law prohibited the hospital from discharging patients until they could breathe on their own. He asked me to set a goal for time out of the tank.

"Fifteen minutes," I said. "That'll give me time to get up and go home in an ambulance."

I got up to six minutes, but it seemed as though I would stay at that level forever. On my birthday, July 31, when I had been in the hospital for nearly a month, Doris asked one of the nurses to help her change my sheet. I was in my third minute out and feeling okay.

"Today's Mark's birthday," Doris told the nurse.

"Oh, yeah? How old are you?"

I mouthed, "Forty-two," but no sound came out. They laughed. Although I was frustrated that I still couldn't talk out of the iron lung, I saw the humor in the situation. If I could have laughed, I would have. Polio killed the nerves that control my diaphragm, so, when I laugh, no sound comes out.

A week later, they took the catheter out. I'd drunk a lot of water beforehand to make sure I could pee. I never wanted to be catheterized again, so I was glad an hour later when I urinated easily into the bag. At the same time, they disconnected all the monitors and moved me in my iron lung to a larger room. The next morning, I saw Flann heading for my old room. When I called his name, he turned to look at me: we were both surprised that I could yell that loudly.

Eight minutes, ten minutes: I was getting stronger. I was beginning to have erotic dreams and developing a crush on Mrs. Tadazreuski, a dark-haired, efficient nurse who told me silly jokes.

One morning, I passed the fifteen-minute mark without turning blue or fainting. My voice was weak, and I was tired but overjoyed that I had done it. It was a Thursday. I thought I would be allowed to go home the next day, but Dr. Falcone wanted to keep me over the weekend to make sure I was strong enough.

The next Tuesday, Flann dressed me and put me on an ambulance gurney. An ambulance attendant pushed the gurney while Mrs. Tadazreuski trailed. I eyed her longingly until I knew I had to give it up. After six weeks, hospital time was over. We went into the elevator and down to the first floor.

Outside, I was blinded by the noon sun: I'd forgotten how bright it was. A respiratory tech held up a copy of the *Daily Californian* to shield my eyes. Once inside the ambulance, he pushed air into my lungs with a little accordion-like bag. The nurse in the ambulance seemed interested in Flann and began chatting him up. As we pulled up in front of my building, she asked, "So what year of medical school are you in?"

"Oh, no, no. I'm not in med school. I'm a Celticist."

I couldn't see her face, but I assumed her jaw dropped.

The attendants pushed me into my apartment, and Flann put me in my old familiar iron lung. I was glad to be home, but I didn't know how homelike it could be without Kerry. Then, and since, I've often wondered why God wanted to keep me alive.

Three Reasons to Live

THE PRACTICAL

O God, it was boring
but there was nothing else
so I did it
got it out of the way

THE SPIRITUAL

we had this deal going
like God gave me life
for a while
I gave him gratitude
for a while and
it worked ok

THE INTELLECTUAL

things just kept happening
you know how every day is different?
and I just wanted to see
what would happen next.

Afterword

(August 1991–May 1997)

I never returned to the California Shakespeare Festival. The festival apologized for the problems I'd had on my last visit there, but it didn't matter. The illness had kicked the stuffing out of me, and I was never again able to stay out of the iron lung longer than three hours. There was no way I could stay up for the five hours necessary for trips to the Shakespeare Festival or to Candlestick Park.

Everyone said I would need a live-in attendant after Kerry moved out. After interviewing several people, I picked Diego, a quiet, intelligent man who was interested in politics and basketball. One of his hobbies was growing orchids, and soon the windowsills in the house were covered with the light, delicate flowers.

My sister's husband died in 1992, at age twenty-eight. It seemed inconceivable. When Jeff and Rachel had gotten married in 1985, she had been twenty-two and he a young-looking twenty-one. He had a rare kidney disease that forced him to use dialysis. He died of a blood clot in the heart, which the doctors later conjectured was an indirect result of the dialysis. Everyone in my family missed Jeff, and Rachel was devastated.

Northern California was battered by storms during the winter of 1992–1993. Diego, seeing how scrawny and tired Cosmo was, declared, "I'm going to turn him into a real cat."

He brought Kerry's old outdoor cat indoors, bathed him to get off all the street grime, and started feeding him twice a day. I paid for

Cosmo's food and appointments at the Berkeley Dog and Cat Hospital. After a month, Cosmo had gained enough weight so that you could no longer see his ribs protruding. His brown coat shone with health.

An elderly, arthritic cat, Cosmo slept under the iron lung at night. In the morning, we'd exchange meows. He'd look out the window, use the litter box, eat breakfast, and pad around the apartment until noon. We both rested in the afternoon. He accompanied me through my days. Some days, he was the only creature I saw besides my attendant. He wasn't frisky and adorable, like cat food–commercial kitties. He seldom leapt up on my desk as Calloo and Bumpkin had, although he would for special occasions. But I was very glad to have him, and Kerry was happy that we had taken him in.

Cosmo

He seems to understand the deal—
I buy him food, take him to the vet;
he pretends to be my cat.
At supper,
he jumps up on my desk,
sniffs my mustard chicken,
his nose expanding and contracting like .
a heart gone mad with love.

In June 1995, Cosmo was sleeping all day and all night. The vet said he had kidney failure and that nothing could be done for him. I called Kerry and Flann for help, which they had previously offered for such a time, and Flann came over. He put the cardboard cat carrier on the bedside table and lifted Cosmo into it. I thought the cat's face looked trusting—he had no fear of the vet—and I hated myself for betraying him.

I knew I didn't want him to suffer, knew that I had to make the decisions because Cosmo couldn't. Still, I could picture someone putting me to death "for my own good," and I felt terrible. When Flann returned with the empty carrier, he said, "As soon as the needle went in, Cosmo just went down. I think he was ready."

Cosmo had not been a spectacular animal, just an old cat near the end of the line. But I admired him. After all the abuse he had suffered, he was still eager to love and to be loved. I felt grateful for his presence and for having had the chance to prolong his life by making him an indoor cat.

In March 1993, a *Los Angeles Times* journalist named Brenda Bell called me, saying she would like to interview me. Surprised, I asked how she knew about me. She explained that she was from Texas and knew Pat LittleDog, publisher of my chapbook. That June, Brenda came to Berkeley and interviewed me over three days. I found her not only charming but intelligent: she shared my loathing for Raymond Carver's stories.

The article was the cover story of the *Los Angeles Times Sunday Magazine* on my birthday, 31 July 1994. John Callahan, the disabled cartoonist and writer, called with congratulations. I was pleased to hear from him, but I didn't expect much more to come from the article.

Boy, was I wrong.

I received a lot of phone calls, one of them from Daniel Zwerdling, of National Public Radio's *All Things Considered*. He had read Brenda's article and wanted an interview, which I was happy to grant. We met on Labor Day weekend, and I enjoyed talking with Zwerdling, thrilled to be calling him "Danny." The interview was to air the following weekend, but it had to be postponed because of developments in the news.

That Monday, early in September, I had just finished my morning routine when I saw my brother, Ken, outside the window, waving. I was surprised, since he had always called before visiting me. When he came in, I showed him my new computer, babbling about how great it was. He interrupted, saying he had tried to call me the night before, but he kept getting a wrong-number message. He recited what he thought my phone number was; he had the right number but the wrong area code.

Sitting down, he said he had some bad news. "Helen died last night."

Instantly, I felt tears coming as he explained that she had woken O'Bie at 5 A.M., saying she was having problems breathing. O'Bie called 911, and the ambulance took her to a hospital, where she died. "She probably would have died in the ambulance if it hadn't been for all the things the medics did," said Ken. He assured me that her death had been quick and painless.

A few minutes later, Rachel and her boyfriend, Mike, arrived. Ken had to go back to Sacramento to be with O'Bie, to make the funeral arrangements, and to work on Helen's will. O'Bie had left papers in case he died before Helen, but he had never considered that Helen might die first.

I called and spoke to my father, who sounded confused. Rachel and Mike spent the day with me. Neither Rachel nor I felt hungry, but Mike insisted we eat and bought us sandwiches from a restaurant. The sandwiches were superb, maybe because they reminded us we were alive. We talked all day, crying off and on. Although I couldn't go to Helen's funeral, Ken asked me to write part of the eulogy, and I felt privileged to contribute. He wrote and gave a wonderful eulogy, including a few jokes.

"I should tell you of my mother's faults," Ken said at the funeral, "just so you won't think I'm making this up. She always overcooked the swordfish."

A long pause followed, then laughter from the mourners.

More soberly, Ken continued, "I sat in the hospital with my father the morning she died. I asked him about the day he met Helen. He told me about it, how they'd been set up for a blind date by my uncle Don. Then he said, in the softest voice, 'It was the most wonderful day of my life.'"

I contributed the following:

Helen was my mother and, of course, I loved her. But she was also the woman who fed me, washed me, and lifted me every day for nineteen years. After I got polio in 1955, I lived in hospitals for two years. Both my parents, Helen and Walter, wanted me to live with them again, so in 1957, I returned home, to a new home in Stoughton, a suburb of Boston. That's when she began the extraordinary task of taking care of me.

She gave me the greatest gift a parent can give a child, independence. With her encouragement, I've lived on my own, attended the University of California at Berkeley, graduated, written a book of poetry and many articles for newspapers and magazines.

Through all the hard times, Helen never lost her talent for love. Instead, she strengthened and refined it into a miracle of love. This miracle of love is her great achievement and her enduring triumph. The world is a little colder without her.

Later, when I thanked Ken for taking care of everything, he said, "I had to. O'Bie was counting on me."

The NPR interview aired the following Sunday, and I regretted very much that Helen couldn't hear it. I consoled myself a little by thinking that she had seen the article.

The following month, Rachel married her new partner, Mike. They had the service in O'Bie's back yard, where he gave Rachel away for the second time.

A filmmaker named Jessica Yu began filming me on the first day of 1995. She had written for Pacific News Service, as I had, and the PNS editor Sandy Close had suggested that Jessica make a documentary about me. She had given me videos of her other films, and I liked them. Her technique differed from that of most documentary filmmakers in that Jessica let her subjects do all the talking. She never narrated. Sitting next to the camera, which was pointed at me, she'd ask me a series of questions. The microphone could pick up only my voice.

Jessica finished filming the documentary in July 1995. After the last reel of film was shot, she told me she had met the builder of a new, accessible building in downtown Berkeley. The builder had said he wanted me to move in.

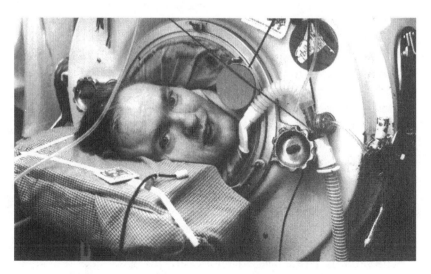

Mark was the subject of the Academy Award–winning documentary
Breathing Lessons, by Jessica Yu.
Photo courtesy of Jessica Yu, 1995.

In September, after the elevator was installed, Diego took me to see the building. We met the builder outside as a fire engine roared by. "Life in the city!" he said over the noise. The apartments were bright and lovely, brand new, with touches that my old apartment didn't have. Sunlight poured in through huge windows, whereas direct light had been a rare occurrence in my old place. There was an outside balcony I could be wheeled to easily, and Diego's orchids would flourish in the sun from his bay window. Diego and I moved into a one-bedroom unit in November.

Jessica gave me a video of her film, *Breathing Lessons: The Life and Work of Mark O'Brien*, a month before it premiered in December 1995. Watching it with me, Diego said the film should win an Oscar.

Jessica asked me to speak to the audience after the film's premiere. At the opening, Sandy, who had financed the film through Pacific News Service, stood behind a podium and introduced me as "one of the sexiest men I know." I was overwhelmed by the compliment and by an ovation from the audience. There were more than a hundred people in the theater, including several WELLbeings (people in the WELL computer network) whom I had invited. Jessica and I waited for questions. None came until her husband, the writer Mark Salzman, asked why I didn't like to be called brave. That loosened up the audience and me.

After the twenty-minute Q & A, several people introduced themselves to me. One woman greeted me with "Betcha don't recognize me!"

I didn't. It was Cheryl, the sex surrogate. Her long, brown hair had been replaced by a blonde punk cut. She knelt on the floor so that she could be at eye level with me. When she rested a hand on my shoulder, I felt attracted to her, and I wanted to see her again.

I also met Susan, a WELLbeing I had exchanged email with but never met. We talked vaguely about getting together.

Later, Diego and I went to the reception. The coconut cake, molasses cookies, and the rest of the food had been made that morning by Jessica's mother. Shouting over the crowd noise, I talked with the moviegoers. As Diego pushed me home, I was struck by the contrast. At the Pacific Film Archive, I had been treated as a celebrity. Now I was just another Berkeley cripple, as anonymous as the trees.

I invited Susan over to visit the next week, and she continued to see me once every week or two. I liked her. Bright and cheerful, she excelled at word games on the WELL. She, like me, was interested in religion, writing, and Shakespeare. Then, one day in April, she visited me and asked, "Aren't the Giants on TV now?" Perhaps it was a coincidence, but later that month I decided I loved her. Or perhaps it was the poem she wrote for me:

If I Were Able

I might collect a comet and several stars for you
I might wrap them in the clover-scented breeze for you
I might bottle the seaweed smell of the bayside rocks for you
I might wrap that in a square of sky for you
Perhaps with clouds like crumpled cotton,
Or the robin's-egg blue that happens after sunset.
I might throw in the midnight song of the mockingbird,
Or the smell of the wild carrots,
Or the crazy dance of the cedar branches in a storm.
I would bring all these to you.
I would kiss you
Like the fairy kissed the Velveteen Rabbit, and
I would let you lead me, summer in our legs,
To the place where the night wind whispers,
"Wake up. You were real all along. No excuses now."

No one had ever written a poem for me. I cried when she read it aloud, and later I kept a copy of it pinned to my wall, where I could see it.

As my forty-seventh birthday approached in July 1996, Susan asked me whether I was going to have a party. I hadn't had a party in over a decade. Throwing parties always made me anxious—what should I buy? Whom should I invite? What if no one came? But she offered to set the whole thing up. Together we planned a guest list, and Susan sent invitations she'd made on her computer.

Twenty people packed into my apartment. Helium balloons bobbed from the ceiling, and we popped open and drank champagne that Jessica sent. Casey brought a cake from her sister's bakery. There were three guests in wheelchairs—my neighbor Bill, the playwright Neil

Marcus, and the Berkeley City Council member Dona Spring. At the height of things, somehow, Dona got everyone to shut up.

Holding up an official-looking piece of paper, she said, "I want to read this proclamation." Passed by the Berkeley City Council and signed by the mayor, it declared August 3, the day of the party, Mark O'Brien Day in Berkeley.

A week after the party, I was listening to a Giants game on the radio, when suddenly the sound stopped; the power had gone out. It was eight in the evening, dark in my apartment, and I was alone. Without electricity, the iron lung stopped. As my breath grew weaker and weaker, I telephoned Susan and Diego, hoping one of them could come and switch on the battery-powered respirator on my wheelchair. I kept hoping the electricity would come back on, but it didn't. The operators had problems understanding me as I strangled in the collar of the iron lung. No one was home. I remember feeling terrified before I passed out, thinking, "So this is how it ends, alone, with all my backup systems gone."

I woke up in a bed early the next morning, confused and uncomfortable. I hadn't slept in a bed since the days I lived with my parents and used the turtle shell respirator. It felt strange to be without an iron lung. Even stranger, there was an oxygen mask strapped on my face. Dimly, I remembered that during the night I had asked a nurse to take the mask off, but she had refused. I had an irrational urge to shake it off, even though it was keeping me alive. It pinched my nose and would, I knew, make it impossible for people to hear me talk.

I wondered what had happened and where I was. Outside the window, the sun shone a dim orange on the Alta Bates Hospital parking garage. *Alta Bates*, I thought. *I must be in Berkeley.*

Then Susan and Diego appeared at my bedside. They had stayed most of the night at the hospital. Someone I'd called before passing out had phoned 911, and the two of them had arrived at my apartment right after the emergency medical team.

"They were trying to figure out how to open the iron lung," Diego said. "So I showed them, and they put you on a stretcher and carried you down the stairwell in the dark."

"There was no emergency lighting in the stairwell," Susan said. "I carried a flashlight they had."

"Your arms dangled off the sides of the stretcher," Diego said, munching a Mars bar. "You would've screamed if you'd been conscious."

"My God," I said. They strained to hear me through the mask.

"They put you in an ambulance," Diego continued. "We followed in Susan's car, and we stayed here till they got you a room. We've been waiting for you to wake up."

"We weren't sure you would wake up, honey," Susan said.

"My foot feels funny," I said through the mask. "I can't raise my left knee."

"That IV probably saved your life," said Diego. "The medics stuck it in you when you were in the ambulance. They couldn't find any other vein."

"Why didn't they put me in an iron lung?" I asked. "They had one the last time I was here."

"Well, they have one, and the respiratory people were ready to set it up," Susan told me, "but it hadn't been used since the last time you were here, and the doctor didn't trust it."

Later that day, my attendants put me in an iron lung. Two days later, I was discharged, and Susan and Diego were sternly warned about a backup system to use during power failures. Diego decided he would switch on the portable respirator whenever I was alone. In an emergency, that would give me an hour or two.

After that adventure, I was tired and sore for a month. I didn't go out again until September.

Susan took me to a party given by my disabled neighbor, Bill. I felt out of place and tired quickly. Afterward, Susan and I took the elevator to the roof to watch an eclipse of the moon. We kissed between puffs of my portable respirator. I didn't catch much of the eclipse.

For the second time in six years, I had come close to dying. I didn't know what to make of it except that I wanted to do as much as I could with the rest of my life. Susan wrote another poem for me.

Evening

i.

In the fading light, we've created a
Miniature, manageable universe.
With our fireplace a votive candle,
Our garden a vase of pale roses,
You weave for me glowing yesterdays:
The Japanese tea garden with Jo

A Giants game at Candlestick
Shakespeare in the round.
Together we've almost plotted new forays.
What would it be like, we wonder, to visit
The coliseum
The campus
The couch?
Your life flame, so capricious, teases me—
Now leaping high to throw a
Laughing shadow on the wall,
Now dwindling down to barest, faintest glow.
I don't know what to hope for.

ii.

In between
Seeing your bright smile of greeting and
Discerning only your faint outline as I leave,
In between
Jokes over dinner and
Later softer laughter,
In between
Bruce's arrival with the groceries and
When he closes his door,
In between,
There is a moment when the setting sun
Slides in from my right,
Blinding me almost as completely
As my love for you.

Later that month, anticipating the "visit to the couch" mentioned
in her poem, I gave Susan money to buy a futon. She bought one that
had to be assembled by the user. Amused by the title of the futon's
manual, I used it in a poem.

How to Operate Your Futon Frame

For the first anniversary of our meeting, December 17th, 1995, a date that will live
in famy.

Certain items are necessary:
the base, the back, the arms, all made of oak,
nuts, screws, bolts of stainless steel,
a mattress made of foam, a cotton cover.
Most important: a woman made of love and courage.

She is needed to assemble
the less important materials
with skill and patience,
to laugh at the impossibilities
that arise whenever anyone
assembles the less important parts.

To operate the futon,
the woman needs a man
to tickle, kiss and carry on
when the futon is in Flat Mode (see pg. 7).
If the man is paralyzed,
the woman must do the tickling, kissing
and so forth,
until they both become too tired,
until they make each other real.

Early in 1997, a friend told me that *Breathing Lessons* was up for
an Oscar, nominated for best short documentary. Excited and pleased,
I remembered Diego's comment the first time we watched it: "That
movie's gonna win an Academy Award."

Susan and I gave several interviews about the movie. Predictably,
the questions focused on my alleged heroism. The conversation with
a KGO-TV reporter was typical and exasperating. Near the end of the
interview, during which I had discussed the political aspects of disability, she asked me, "What special qualities enabled you to get out of
the nursing home?"

She still hadn't gotten it. I exploded. "Look, it doesn't matter how
brave you are, how intelligent you are. If you're in a nursing home and
your state has no provisions for independent living, then you're stuck!"

I watched the interview later that day. My final outburst had been
cut, along with everything else political.

Though I was nervous about the Oscar broadcast, I invited friends over, and we joked around, watching it. We had fun looking in the crowd for Ken, O'Bie, and Rachel, who had gotten tickets from Jessica. Conversation turned to the news media and how terrified they are at letting go of the "heroic cripple" stereotype.

Prepared for the movie to lose, I felt like bouncing off the ceiling when Will Smith announced that it had won the award. Everyone screamed. I yelled, "There's Jessica! There's Jessica!," amazed to see her on TV. She looked beautiful, and, after she made her speech, Channel Five reporters called me from the front door of my apartment building, asking if they could come up.

"No!" I said.

Friends gather in Mark's apartment to celebrate the Oscar win in 1997. Clockwise from bottom left are Mark's attendant, Diego, Jessica Yu (with the Oscar), Susan Fernbach, Mark (in iron lung), and Sandy Close, executive director of the Pacific News Service, who introduced O'Brien and Yu.

"No?" said the voice, sounding puzzled, as though they were seldom turned down.

Not wanting my privacy invaded, I stuck with my refusal. It had always been hard for me to say no, but this time it was easy. I was becoming wary of the mass media.

Jessica and many other friends called that night, people wandered in from Bill's party down the hall, and we had a wonderful evening.

I was surprised when the chairman of the Berkeley English department called me in April 1997. I was even more surprised when he asked me to give the commencement speech for the graduating class of English majors that May. At first, I thought it was a joke a student was pulling. Eventually, when I believed he really was the chairman, I told him I couldn't give the speech because I can barely be heard when I'm outside the iron lung. He said the department could tape my speech when I was at home, then play it back while I sat on the stage. It sounded crazy to me, but I agreed, asking only that a microphone be placed beside my wheelchair in case I felt like saying anything after the tape was played.

An attendant drove Susan and me to the Hearst Theater in the hilly part of campus on a clear, hot day. Positioned in a fold of the hills, the classical Greek-style auditorium has been the scene of many events, especially rock concerts. Waiting offstage, Susan and I heard the distorted warbles of introductory speeches echoing off the hills. I felt amazed to be there. It had been fifteen years since my own graduation. Was fifteen years a long time? It seemed so in the day-to-day sense. Was it a short time? It seemed so when I thought of the recognition I was getting.

Back then, at my graduation, I had driven the power-chair across the stage of Zellerbach Auditorium. Helen had been sitting in the front row, Tracy jumping up and down backstage, and O'Bie flashing his camera. Now, fifteen years later, Susan pushed me on stage in my wheelchair. People cheered, just as they had at that first graduation. The tape recorder was switched on. I smiled and looked at the crowd while my voice boomed out over the loudspeaker. Here is the address I gave.

I want to thank Jeffrey Knapp, the Chair of the Department of English, for inviting me to give the commencement speech. I also want to thank professor emeritus Peter Dale Scott for suggesting me as a commencement speaker to Dr. Knapp.

A few years ago, no, several years ago (you English majors know the difference between "few" and "several." No one else does), I was on your side of commencement. I sat in the wings of Zellerbach Auditorium listening to a well-known writer give a rambling, confusing commencement speech. I couldn't help thinking, "The History Department got Tom Wicker as their commencement speaker. Why couldn't we get someone better? The Journalism School got Walter Cronkite. Why couldn't we get someone better?" Today I imagine you're all thinking, "Why couldn't we get someone better?" So if you will forgive me this weird piece of performance art, I'll continue.

Now, the commencement speech has three functions. The first is to give the professors an opportunity to congratulate themselves for turning out another crop of students. I'm sure you'll agree the professors deserve such a measly perk. The second is to give the parents time to take a nap, and the third function is to subject you to a final rite of passage, another boring speech from yet another boring adult. Don't worry, you won't have to write a paper on it.

I admire you. I admire you for having the courage to major in English. While your friends in other departments have been pestered these past weeks by recruiters from Boeing, Bechtel, and IBM, you have been left free to complete your studies in peace and to consider your future in burger flipping. It took courage for you to choose English, and it took more courage to stick with it, so I congratulate you. You have chosen the word as the focus of your studies.

Language is our greatest achievement. While there are many forms of language—mathematics, music, gesture—only the word, written and spoken, combines the precision of mathematics with the immediacy of gesture. It can even aspire to possess the beauty of music.

We who live by the word know how powerful it is, know that it can corrupt and destroy as much as it can edify and enlighten. To make sure that we use the word for its highest purposes, we must obey three conditions.

We must be humble. The words we use are old and powerful. Most of the words we use in everyday speech can be found in Chaucer. We must never refrain from using a word merely because it's old. Old words are often the best words, more precise than current slang, more powerful than jargon. Old words are powerful; they are the words we grew up with and that stir us most deeply. A study of Winston Churchill's "We will fight them on the beaches" speech showed that more than 80 percent of the words in the speech were from Anglo-Saxon. Of course, we should also have the humility to welcome new words such as "fubar," "cyberspace," and "interface." These words fill the gaps in the language and allow us to express ideas we didn't know we had.

We must be honest. Whenever I hear the dishonest use of words in a commercial or a political speech, I say, "Bullshit." I say "Bullshit" as emphatically as I can because there is a part of me that believes everything I hear. I've found that if I don't say "Bullshit," that part of me will take it in, and I will become polluted by lies. It is easy to detect the bullshit in a jingle or an official euphemism for murder, but the difficult part of this condition is that I must apply it to myself. I must keep my bullshit detector on when I say or write that I'm only a good person who only wants peace and justice. Bullshit. I'm also a greedy person who wants a snazzy computer and a place in the country. I'm a demanding person who wants a clean environment, safe streets, and lower taxes. I'm an impossible person who wants instant nirvana, heaven on the cheap, sainthood in ten easy lessons. Perhaps you know people like me. So all of us had better watch ourselves before we start criticizing the transparent lies of public life. Such self-criticism will keep us sensitive to the bullshit all around us.

We must be grateful. Of all the creatures on this planet, only we have been given this subtle and marvelous gift of the word. When we are grateful, we will be happy, and happy people feel less need to lie, less need to think they invented words. In the Christian bible, the Gospel according to John says, "in the beginning was the word, and the word was with God, and the word was God." I quote this to show you how important the word is in the West. We identify it with our highest concept. Let us remember how close these two ideas are, God and the word. Let us show gratitude through the words we speak, the songs we sing, the poetry we write. I am grateful to you for listening to me today.

When the tape ran out, a microphone was placed near my mouth. I said the only words I could say, the only words I needed to say, "I love this university! It saved my life. *Fiat lux.*"